CAN AMERICAN DEMOCRACY
SURVIVE COLD WAR?

HARRY HOWE RANSOM teaches political science at Vanderbilt University. He has also taught at Harvard, Princeton, Vassar, and Michigan State University. Born in Nashville, Tennessee, he received his B.A. degree from Vanderbilt, his M.A. and Ph.D. degrees from Princeton. During World War II he was a member of the United States Third Army in five major military campaigns in the European Theater of Operations, and for ten years after the war he was an officer in the Army Reserve. In 1953–54 he was a Congressional Fellow of the American Political Science Association, and from 1955–61 Research Associate and senior staff member of the Harvard Defense Studies Program. He is author of *Central Intelligence and National Security*, which Walter Millis in the New York *Times* called "the best study I have encountered of a phenomenon of American government of the utmost interest," and of numerous articles in the New York *Times Magazine* and various political science, international affairs, and military journals.

Harry Howe Ransom

CAN AMERICAN DEMOCRACY SURVIVE COLD WAR?

ANCHOR BOOKS
Doubleday & Company, Inc.
Garden City, New York
1964

CAN AMERICAN DEMOCRACY SURVIVE COLD WAR? was originally published by Doubleday & Company, Inc., in 1963.

Anchor Edition: 1964

ACKNOWLEDGMENTS

Neither the names I shall note here nor the many footnote references published with each chapter can be an all-inclusive list of all those who helped me produce this book, personally or through their published writings. The book took shape during my years with the Defense Studies Program at Harvard University, 1955–61. I am indebted, most of all, to W. Barton Leach, Professor in the Law School, whose ideas and energy created the Defense Studies Program. I wish to thank also Henry A. Kissinger, Edward L. Katzenbach, Jr., Maury Feld, Bernard K. Gordon, Morton H. Halperin, Timothy W. Stanley, Donald Keesing, Bayley F. Mason, Robert W. Berry, Laurence W. Levine, John Ballard, Audrey Plimpton Schlick, Elizabeth Theiler, and Deirdre Henderson, all associated at one time or another with the Defense Studies Program. A few chapters in this book, in their earliest draft, were read critically by Professor V. O. Key, Jr., of Harvard, and by Anthony Pearce. I should like to thank also the several score of scholars, diplomats, and government officials—civilian and military—whose lectures to the Harvard Defense Policy Seminar added to my knowledge, as did my contact with about 250 graduate students enrolled in the Seminar between 1955 and 1961. A note of thanks is due Professor Robert R. Bowie, Director of the Harvard Center for International Affairs, and his associates, whose hospitality during my last three years at Harvard was most beneficial, particularly in the contacts it afforded with many Visiting Fellows from high diplomatic and military positions in American and foreign governments. If this book has some order and clarity, the reader shares my great indebtedness to Anne Freedgood of Doubleday. In various phases of this study the beneficence of the Ford Foundation, the Carnegie Corporation of New York, and the Institute of Research in the Social Sciences, Vanderbilt University is appreciated. I also thank all of my new colleagues at Vanderbilt University for tolerating my absent-mindedness. The same goes for my wife, Nancy A. Ransom, who not only has been similarly tolerant but has helped immeasurably at every stage in this book's preparation.

H.H.R.

CONTENTS

To
M. H. R.
F. O. A.
and
to the memory of
S. B. A.

. . . it seems to have been reserved to the people of this country, by their conduct and example, to decide the important question, whether societies of men are really capable or not of establishing good government from reflection and choice, or whether they are forever destined to depend for their political constitutions upon accident and force. . . . the crisis at which we are arrived may with propriety be regarded as the era in which that decision is to be made; and a wrong election on the part we shall act may . . . deserve to be considered as the general misfortune of mankind.

ALEXANDER HAMILTON
The Federalist, NO. 1, 1787

Before my term is ended, we shall have to test anew whether a nation organized and governed such as ours can endure. The outcome is by no means certain. The answers are by no means clear.

JOHN F. KENNEDY
STATE OF THE UNION MESSAGE
JANUARY 29, 1961

DEFENSE AND DEMOCRACY

Primo vivere deinde philosophari is an enduring rule for all societies: think first about survival, then about other things.

Survival is a categorical imperative for any government. The writing of this book has been stimulated, however, by my strong preference to think concurrently about national survival and the survival of American democratic values and institutions, both of which are gravely challenged by the contemporary world political environment.

I believe that America's defense and democracy are threatened partly because we may fail to recognize and to cope adequately with what I shall call the problem of organizational lead-time. Our governmental system resists rapid structural change. My greatest concern is that in periods of obsessive fear or true national emergency, radical changes will occur in our institutions—in the name of national security—that will severely damage the democratic framework. My thesis is that this can be avoided by organizational foresight.

Communist imperialism and subversion around the world constitute one major threat we face. Reacting to this, the United States has undertaken enormous commitments to preserve the security and promote the democratic development of the non-Communist world. But even without world communism, the innovations of this century—an accelerating technology which has vastly magnified military power; the "revolution of rising expectations" among three-score new nations; and other revolutionary features of the great transformations in international politics in the mid-twentieth century—would challenge American sovereignty, security, and way of life.

Americans seem inclined to regard such agencies as the National Security Council, the Department of Defense, the Central Intelligence Agency, and other sectors of the national security apparatus as bulwarks of the common defense. But how these complex, partially secret bureaucracies impinge upon the ideals of democratic government *or*, conversely, how the American democratic system impinges upon the efficient functioning of these agencies in the performance of their mission of providing for the common defense, are questions inadequately discussed.

The basic paradox is this: an efficient strategy for survival and security in the years ahead may be dangerously threatened by the forms and processes of American constitutional democracy. At the same time, the requirements and values of American democracy are themselves threatened by the organizational and policy responses already made to Cold War.

The compatibility of the requirements of defense and democracy is an old question that has assumed a new urgency. Alexis de Tocqueville, observing American democracy in the 1830s, concluded that in the conduct of foreign relations democracies are "decidedly inferior to other governments." Democracy, he wrote, was better adapted to peace than to war or to prolonged crisis. In a world radically different from Tocqueville's, the United States maintains virtually the same constitutional structure that the perceptive Frenchman found so deficient.

A democracy, Tocqueville wrote,

. . . can only with great difficulty regulate the details of an important undertaking, persevere in a fixed design, and work out its execution in spite of serious obstacles. It cannot combine its measures with secrecy or await their consequences with patience.[1]

America's incipient crisis involves the confidence of Americans in both themselves and their governmental system. President Kennedy's assertion in his first State of the Union

[1] *Democracy in America*, ed., Phillips Bradley, New York, Knopf, 1945, Vol. I, pp. 234-35.

message that "we shall have to test anew whether a nation organized and governed such as ours can endure," suggests that
the confidence is uncertain. There is also the more objective
question whether our open, democratic system can produce
the required security and compete effectively in protracted
cold warfare with a closed Communist society.

The Communist leaders have the advantage of being able
to pursue their world-wide objectives with an intense ideological purpose and a refined doctrine implemented by a disci-
plined, centralized regime. There is no free press within the
U.S.S.R. or China to disclose prematurely details of secret
operations; and despite internecine party strife, no opposition parties exist outside the Communist Party to question
the wisdom of policies or the competence of operations. No
autonomous legislature reviews policy recommendations or
investigates failures. The people learn only what their government wants them to know.

Against such a competitor, the basic problem is not
whether the American system can continue to provide both
defense and democracy, but whether it can provide either.

Alexander Hamilton, writing in *The Federalist*, No. 8,
early foresaw the dilemma:

> Safety from external danger is the most powerful director
> of national conduct. Even the ardent love of liberty will
> after a time, give way to its dictates. . . . To be more safe
> . . . [nations] at length become willing to run the risk of
> being less free.

Abraham Lincoln also grasped the critical question in a later
national crisis when he rhetorically asked Congress, on July 4,
1861: "Must a government of necessity be too strong for the
liberties of its own people, or too weak to maintain its own
existence?"

The American people emerged from the crises of 1776–87
and 1860–64 with their democracy expanded and more secure, but also with greater authority and power in the national government. As we approach the end of the Republic's
second century, we find the nation involved in a more tenu-

ous, long-term crisis, a crisis in which Lincoln's question remains relevant and urgent.

Surely a government that is insecure, or believes itself to be insecure against external (or internal) enemies will be currently unwilling and ultimately unable to dispense the "Blessings of Liberty" to its citizens. Conversely, unrestrained individualism and rampant pluralism can prevent a government from responding adequately to either common dangers or great opportunities.

The American system is designed to preserve a delicate balance between authority and freedom. In exploring the current security-liberty dilemma, this book focuses upon the organization, procedures, and major features of the national security bureaucracies spawned by contemporary world-affairs crises. It does not attempt to encompass all the dimensions of the problem of preserving American democracy in the modern world, neither is it a survey of all of the departments and agencies concerned with, nor of all of the ramifications of, national security policies. American democracy is profoundly threatened in many ways by the new role of scientists, technologists, and managers of the Cold War apparatus in a world we cannot fully understand. This book considers but one slice of a much larger problem: the structure and process developed for defense policy making, particularly in the period since World War II.

To understand and describe this process, and the impact of the Cold War upon it, is a formidable task. It is particularly challenging in the national defense field, not only because of the increasing complexity and dynamism of policy making, but because most of the crucial institutions and processes are shrouded by at least partial secrecy. By examining in the following chapters the American system for coordinating defense policy, the defense organization, the defense budget, problems of secret intelligence organization, policy and control, and the more general policies of government secrecy and disclosure, I hope to illuminate some of the significant sectors of a vast new gray zone of government.

The purpose throughout is not to give final answers to the

perplexing and significant questions that arise, or to solve the central problems they represent, but rather to define some of the major issues facing the American Constitutional system as it attempts to sustain defense and democracy during an indefinite period of neither war nor peace.

The success of democracy depends ultimately upon the personal initiative of its citizenry and the application of intelligence and will power. My bias is toward a voluntaristic rather than fatalistic theory of man and society. We can survive with our democratic values essentially intact if we have the will to do so. Greater public awareness and understanding of the defense-democracy dilemmas are the first steps toward a proper perspective for arriving at a national consensus on the adjustments that are required for the survival of the American system.

As this is written there is no national consensus on the requirements of defense, or the prerequisites of democracy, or, indeed, on the ways in which defense and democracy are threatened. Only posterity can judge the success with which the United States manages to balance security with liberty, or whether the nation's survival, or demise, will be attributable to too much or too little democracy. The plausibility of the democratic ideal is always on trial. Democracy's premise is that the people shape their own instruments of governance. Therefore it is essential to keep an information spotlight on government institutions, to watch the nature and direction of their growth, and to attempt to judge their impact upon the viability of the democratic ideal. It may not be an exaggeration to suggest that the fate of mankind rests upon the success of the United States in uniting purpose, policy, and organization.

In the early days of the Republic, James Madison, writing in 1798 to Thomas Jefferson about foreign affairs, remarked that "Perhaps it is a universal truth that the loss of liberty at home is to be charged to the provisions against dangers, real or pretended, from abroad." Our contemporary dangers are not imaginary, and the efforts to meet them are endangering liberty at home. Yet faith in the power of the democratic idea inspires the belief that liberty need not be lost and a relatively high degree of national security need not remain beyond reach, if the citizenry make an effort to understand and help to solve the modern version of the old problem of balancing security and freedom. The pages following propose to aid such an understanding.

H.H.R.

December 1962

CHAPTER I

COORDINATING POLICY AND
MILITARY POWER: 1900–1945

I

Early and late in United States history, prime responsibility for the common defense has been the President's. The Constitution made the President Commander in Chief of the armed forces and sole agent in foreign relations, although Congress was given the power of the purse and a veto in foreign relations. But although the common defense is today more than a full time job, it is only one of the President's tasks.

The 1937 Report of the President's Committee on Administrative Management succinctly described the scope of the President's office:

> Our Presidency unites at least three important functions. From one point of view the President is a political leader—leader of a party, leader of the Congress, leader of a people. From another point of view he is head of the Nation in the ceremonial sense of the term, the symbol of our American national solidarity. From still another point of view the President is the Chief Executive and administrator within the Federal system and service.[1]

From this report emerged the concept of the Executive Office of the President, designed to supply him with the help needed to perform these tasks. Like the rest of the government, the office has continued to grow, from several score employees in 1938 to one thousand in 1947, to more than

[1] Washington, D.C., Government Printing Office, 1937, p. 2.

two and a half times that number in 1961, exclusive of the many thousands of Central Intelligence Agency employees who have been added since World War II. The President has come to have a personal staff of more than four hundred (the White House Office) in addition to the sizable staffs of his Bureau of the Budget, National Security Council, Council of Economic Advisers, and Office of Emergency Planning. The Presidency, it may be said, is now twenty-five hundred men—fifteen thousand if the CIA is counted. Contrast this with the picture of Grover Cleveland with one secretary; or Woodrow Wilson typing some of his own letters.

Each of the ten Cabinet departments of the Federal Government and eighteen independent agencies are now directly involved in national security policy. In the field of foreign economic assistance alone, as of 1961, four American government agencies and six international financial organizations were at work. In 1960 there were some 160 formal interdepartmental or interagency committees within the American governmental structure, a sizable majority of them dealing with some aspect of national security.

The Presidential task of performing all of his roles and "coordinating" all this and much more bureaucratic activity becomes increasingly formidable as foreign and domestic policies intermesh more closely and the sharp distinction between political and military affairs fades. Who would claim that matters of health, education, welfare, national and international trade, and agriculture, to cite but a few, do not impinge upon national security?

A central problem is how to organize the national security policy "machine" so that the President may translate the national will—a will he must help to shape and interpret—into effective action. The President has the challenging task, as the one elected executive representative of all of the people, of building a coherent, responsive, and efficient national program within the framework of federalism, pluralism, separated or shared executive-legislative powers, and a highly fragmented bureaucracy.

The basic features of this framework, set up in the eighteenth century, were designed for an age when centralized executive power seemed to endanger the values of the existing society. Congress was expected to be the principal branch of government. The Founding Fathers recognized that the President would provide the energy and responsibility required for good government, particularly in foreign affairs,[2] but the constitutional structure deliberately divided powers and functions between the President and Congress ambiguously. Today, when the common defense demands unitary direction and leadership, tradition-oriented American governmental institutions and the old-fashioned American approach to policy making are inadequate.

The American President's constituency has been expanded far beyond America's continental shores; American national interest has become inextricably entwined with the interests of scores of other nations. Collective security commitments have bound the United States to the defense of territory thousands of miles beyond our national boundaries. Modern technology, the dynamics of world politics and the multipronged nature of the Sino-Soviet threat have created a new environment in which positive action for the common safety can only come from a central leadership.

To create and implement a national policy the President must act with full awareness of the political setting in which he operates.[3] He must simultaneously contend with purposeful, relentless, and resourceful foreign adversaries and mold a consensus from not only a disparate world alliance but the often competing bureaucratic units within his own governmental system, the competitive character of the two great American political parties, the countervailing political power on Capitol Hill, and many conflicting pressures from within America's plural society. Even with an ideal administrative structure, such a task would be formidable. With an anachronistic structure, shaped by the attitudes and requirements of an earlier age, it could prove impossible.

[2] See particularly Alexander Hamilton's *The Federalist*, NO. 70.
[3] The best treatment of the strategy of Presidential power is Richard E. Neustadt, *Presidential Power*, New York, Wiley, 1960.

Providing for the common defense is but one segment of a broader problem, if perhaps the most crucial one. To understand the dimensions of the problem and the strengths and weaknesses of the present American national security system we must first trace its historical evolution, which proceeded along two main lines of organizational development: first, centralized organization of separate armed services, and second, the coordination of military power and foreign policy.

II

The concept of military unification is at least as old as Federal Union armed forces. This nation started out with a War Department which "unified" the meager land army with the virtually non-existent sea forces maintained by the young Republic. But once the fledgling Navy was supplied with ships, their care, management, and operation seemed so different a function from the management of foot soldiers that the pressure for separation mounted. The Navy Department was created by Congress in 1798. Since then, any unified direction of armed forces had to come from the Constitutional Commander in Chief, the President.

For more than a hundred years, the War Department (Army) and the Navy went their own ways, the functions, missions, and doctrines of each defined by its weapons, modes of transport, and the demarcation between land and water. The two services rarely came in contact. They developed separate organizational structures, weapons, educational systems, and service traditions.

At the end of the nineteenth century the war with Spain projected the United States into world politics, and the resultant assumption of defense responsibility for island outposts brought into existence, in 1903, an Army-Navy Joint Board—the organizational ancestor of the Joint Chiefs of Staff —to deal with problems of interservice coordination.[4] The

[4] Louis Morton, "Interservice Cooperation and Political-Military Collaboration, 1900–1938," *Total War and Cold War*, ed., Harry L. Coles, Ohio State University Press, 1962.

Navy had already established its General Board in 1900, and now, after a bitter intra-Army controversy, the Army General Staff was created.[5] Here, for the first time, central war plans, based on various contingencies shaped in peacetime, were worked out. From the start, vested interests opposed the establishment of either general staffs within the services or higher councils of national defense. These interests, which still exist today, often reflect either local or industrial groups, which benefit from subjective rather than objective determination of defense requirements—shipbuilders who want a big Navy or state-based National Guard units that favor the perpetuation of anachronistic military units. Such proponents of continuing decentralization have always found support in Congress, itself a body reflecting local or particular interests. Indeed, many of the centralizing reforms proposed have seemed to threaten Congressional power itself.

Early in its life the Army-Navy Joint Board demonstrated its inability to reconcile the divergent interests and strategic concepts of the Army and Navy. The two services were simply unable to come together on a joint war plan. Presidents Theodore Roosevelt, Taft, and Wilson made little use of the Board, and by not forcing truly joint planning allowed the services to go their separate ways. Actually, few fundamental issues existed on which coordination seemed to be required until the advent of a new dimension of warfare—the air.

The rugged independence of each of the armed services in the Wilson Administration prior to World War I was illustrated by Secretary of War Garrison's reply to Secretary of Navy Daniels' offer of interdepartmental cooperation: "I don't care a damn about the Navy and you don't care a damn

[5] For a general account, see Paul Y. Hammond, *Organizing for Defense*, Princeton University Press, 1961, Chs. II, III; also see Charles Paullin, "A Half Century of Naval Administration in America, 1861–1911," *U. S. Naval Institute Proceedings*, Vol. XL, (1914), pp. 111–28. For the Army, see Otto L. Nelson, *National Security and the General Staff*, Washington, D.C., Infantry Journal Press, 1946, especially pp. 112–66; and Harry Howe Ransom, "Defective at the Top," *Air Force and Space Digest*, March 1961, pp. 59–63.

about the Army. You run your machine, and I'll run mine."[6]
Even within the Army and Navy themselves, internal unification came slowly, often over Congressional opposition. Not
until World War II, for example, was internal unification
achieved in the Navy Department's command structure.[7]

Although proposals for a department of national defense
had been made in earlier years, the question of unification
became really active in the 1920s. Two main arguments supported this concept: first, that the airplane had blurred the
distinction between land and sea warfare. Brigadier General
Billy Mitchell and other proponents of air power were out-
spoken in their belief that aviation had revolutionized the
nature of warfare. Mitchell and his band of brilliant, vociferous air radicals argued that aviation required new military
doctrines as well as a new defense organization. Out of this
belief grew the argument that the air arm ought to have a
separate organizational status. If a third department was to
be added, it followed that a fourth agency—a coordinating
secretary within a department of defense—was needed. Air
power proponents seemed to believe that since the airplane
was the weapon of the future, whoever was to be secretary of
defense would, in the future, be "air-minded."

The second important argument for a department of defense was that unifying certain military services and thereby
ending costly duplication would save money. This was the
motive behind President Warren G. Harding's half-hearted
proposal in 1923 of a single department of defense. Congress
rejected it. But it was the idea of saving money, rather than
the technological impact upon strategy and military force requirements that aroused the greatest public interest in and
Congressional support for unification. Between 1919 and
1939, reorganization of the defense establishment was considered by nineteen major boards or government study groups.

[6] Josephus Daniels, *The Wilson Era*, University of North Carolina
Press, 1946, Ch. I, p. 541; quoted in Richard F. Fenno, Jr., *The
President's Cabinet*, Harvard University Press, 1959, p. 133.

[7] A good account of these developments is found in Hammond,
loc. cit.

Usually the central issues were a separate air force and a department of defense.

In the numerous hearings, studies, and special reports in the 1920s on the question of the organizational and strategic implications of air power, only one group, a Select Committee (Florian Lampert, Chairman) of the House of Representatives advocated, in 1925, greater defense unification. The more influential groups, such as President Coolidge's Aircraft Board (Dwight Morrow, Chairman) and the House and Senate Military and Naval Affairs Committees—backed by the War and Navy Departments—were staunchly opposed to the idea.

During the 1920s and 1930s the Army and the Navy developed stock answers against a separate air force and a unified defense department. Until the outbreak of World War II the Army continued to insist that no cogent reasons existed "to warrant the belief that either a Department of National Defense or a Department of Air would improve our organization for the nation's defense, or reduce its net cost."[8] Indeed the Army could produce almost automatically upon Congressional inquiry a well-prepared argument that "unification" would do more harm than good to the armed forces.[9]

The prophetic findings of the Morrow Board in 1925 reflected the predominant view of ranking Army and Navy officials.

> If the two present service organizations were consolidated under a single secretary, it would at once become necessary to create a super staff. No secretary of national defense could operate the two organizations without subsecretaries or technical advisers. This super general staff, which would be in addition to the present service staffs, would necessarily comprise Army and Navy advisers who had been

[8] Brigadier General George V. Strong, Memorandum for Chief of Staff, 3 February 1939. Quoted in Morton, loc. cit.

[9] See Ray S. Cline and Maurice Matloff, "Development of War Department Views on Unification," Military Affairs, Summer 1949, and Hammond, op. cit., Ch. IV.

educated not only in their own particular schools but who would be required to have taken courses in schools of the service to which they did not belong. It is difficult to see how any such superorganization would make for economy in time of peace or efficiency in time of war.[10]

Nevertheless—in the early years of the great depression significantly—a "unification" bill came close to passage in Congress. Its appeal stemmed from the patently mistaken belief that economy in government was the key to solving the nation's economic problems. In April 1932, the House narrowly defeated such a proposal by a vote of 153 to 135.[11]

The dimensions of the 1932 Congressional debate indicate the persistence of basic elements in the unification debate through the years. One of the arguments against a department of defense in 1932 was that the secretary of defense would become a dangerous "superman" if he had such amalgamated military power at his command. In the same breath it was also argued that such a job was too big for any one man. A "new militarism" was said to be another probable outgrowth of a concentration of decision-making power. Any economies would be offset by the new superstaff of a secretary of defense. Combat on land and at sea were said to require sharply different skills, and to involve such distinct functions that they could not be effectively combined in a single directing organization. Further, it was denied that a separate, independent function existed for military aviation, which was still thought to be a purely auxiliary instrument for the Army and Navy. And, in fact, no national strategic concept then existed that required a force for strategic bombing. Agitation for change was said to be impairing service morale. If better coordination of the Army and Navy were needed, this could be accomplished through the Presidency. The final argument always was that the existing system had served the country well through six major wars. Why change?

[10] Report, President's Aircraft Board, Dwight Morrow, Chairman, Washington, D.C., 1925.
[11] *Congressional Record*, April 30, 1932, p. 9339.

Those favoring unification in the early 1930s insisted that duplication and costly overlapping of functions were rampant; that millions of dollars could be saved by unification, through standardization of equipment, common services, and unified planning; and that the number of civilian personnel serving the armed forces could be sharply reduced. The existing system was also said to be productive of service rivalry which was sapping the nation's morale and strength. At Hawaii, it was alleged, the Army and Navy commanders were not on speaking terms. Neglect of air power would be ended by unification, and the independent military function of aviation would benefit from organizational reform. But the closing argument was always a reiteration that the taxpayers' money could be saved through unification; economy and efficiency would be promoted by a rationalized defense organization. Similar arguments on both sides of the issue were heard again fifteen years later, when the National Security Act of 1947 was debated.

The advice of the Army Chief of Staff, General Douglas MacArthur, on the 1932 proposal was that the Army and Navy must be each left "free to perform its mission unhindered by any centralized or ponderous bureaucratic control. Fighting on the sea and on the land have no elements in common except insofar as they are both engaged in the ultimate mission of victory." MacArthur added, "Pass this bill and every potential enemy of the United States will rejoice."[12] Similar advice came from the Navy Secretary Charles Francis Adams on grounds that the proposal threw overboard "all past experience."

The unification idea was rejected again in 1935.[13] Mean-

[12] Letter to Representative Charles H. Martin (D., Ore.) February 18, 1932, in House Committee on Expenditures in the Executive Department, *Hearings* on H.R. 4742, 72d Congress, 1st Session, 1932, pp. 249–50.

[13] The unification question had been debated again in 1934 by the Baker Board, composed of distinguished civilians headed by former Secretary of War Newton D. Baker, to consider the utility of air power in warfare and the proper status of military aviation. Created in part to quell the agitation for a separate air force, the board con-

while Army Air (by now the Air Corps) was moving slowly toward independence, as aviation technology progressed and increased amounts were appropriated for military aviation.

In 1941 both the Army and the Navy began to express official interest in a defense reorganization that would provide a defense department and joint chiefs of staff. Various boards and committees began to study alternative reorganizational proposals. Controversy quickly developed over the degree of centralization. Navy support, expressed by the General Board in 1941 and traceable back to the Wilson Administration, soon evaporated as it became apparent that Navy control of aviation, the future of the Marine Corps and the Navy's departmental status within the government were threatened by the proposed unification.

In 1943 the War Department became the advocate of a highly centralized system, with a powerful defense secretary, a single armed forces chief of staff with a general staff, and virtual elimination of separate civilian secretaries for each of the armed services. This position was supported by General George C. Marshall, General Dwight D. Eisenhower, and Henry L. Stimson, Secretary of War. World War II experience convinced General Marshall that "even under the stress of war, agreement has been reached in the Joint Chiefs of Staff at times only by numerous compromises and long delays. . . ." Under such a military confederation, said General Marshall, "local service enthusiasms become a source of weakness instead of a source of strength."[14] Meanwhile the requirements for close collaboration with the British military planners had prompted the establishment, by Executive directive, late in 1941 of a Joint Chiefs of Staff, including a representative of the increasingly "independent" Army Air Corps.[15]

---

cluded that a single defense department was unnecessary. See War Department, Special Committee on the Army Air Corps, *Final Report*, July 18, 1934.

[14] *Hearings*, "Department of Armed Forces," Senate Committee on Military Affairs, October 18, 1945, p. 50.

[15] For a detailed account of JCS in World War II, see Hammond, *op. cit.*, Ch. VII.

COORDINATING POLICY AND MILITARY POWER   11

From 1943, when the War Department began to press in earnest for further unification, to 1947, when the National Security (Unification) Act became law, the subject of defense organization was hotly debated. Numerous committees, in the Executive Branch and in Congress, studied and made proposals on the subject. The Navy, the principal antagonist of highly centralized schemes, nurtured powerful support on Capitol Hill. There is no need to present in detail here all the plans, reports and committee hearings on the subject.[16] The basic issue was the degree to which civilian and military authority would be centralized for strategic planning, force levels, and assignment of service missions. The Navy was concerned with the preservation of the Marine Corps, the Naval air arm—particularly land-based naval aviation—and the integrity of adequately supported naval combat forces. It feared the dominance of air power concepts of warfare. The Army seemed, somehow, less concerned about preserving a vested interest than about eliminating the wartime frustrations attendant on attempts to "coordinate" strategy and forces, and was apparently eager to apply its traditional doctrine of unity of command to the over-all defense structure. The Air Force, long a neglected stepchild, was primarily anxious to get independent status for a strategic bombing function, which its leaders believed was most important both then and for the future of warfare. Unification was regarded as a means to this end. The way in which these issues were resolved will be discussed in Chapter III.

III

The unification of the armed services effected in 1947 was achieved by the persistent and vociferous efforts of many in-

[16] Good accounts can be found in Timothy W. Stanley, *American Defense and National Security*, Washington, D.C., Public Affairs Press, 1956; Hammond, *op. cit.*; Murray Green, "Yesterday's and Today's First Line of Defense," *Air Force and Space Digest*, Parts I and II, June and July 1961; and Francis W. Laurent, *Organization for Military Defense of the United States*, University of Wisconsin National Security Studies, Monograph No. 1, 1959.

dividuals and groups. Political-military coordination in the top
policy-making echelons of government had a different history.
Until America's entrance into World War I, whenever military and foreign policy had to be coordinated, this was executed through the Office of the President, possibly in a
Cabinet meeting or by formal correspondence among the
Secretaries of State, War, and Navy. For example, the Secretary of the Navy, upon advice from his General Board, would
write to the Secretary of State, proposing acquisition of a
certain foreign naval base. After considering the proposal and
seeking expert advice, the Secretary of State would arrive at a
recommendation, either killing the idea or forwarding it for
Presidential decision.[17] Though the armed services usually
deferred to the Secretary of State in such matters, political-
military consultation on matters of national strategy was anything but a standard procedure.

As one scholar has noted:

> In the archives of the McKinley, Roosevelt, and Taft Ad-
> ministrations, I have yet to find a letter from a Secretary of
> State, asking for a military cost accounting before some
> diplomatic stroke. Although Taft's Secretary of State did
> occasionally ask the fleet to bolster his diplomacy, he never
> inquired ahead of time about the fleet's location and
> make-up. Thus, in May 1912, when unrest was sweeping
> Cuba, the Secretary asked for a "considerable naval force
> . . . in the vicinity of Havana." Only by chance, or as a
> result of naval clairvoyance, did nine warships happen to
> be handy at Key West.[18]

The archives, of course, may not contain the full story of
informal discussions among State-War-Navy leaders, all of
whom then inhabited the same building in Washington. But
the evidence suggests that even with this physical proximity
of headquarters, very little mutual consultation occurred. For-

[17] Ernest R. May, "The Development of Political-Military Consultation in the United States," *Political Science Quarterly*, June
1955, p. 163.
[18] *Ibid.*, p. 164.

eign policy and the planning and management of military
forces were two isolated functions.

Involvement in and conduct of the war with Spain illustrates the lack of policy integration. The comic-opera nature
of this "splendid little war" in which American troops were
sent to tropical battlefields in Cuba clad in heavy winter uni-
forms with grossly inadequate equipment is an example of
the American tradition of preparing for war only after war
has begun. Over most of our history our lack of military preparedness demonstrates the fact that policy and power were
poorly coordinated, if at all.

In 1911 a Council of National Defense was proposed and
seriously considered. Although it had the support of both
Army and Navy officials, its functions and composition were
a heavily contested issue. The Navy wanted to include the
Secretary of State on the Council; the Army did not. The
Navy apparently viewed the Council as a source of national
strategy; the Army considered it "a tool which could be used
to protect it against the inconstancy and parochialism of politics."[19] Such proposals and controversies over functions continued down through World War II and into the postwar
"unification" debate.

Professor Louis Morton reminds us that Wilson appointed
a Quaker as his Secretary of War and a pacifist as his first
Secretary of State. The latter, William Jennings Bryan, when
the Joint Board proposed a fleet movement during the 1913
crisis with Japan, thundered that "Army and Navy officers
could not be trusted to say what we should or should not do,
till we actually get into war. . . ."[20] Ironically, most Army
and Navy leaders were in agreement with Bryan. It was official
doctrine that policy making was the province of the politicians. "The work of the statesman and the soldier," wrote the

[19] Hammond, op. cit., p. 67. See, for details, House Naval Affairs
Committee, Hearings, "Council of National Defense," 62d Congress,
2d Session, 1911.

[20] Quoted in Morton, op. cit., from David F. Houston, Eight
Years with Wilson's Cabinet, Garden City, New York, Doubleday,
1926, Vol. I, p. 66.

Army Staff planners, "are . . . coordinate; where the first
leaves off the other takes hold."[21] The Navy was in general
agreement.

Even President Wilson at one period seems to have been
convinced that long-range war contingency planning had no
place in the national scheme of things. "When history is written eighty or a hundred years from now," he once said to
Franklin Roosevelt, then Assistant Secretary of the Navy, "I
don't want to have it possible for any one to say that America
prepared before the act of war."[22]

Woodrow Wilson devoutly hoped to avoid war and dog-
matically opposed the idea that the United States engage in
war planning. In the autumn of 1915, he summoned Henry
Breckinridge, acting Secretary of War, to his office. The Secretary found the President holding the Baltimore *Sun* and
"trembling and white with passion." Wilson pointed to an
item in the newspaper which reported that the Army's General Staff was preparing a plan in the event of war with Germany. The President asked Breckinridge if this were true. As
later recorded by Major General Tasker H. Bliss, then Acting
Chief of Staff: "The President directed him to make an immediate investigation and, if it proved true, to relieve at once
every officer of the General Staff and order him out of Washington."[23]

General Bliss was assigned the task of investigating and explaining the situation to the President:

> I told him that the law creating the General Staff made
> it its duty "to prepare plans for the national defense"; that
> I was President of the [Army] War College when the Gen-

[21] "A Proper Military Policy for the United States," by War College Division, General Staff, Army War College, Washington, D.C.,
Government Printing Office, 1915, p. 10.

[22] Quoted by Hermann Hagedorn from F. D. Roosevelt, New York
Herald Tribune, December 29, 1928, in *Leonard Wood: A Biog-
raphy*, New York, Harper, 1931, Vol. II, p. 205.

[23] Quoted in Frederick Palmer, *Newton D. Baker*, New York,
Dodd, Mead, 1931, Vol. I, p. 40; see also Arthur S. Link, *Woodrow
Wilson and the Progressive Era*, New York, Harper, 1954, p. 168.

eral Staff was organized in 1903; that from that time until then [1915] the College had studied over and over again plans for war with Germany, England, France, Italy, Japan, Mexico, *etc.* I said that if the President took the action threatened, it would only make patent to everybody [that] which pretty much everybody knew and would create a great political row, and, finally, it would be absurd.

I think the President realized this in a cooler moment. Nothing further was said to him about the matter, nor did he again mention it. But Mr. Breckinridge directed me to caution the War College to "camouflage" its work. It resulted in practically no further official studies.[24]

Certainly many informal meetings between soldiers and diplomats occurred during the prewar Wilson Administration, as, for example, when tension mounted with Mexico. But until American involvement in World War I, the system for political-military consultation was makeshift. Indeed, the planning staffs of both the armed services and the State Department were clearly deficient in organization and in trained personnel.

World War I revealed these defects, and the immediate postwar period saw numerous proposals for reform: for internal reorganization within the several departments and for higher-level policy-coordinating machinery. The Army General Staff again was reorganized; the Office of Naval Operations went through several structural changes; and the Rogers Act of 1924 radically altered the personnel policies of the Department of State by professionalizing the foreign service corps.

The first and most comprehensive proposal for national policy coordination in the postwar period came over the signature of Franklin D. Roosevelt, as Assistant Secretary of the Navy. On May 1, 1919, a Roosevelt letter to the Secretary of State declared:

. . . the foreign policy of a government depends for its ac-

[24] Palmer, *op. cit.*, Vol. I, pp. 40–41.

ceptance by other nations upon the naval and military force that is behind it.

Hence . . . in the framing of our policies, it is necessary for the State Department to know how much they [foreign policies] will cost to maintain by force, in order to assign them their relative importance.

Conversely, it is necessary for the Navy Department to know what policies it may be called upon to uphold by force, in order to formulate plans and building programs.[25]

Roosevelt's proposal was apparently derived from Naval War College studies and drafted by a Navy staff group known as "OP-56". Attached to his written suggestion was a large organizational blueprint for national policy making and strategic planning. For more than a decade, naval strategists had been convinced of the need for a formal structure to determine national policy and strategy.

Exploring the fate of this 1919 recommendation, Professor Ernest R. May discovered three decades later that Roosevelt's letter and blueprint were missent to State's Division of Latin American Affairs and finally found their way into the Navy's general files. Apparently they were never seen by the Secretary of State. When the original of Roosevelt's letter was found in the State Department archives, the blueprint was stapled to it, and apparently never had been unfolded.[26]

Other proposals with a similar aim but of different design were under study at this period. They reflected military concern about the vagueness of national foreign policy objectives. Those charged with strategic planning were constantly frustrated by their inability to elicit a clear response from the State Department on such questions as: What are America's interests and objectives in the Western Pacific?

Another proposal was made some two years later, this time under the joint sponsorship of the Secretaries of War and

[25] Quoted in May, op. cit., p. 167; see also Frank Freidel, Franklin D. Roosevelt, Vol. 2, The Ordeal, Boston, Little, Brown, 1954, pp. 19–20.
[26] May, op. cit., p. 168.

Navy. Less elaborate than the original Navy suggestion, the 1921 proposal suggested routine collaboration between the State Department and the Army-Navy Joint Board, which had been revitalized in postwar reorganizations, given a permanent civilian secretary, and, more importantly, a Joint Planning Committee with representatives from the Army and Navy War Plans Divisions and the State Department. Under this scheme the State Department would refer to the Joint Board national policies under consideration that might require military support, with the Secretaries of State, War, and Navy, acting as a kind of war planning council, or final tribunal.

Military proponents of better coordinating machinery were on logical ground in their suggestions, even though they may have been motivated by fear of disarmament maneuvers by statesmen or that foreign policy commitments would outrun defense appropriations. But Secretary of State Charles Evans Hughes opposed the proposal. To him it seemed to give the armed services a role in foreign policy outside their proper jurisdiction. Further, he was unwilling to delegate the responsibility in this matter to lower ranking officials in the State Department. And perhaps, too, he feared the effect of military foot-dragging on disarmament schemes in the wind. In any case, he wrote vetoing the proposal, concluding:

> Should a crisis arise in our national affairs, where it may seem to this Department advisable to consult and cooperate with the Joint Board, I shall certainly avail myself of the opportunity to do so.[27]

War and Navy Department strategic planners countered with a new proposal: that the Army-Navy Joint Board routinely inform the State Department whenever, in their strategic planning, military officials encountered material with definite foreign policy implications. In such an event, the Secretary of State or his representative could meet with the Joint Board to work out a mutual agreement for policy recom-

[27] Hughes' letter to the Secretaries of War and of the Navy, January 17, 1922. Quoted in Morton, *op. cit.*

mendation. Hughes agreed to this arrangement "in principle." But there is little evidence that such collaboration, agreed upon in 1922, ever actually took place in the decade that followed. At the Washington Limitation of Armaments Conference in 1921–22, and at subsequent international conferences, the State Department often rejected or failed to seek the advice of military leaders.

The national spirit of the 1920s did not engender political-military consultation. America's defense interests were narrowly conceived. "Who's gonna fight us?" President Coolidge often asked those who came to him to plead for a bigger Army or Navy. Continental defense was the main objective of national policy, and American shores seemed invulnerable to foreign invasion. Brigadier General Billy Mitchell's preachments on the strategic implications of progress in aeronautical science caused a ripple of concern. But it did not run deep.

When Herbert Hoover assumed office in 1929 he summoned the Army and Navy chiefs to the White House and, by his own account, addressed one question to them: "Are our defenses strong enough to prevent a successful landing of foreign soldiers on the continental United States and ultimately on the Western Hemisphere?" When Mr. Hoover received the emphatic reply of "Yes," he seems to have felt assured that the nation's defenses were adequate and that the basic mission of the armed forces was being fulfilled.[28]

To be sure, the question of the size of the Navy and the naval competition with Great Britain and Japan were matters of national concern. But these were issues to be decided finally by the President and the civilians of the State Department. At the London Naval Conference of 1930, the recommendations of the Navy's General Board were again unheeded or overruled.

Despite the temper of the times an inevitable interchange began to occur among Army, Navy, and Foreign Service officers. The latter, in 1922, started to attend the war colleges of the Army and Navy. Simultaneously the advent of mili-

[28] Herbert Hoover, *Memoirs*, New York, Macmillan, 1952, Vol. II, p. 338.

tary aviation stirred up bitter controversies between the Army and Navy. Even so, the interchange stimulated little thought about the crucial relationship between military power and diplomacy.

The isolationist attitudes of America in the 1920s were altered by the changing international atmosphere of the 1930s. The rise of Hitler, Mussolini's muscle flexing, and an increasingly hostile and aggressively minded Japanese leadership ultimately had impact upon the American outlook and upon policy-making institutions as well.

The Administration of Franklin D. Roosevelt, though initially preoccupied with domestic economic crises, found it necessary to have more than a theoretical interest in coordinating foreign and military policy, particularly in Roosevelt's second term. Secretary of State Cordell Hull had the frustrating assignment of trying to oppose early Japanese moves by insisting upon the rules of good conduct and proclaiming America's opposition to aggression. In this period, he could do little more. The American Army and Navy were incapable of fighting in the Western Pacific, even if the nation had been willing to attempt to halt patent aggression.

Secretary Hull, theoretically the President's chief foreign policy adviser, began to learn the hard facts of international life. As he later recounted to a Congressional committee investigating the attack on Pearl Harbor:

> . . . when I would be talking with the representative of the thugs at the head of governments abroad [Germany, Japan, Italy] . . . they would look at me in the face but I soon discovered they were looking over my shoulder at our Navy and our Army and that our diplomatic strength . . . goes up or down with their estimate of what that amounts to.[29]

Administration officials under Roosevelt gradually began to take a more solicitous attitude toward the armed services.

[29] From *Hearings*, Joint Committee on the Investigation of the Pearl Harbor Attack, 79th Congress, 1st. Session, Part II, p. 455. Quoted in May, *op. cit.*, p. 171.

Navy views were well represented and influential at the 1935 Naval Conference in London. A high-ranking State Department official was assigned, at the request of the Secretaries of War and Navy, to regular participation in the work of the Planning Committee of the Army-Navy Joint Board.

Moves by the Axis powers toward establishing military influence—through military training missions—in certain Latin American nations, as well as Japanese actions in the Far East, prompted the State Department, in 1938, to propose a more effective system for political-military consultation. Secretary Hull recommended to President Roosevelt the establishment of a standing liaison committee composed of the second ranking officers of the State, War, and Navy Departments to discuss, and make recommendations on, matters of policy of interdepartmental concern. Secretary Hull's suggestion was approved "heartily" by the President and put into effect with one major change: the Army Chief of Staff and the Chief of Naval Operations instead of civilian assistant secretaries represented the armed services. Thus in 1938 a formal mechanism was created to coordinate the government's military, naval, and diplomatic arms.[30]

As the implications of the war in Europe on America's national interest became more obvious in 1940, the Standing Liaison Committee broadened the boundaries of its discussions. Its importance in national decision making actually decreased, however, after Henry L. Stimson was appointed Secretary of War in 1940. Under the leadership of this very able former Secretary of State, an increasing number of pressing military-foreign policy questions were handled at the Secretarial level.[31] Shortly before the outbreak of war in Europe, the Army-Navy Joint Board had begun to report directly to the President, making much of the SLC's initial activity meaningless.[32]

[30] Mark S. Watson, *Chief of Staff: Prewar Plans and Preparations*, Washington, D.C., Department of the Army, 1950, p. 90.

[31] See Elting E. Morison, *Turmoil and Tradition*, Boston, Houghton Mifflin, 1960, Ch. 26.

[32] Watson, *op. cit.*, p. 91.

Secretary Stimson was nonetheless successful in his efforts
to coordinate general policy among the leadership of the War,
Navy, and State Departments. Soon after his arrival in Washington in the summer of 1940, he invited Navy Secretary
Frank Knox and Cordell Hull to meet with him regularly on
matters of joint official interest. By the close of 1940, such
meetings, to be continued through the war, had assumed a
formal status and permitted the three Secretaries to recommend agreed policy to the President. But, as a Stimson biog-
rapher has observed, "whether the President acted on these
recommendations remained, throughout the war, quite another matter."[33] As the war progressed, Stimson, Knox, and
Hull, particularly the last, often found themselves on the
periphery of the discussions from which the grand strategy
of the war was derived.

From 1939 onward, the President was ahead of most members of his Administration, Congress, and public opinion on
the question of intervention in what was fast becoming a
world war. According to Professors Mansfield and Stein:

> Throughout the 1938–41 period the military, so far from
> pushing the country toward war, rather lagged behind the
> changing trend of public opinion. Except for the beginning
> of naval stag conversations with the British, all of the major
> policy moves that marked the successive stages in the shift
> appear to have had a civilian origin; and all except selective
> service depended on Roosevelt's active approval and sup-
> port, or even on his initiative.[34]

Ironically, this suggests that if Roosevelt's 1919 Navy
proposal for closer political-military coordination had been
adopted, the results might have been disastrous to the nation.
Given the preoccupation of the country at large with isola-
tionism and neutrality, and military plans that stressed continental, or at best hemispheric, defense, an elaborate ma-

[33] Morison, *op. cit.*, p. 508.
[34] Walter Millis, with Harvey C. Mansfield and Harold Stein,
Arms and the State, New York, Twentieth Century Fund, 1958, pp.
42–43.

chinery for coordinating national policy might have hampered Presidential leadership. As it was, a sometimes wavering Roosevelt faced a tremendously difficult task in awakening many of his political associates as well as Congress and the public to the perils of growing Axis power. His political environment forced him to walk a tightrope between the conflicting and powerful demands of interventionists and isolationists. A more precisely defined and elaborate national security machinery could conceivably have made him its prisoner. Perhaps herein lies a lesson for the future. Alternatively, if the national leadership had followed the "will of the people," the nation would most likely have been led down the wrong path. Here is one of the paradoxes of democratic government.

Roosevelt's main tactic in the face of existing machinery and personalities was to "divide and rule." To this he added "a considerable measure of secretiveness and an occasional dash of talkativeness, and a readiness to reach directly into operating agencies below the level of their chiefs."[35] In the situation little time existed for grand strategy, so it was often neglected for the immediate tactical problem at hand. This was the case throughout much of the war.

By autumn of 1941 the President was, in effect, operating his own War Council. Its members included the Secretaries of War, Navy, and State, and the armed services chiefs. But this council did not function, at the highest level, in a formal fashion with a set agenda, for this was not Roosevelt's style. Rather it served as a sounding board against which Roosevelt would cast decisions reached through personal dealings with the military chiefs of staff or allied foreign leaders. It was a medium more for communication than for decision making.

IV

When the United States declared war, the country lapsed into what has been called a "Presidential dictatorship." In this "dictatorship" the virtual elimination of the Secretary of

[35] Millis *et al., op. cit.,* p. 44.

State from the highest policy and strategy councils was perhaps the most significant change. On many of the most important strategic decisions, Secretary Hull sat on the sidelines while Roosevelt worked closely with his small informal "war cabinet": James F. Byrnes, Samuel Rosenman, Harry Hopkins, Admiral William D. Leahy, serving as the President's personal military chief of staff, and, sporadically, the Army and Navy chiefs. Victory by defeating the enemy's armed forces became the basic aim of national policy, with little thought given to the longer-range political goals beyond this immediate objective. The State Department, until late in the war, clearly had little influence in forming and applying national strategy.

Initially this produced a serious policy vacuum; military officers were by training and experience very reticent, even inhibited, when it came to political affairs. Traditional military indoctrination, in spite of the more sophisticated views held in the war colleges, had conditioned officers to assume that political and military factors were separate compartments of national policy: "their code was that the Army, when asked, would advise 'how' to achieve stated military objectives, but would not otherwise influence decisions about 'what' to do."[36]

Early in the war, President Roosevelt encouraged this somewhat narrow view by making it clear to military leaders that his aim was to defeat the enemy in the most militarily efficient way. But when American forces were deployed overseas their commanders came to realize that almost every major military move raised political questions. Military professionals were moved to action by the realization that the British Chiefs of Staff always seemed better advised and guided on political questions than the Americans. The British seemed to have a better integrated national policy and a better system for orderly communication between political and military leaders. In contrast, the flow of strategic information from and to the American President was haphazard, and sometimes

[36] Ray S. Cline, *Washington Command Post: The Operations Division*, Washington, D.C., Department of the Army, 1951, p. 313.

non-existent. On more than one occasion Roosevelt sent messages with serious military ramifications to Churchill or Stalin
without even informing his military chiefs. Or he consulted
with his military chiefs while leaving his War and Navy Secretaries in the dark.

Through various informal organizational devices the Army
attempted to breach the informational gap by conducting, in
effect, intragovernmental espionage. But important military
decisions—like the North African campaign of 1942—were
made by Roosevelt without the prior advice of military
leaders.[37]

A major development in political-military consultation occurred toward the end of 1943. After the Foreign Ministers
Conference in Moscow, a European Advisory Commission
was created by the United States, Great Britain, and Russia,
and the American delegation was put under State Department leadership. Later, in mid-1944, the Joint Chiefs of Staff
created their own Joint Postwar Committee, further complicating the planning machinery. It was soon apparent that a
more orderly interdepartmental planning system was necessary. The inactive State-War-Navy Committee of the three
Secretaries was revived, and, more important, the State-War-
Navy Coordinating Committee was established in November
1944. On it were assistant secretaries from each of the three
departments. SWNCC also formed area subcommittees for
Europe, Latin America, the Middle and Far East.

While committees were being formed in Washington, military leaders in the field were conducting the most important
operational business: negotiations with allied governments.
Generals Eisenhower, Stilwell, and Wedemeyer were up to
their ears in what were essentially political missions. At another level, the American Joint Chiefs of Staff were, in effect,
negotiating international treaties with their allied counter-
parts. The Joint Chiefs of Staff, with Army Chief General
George C. Marshall usually dominant, acted as Presidential
agents and had only tenuous communication with the State

[37] See Morison, *op. cit.*, p. 589.

Department. "Thus," one scholar has observed, "during World War II, the strategists took command, and the military-State Department relation was reversed. No longer were the military leaders seeking parity with diplomats; on the contrary, the diplomats were looking for space alongside the chiefs of staff."[38]

General Marshall was a soldier of great integrity with administrative genius and the eye of a statesman. Yet he seemed inculcated with the Clausewitzian doctrine of concentrating superior power against the main strength of the enemy, apparently forgetting Clausewitz' even more important precept that war should always serve policy. General Marshall seemed to suspect military strategies motivated by political objectives. When it was proposed that Eisenhower's forces be sent to Berlin and Prague before the Russians, he reportedly said he would be loath to risk American lives for purely political purposes. Marshall's sense of military purpose was successful in attaining the immediate objective—victory over the enemy's armed forces. But the separation of military strategy from long-range political objectives represented a misconception of both war and politics.

SWNCC was the true ancestor of the contemporary National Security Council. But by the time "Swink," as it was commonly called, came into action many policy alternatives had been circumscribed by the "purely military" decisions of commanders in the field. This is not to suggest that throughout the war political leaders entirely neglected the problems of post-hostilities policy. The problem of a postwar policy toward Germany was considered by Roosevelt's assistant, Harry Hopkins, in 1942. On Hopkins' urging, Roosevelt requested Secretary Hull to study the question, and Hull set forth proposals at the Moscow Conference of Foreign Ministers in 1943. However, no decisions were made, and this and other matters of postwar policy were referred to the European Advisory Commission. In the detailed and complex negotiations over German zonal boundaries that ensued, the State Depart-

[38] May, *op. cit.*, p. 175.

ment was fully represented in the official committee structure. But the record suggests that the really important decisions were made by military commanders without the participation or knowledge of the State Department. Some State Department officials were apparently awake to the importance of a guarantee in writing of Western access to the Berlin enclave. But their proposals did not prevail in the negotiations. Rather, the "doctrine of pure war" prevailed, leaving little room for decisions based upon political calculations of long-range strategic requirements. This was war, the business of soldiers. The management of the peace would be the task of politicians, later.

During World War II American civilians and military alike showed a lack of comprehension of the fact that war is merely an instrument of policy; that "victory" alone is an inadequate political objective. In the postwar years the nation was to try to apply the lessons learned from this mistake. Perhaps the most important single "lesson," from the standpoint of the American governmental system, was the need for better institutional devices for integrating political and military factors into a single national policy; for matching national power with national purpose; and for achieving this within the framework of responsive and responsible constitutional government.

In attempts to create these institutions the British system was the widely admired model. Because of geography, strategic predisposition and involvement with a world-wide empire, Britain had had to solve the problem of political-military coordination much earlier than the United States. In 1904 the Committee on Imperial Defence had been established, based on the concept that defense policy should be made jointly by the War Office, Admiralty, and top political officers of the government. CID's membership, headed by the Prime Minister, was flexible; its secretariat was primarily military.[39] But in seeking to adapt this idea to the United States' needs, important contrasts between the British and

[39] See Franklyn A. Johnson, *Defence by Committee*, Oxford University Press, 1960.

the American system had to be taken into account—first and foremost the difference between Presidential and Cabinet government. Governmental office and powers are _fused_ within the British Parliamentary-Cabinet-Prime Minister system. In the United States, authority and power are shared or _separated_—some will say con-_fused_—between the Executive and Legislative branches, and the President's cabinet does not and can not bear the stamp of collective responsibility held by the British cabinet. Those who prepared the influential Eberstadt Report, commissioned by the Secretary of the Navy in 1945, which provided the framework for the "Unification" Act of 1947, were presumably aware of these differences. Yet they appear to have been captivated by the British example[40] and sought to transfer to the United States features of the British system that could not in fact be imported without fundamental changes in the American Presidential system.[41] The problems so raised are illustrated in the next chapter in the history of the National Security Council, created by Congressional statute in 1947.

[40] _Ibid._, pp. 315–38.
[41] _The Forrestal Diaries_, ed., Walter Millis, New York, Viking, 1951, p. 145.

CHAPTER II

UNITING PURPOSE, POLICY, AND POWER: THE NATIONAL SECURITY COUNCIL

I

The National Security Council was established in 1947 as a monument to the postwar aspiration that national purpose, policy, and power be better integrated, and that the use of America's foreign policy instruments be coordinated. With the British war council system as a model, and with the lessons of the sudden attack on Pearl Harbor and the deficiencies in politico-military coordination during World War II in mind, the NSC was part of a grand scheme of unification, although the statute that created it was a compromise evolving from the bitter armed forces unification controversies of 1944–47.

Congress specified that NSC's duties were "to advise the President with respect to the integration of domestic, foreign and military policies . . ." among the various government departments and agencies, including the military; and "to assess and appraise the objectives, commitments and risks of the United States in relation to our actual and potential military power. . . ."[1] More than that, NSC was given collective responsibility for assessing military requirements. Perhaps the prime motive of its advocates was to make it difficult for statesmen and diplomats to ignore the military factor in national policies. Some supporters saw NSC as a multipurpose instrument: to insure an effective national strategy, to cir-

---

[1] The National Security Act of 1947, Public Law 253, 80th Congress, July 27, 1947, Sec. 101.

cumscribe Presidential (i.e., political) power, and to perpetuate an autonomous Navy, the independence of which in the
"air power age" seemed to be threatened by unification.[2]

However, the principal role specified for NSC in the statute
was not to make final decisions, but to advise the President;
to make his national security policy and administrative task
more efficient. But whenever the bureaucracy is institutionalized and centralized, there is the risk of minimizing the
discretion and flexible maneuverability of the Presidency.
And this, in turn, can adversely affect both the common defense and the fulfillment of the democratic ideal. Many see
too much unchecked Presidential power as the main threat to
freedom, but this does not appear to be the real danger in
modern American government, with the important possible
exception of Executive control over the flow of information.
It is the President's inability to rise above the decision-making machinery and to exert responsible leadership in the national interest—perceived from the highest level—that places
the basic democratic idea in doubt.

Franklin Roosevelt's leadership, as we have seen, might
have been disastrously frustrated in World War II had a central coordinating mechanism existed for war planning and
policy. On the other hand, some of the failures to give adequate attention, while the war was being fought, to postwar
political objectives might have been avoided by better political-military coordination. The ideal, clearly, is to provide effective integration of policy without vitiating Presidential
leadership.

NSC's development and use between 1947 and 1962 have
been conditioned by the concepts underlying its origin, the
administrative philosophies of the Presidents to whom it has
been available, and the changing world environment. At the
first meeting of NSC in 1947 President Truman indicated
that he regarded it as "*his* council," that is to say, as a purely
advisory body. Later President Eisenhower, although inclined
to regard it as "*the* council," made clear nonetheless that

2 See Hammond, *Organizing for Defense*, p. 84.

NSC was absolved of any responsibility *per se* for national decisions. The NSC advises; the responsibility for decision is the President's, insisted Eisenhower. President Kennedy came to office with an apparent bias against the kind of use Eisenhower had made of NSC. Borne into office amid a great chorus of rhetoric about the need for purposeful, energetic Presidential leadership, Kennedy at first made little use of the Council as a formal advisory body. Following the 1961 Cuban fiasco, however, the NSC was restored somewhat. Since April 1961 there have been more frequent meetings, although the President has been more inclined to the Truman than to the Eisenhower attitude toward the Council. In the tense days of October-November 1962, he made use of a newly designated "Executive Committee" of NSC as a forum for discussing United States reactions to Soviet military installations in Cuba.

Whoever the White House occupant, national policy making is far too complex to divide into an abstract decision-making model. Appraisal of the situation, measurement of national purpose, formulation of policy recommendations, decision, and implementation cannot be made separate functions. A President may say that NSC offers advice only, and that *he* makes the decision. But, as Richard Neustadt has observed, "he never can assume that anyone or any system will supply the bits and pieces [of information] he needs most; on the other hand he must assume that much of what he needs will not be volunteered by his official advisers."[3] The President could, in fact, become an innocent prisoner of an elaborate committee system which denies him the information and knowledge that would allow him to make a meaningful ultimate choice. The Central Intelligence Agency, for example, potentially has this kind of portentous power, a problem to be discussed in Chapter VII. A Presidency without the requirements for real choice has serious implications for democratic government, for it means that responsibility

---

[3] *Presidential Power*, p. 154.

is blurred, and the power of government has become partially invisible.

In practice, many of the most important decisions of national strategy require a thorough "staffing" by interdepartmental committees, so that the policy or action of one government agency will not contradict or counteract that of another. In this elaborate and time-consuming process, policy and strategy are theoretically hammered out, except in a time of crisis. By means of such complex machinery the President is guided to what is often a compromise decision, the Constitutional responsibility for which is his.

Early in NSC's life, according to President Truman, "one or two of its members tried to change it into an operating super-cabinet on the British model."[4] Truman identifies the members as his first two Secretaries of Defense, James Forrestal and Louis Johnson who would sometimes, Truman recounts, "put pressures on" NSC's executive secretary to use NSC authority to see that various governmental agencies were following NSC policy. The executive secretary declined to do this, on the ground that his was an advisory "staff" rather than an executing "line" function. Truman fought to keep the subordinate nature of NSC clear to all, emphasizing that Congress had in fact changed the title of NSC "Director" to "Executive Secretary." Forrestal had, Truman notes, advocated using the British cabinet system as a model for the operation of postwar American government. To change to this system, wrote Truman, "we would have to change the Constitution, and I think we have been doing very well under our Constitution."[5]

Membership of the National Security Council is specified by statute. Statutory members (as of 1962) are: the President, Vice President, Secretary of State, Secretary of Defense, and the Director of the Office of Emergency Planning. The Chairman of the Joint Chiefs of Staff and the Director

[4] Harry S. Truman, *Memoirs*, Vol. 2, *Years of Trial and Hope*, Garden City, New York, Doubleday, 1956, p. 60.
[5] *Ibid.*

of Central Intelligence, who have been regular participants in NSC deliberations, have the special title of "adviser."

Because the ramifications of national security policy are government-wide, its *de facto* membership has considerably expanded from the exclusive statutory list. Whatever the statute says, actual NSC membership will always be determined by the incumbent President. In the Eisenhower years, NSC meetings were normally attended by approximately twenty high-ranking government officials and their assistants. The Secretary of the Treasury, the Chairman of the Atomic Energy Commission, and the Director of the Bureau of the Budget became in effect standing members, as did the Assistant to the President (Sherman Adams), the President's Special Assistant for National Security Affairs and other ranking members of the NSC secretariat (the Executive Secretary and his Deputy), and the President's Staff Secretary. Other officials who might participate in NSC deliberations were the Under Secretary of State, the President's Special Assistants for Foreign Economic Policy, Science and Technology, and Security Operations Coordination,[6] and the Director of the U. S. Information Agency. In addition, the Director of the National Aeronautics and Space Administration, the Attorney General, the Secretaries and Military Chiefs of the Army, Navy, and Air Force were sometimes invited, depending upon the agenda, and the practice was established of using outside consultants and commissioning special purpose study groups on specific security problems.

During the Eisenhower Administration the President acted as chairman at the regular NSC weekly meetings. Gordon Gray has reported that in the first forty-five meetings at which he served as the President's Assistant, the President attended forty-three. By contrast, President Truman's attendance at meetings was irregular.

A somewhat smaller central core of NSC membership was established in the first two years of the Kennedy Administration, which relies more upon individuals than institutions.

[6] This office was abolished early in the Kennedy Administration.

And it is significant that the officials who made up the NSC "executive committee" in the tense "brink of war" days of October 1962, when crucial decisions were made in response to the Soviet Russian emplacement of long-range missiles in Cuba, were: the Director of Central Intelligence, the Attorney General, the Secretaries of State, Defense, and Treasury, the Chairman of the Joint Chiefs of Staff, the President's Special Assistant for National Security Affairs, the Ambassador to the United Nations, the Ambassador-at-large (Llewellyn Thompson), and the President's Special Counsel, Theodore Sorensen.

As is the case in many of the national security sectors of the government, attempts at analysis and evaluation of NSC performance must depend heavily for information upon those who are inclined to give a subjective view. The main body of published, non-secret material on the procedure and effectiveness of NSC has appeared over the signature of Presidential Assistants for National Security Affairs Robert Cutler, Dillon Anderson, Gordon Gray, and McGeorge Bundy.[7] The outside scholar must make his evaluation from these descriptions, with as yet little of such information on the Kennedy Administration. The confusion and controversy surrounding journalistic accounts in *The Saturday Evening Post*, *Newsweek*, *Look*, and *Life* of the NSC meetings in October 1962, and the unwillingness of the President and his aides to clarify these distorted versions, illustrates the problem. The record is reasonably complete on the formal organization and procedures of the National Security Council between 1947 and 1960. The writings of officials who have guided the work of NSC, and various studies by Congressional committees and others in recent years have added to the knowledge of NSC

[7] See also "Organizational History of the National Security Council," a study for the Senate, Government Operations Subcommittee on National Security Policy Machinery, 86th Congress, 2d Session, August 1960; various hearings, staff studies, and reports of this subcommittee, 1959–61; and Burton M. Sapin, "The Organization and Procedures of the National Security Council Mechanism," in Senate, Committee on Foreign Relations, "United States Foreign Policy," Study No. 9, Appendix B, January 1960.

organization and process.[8] This permits at least a description of the formal institutions.

On the organizational chart, the NSC is located in the Executive Office of the President, as a staff organization. It has its own small secretariat (thirty–forty persons), headed by a career Executive Secretary, who works with the President's politically appointed Special Assistant for National Security Affairs. The assigned functions of the Secretariat have included: the analysis of policy questions at the Presidential level, divorced from the operating bias of the government departments but working in cooperation with, and undoubtedly deriving most of its information from, these departments; arrangement of agenda for meetings; keeping the official record of Council meetings and transmittal of Council working papers to participating departments and agencies; and expediting negotiation and conciliation of policy differences among the various government departments concerned.

Under Eisenhower the NSC Secretariat was theoretically

[8] Valuable sources are *Hearings*, "Organizing for National Security," Senate Government Operations Subcommittee on National Policy Machinery, Parts I–VII, 1960. See reports of this committee, including its comprehensive bibliographies, "Organizing for National Security," December 15, 1959, and "Administration of National Security," December 28, 1962; and *Selected Materials*, March 10, 1960. Other useful sources include: Timothy W. Stanley, *American Defense and National Security*; William R. Kintner and associates, *Forging A New Sword*, New York, Harper, 1958; Robert Ellsworth Elder, *The Policy Machine*, Syracuse University Press, 1959; Hammond, *op. cit.*; *The Secretary of State: the 18th Report*, ed., Don K. Price, Englewood Cliffs, New Jersey, Prentice Hall for The American Assembly, 1960; Samuel P. Huntington, *The Soldier and the State*, Harvard University Press, 1957, and *The Common Defense*, Columbia University Press, 1961; Neustadt, *op. cit.*; Laurin L. Henry, *Presidential Transitions*, Washington, D.C., The Brookings Institution, 1960; *Total War and Cold War*, ed., Harry L. Coles; and The Brookings Institution, "The Formulation and Administration of United States Foreign Policy," prepared for the Senate Committee on Foreign Relations, January 13, 1960. As this is written numerous books are appearing which deal with the Kennedy Administration, its personnel, and its administrative style. More of these can be expected as can memoirs by various members of the Eisenhower Administration.

not an originator of policy, strategy, or plans, but a staff middleman between the President (in reality the President's Assistant for National Security Affairs) and the operating departments. In the words of President Eisenhower's Assistant Gordon Gray (1958–60), the NSC Secretariat did "not itself make policy recommendations," rather it scrutinized departmental proposals and suggested policy alternatives or additions meriting consideration.[9] The Kennedy Administration views the NSC staff as exclusively a Presidential instrument, "composed of men who can serve equally well in the process of planning and in that of operational followup."[10]

The principal source of the policy recommendations considered by the National Security Council in the Eisenhower years was the NSC Planning Board, an innovation of the Eisenhower Administration. This powerful element of a potentially invisible government deserves special attention, although the Kennedy Administration has abandoned it. Because the Secretaries of State and Defense and other statutory members and advisers of the NSC are heads of vast administrative bureaucracies, they clearly cannot devote too much time to the time-consuming business of policy planning. Therefore each NSC member and adviser appointed a representative on the Planning Board, normally someone at the Assistant or Deputy Assistant Secretary level. As the size and complexity of national security organizations increased, even this group found it necessary to delegate much of the spadework to "Planning Board Assistants." Expectedly, there were assistants to these assistants. In effect, the process was brought

[9] "Role of the National Security Council in the Formulation of National Policy," paper presented September 11, 1959, at the annual meeting of the American Political Science Association, Washington, D.C., p. 13. See also Robert Cutler, "Defense Organization at the Policy Level," *General Electric Defense Quarterly*, January–March 1959, p. 11.

[10] Letter from McGeorge Bundy, Special Assistant to the President for National Security Affairs, to Senator Henry M. Jackson (D., Wash.), September 4, 1961. Reprinted in *Hearings*, "Organizing for National Security," Senate Government Operations Subcommittee on National Policy Machinery, Washington, D.C., 1961, p. 1338.

down to the day-by-day working level in each of the departments or agencies concerned, and as a result influence over top-level planning was diffused throughout the national security structure.

The principal device in the process was the Planning Board draft paper, and the anonymous assistants who worked on the early drafts of such a paper were influential in determining just what the final draft of the policy recommendation was to be. Similarly the Central Intelligence Agency, which supplied the factual background—the informational appraisal of the situation—for the choice of policy alternatives, was influential in determining the final recommendation, if not the final decision.

Under Eisenhower, NSC papers fell into four general categories: fundamental policy, such as a statement of basic American objectives in the annual national security policy paper; geographical policy with regard to particular nations, such as United States objectives in Franco-American relations; regional policy, such as goals regarding Southeast Asia; or functional papers, such as United States disarmament policy. In each category, many departmental and agency positions had to be "coordinated" or, to put it bluntly, compromised.

President Eisenhower's Special Assistant for National Security Affairs served as chairman of the Planning Board. Under Gordon Gray, in the second Eisenhower Administration, the Board met regularly twice a week for several hours. In an earlier period, under Robert Cutler, the energetic and driving "father" of a highly institutionalized NSC, shorter meetings were held three times a week.

If a topic were of major importance and normal complexity, several Planning Board meetings would occur before the members were convinced that all essential facts had been assembled and the views of all affected departments and agencies had been sought, "debated and integrated."[11] The practice began of attaching a price tag to each policy paper,

[11] Gray, *loc. cit.*, p. 6.

estimating the cost of a new policy or the expenditures involved in policy alternatives.

A Planning Board paper in final draft was discussed by the Joint Chiefs of Staff, who prepared written views to send to NSC before the paper was formally considered in an NSC meeting.

Even with this elaborate procedure, the President, technically at least, made the ultimate decision. In crisis situations the Planning Board could quickly produce a paper on a "crash" basis; and on occasion the NSC is known to have taken action without any participation by the Planning Board.[12] Such highly explosive and secret programs as the U-2 flights over Russia and plans to invade Castro's Cuba in 1960 or 1961 fall into this category. Beyond this, some of the most crucial Presidential decisions were and are made outside the formal NSC structure, such as the decision to defend Korea, the Korean truce, and Berlin policies prior to 1961.

One of the most significant changes in the security policy-making process instituted by the Kennedy Administration, both symbolically and procedurally, was the abolition of the Planning Board in an effort to place greater responsibility and initiative in the major departments, and on particular individuals within those departments, especially State and Defense.

Under Eisenhower, the Planning Board process frequently produced a watered-down, lowest-common-denominator paper, carefully worded so as not to violate the interests of separate, participant departments. The Planning Board did not usually develop imaginative, original policies that offered the President a clear choice of sharply defined alternatives, but rather a negotiated version of recommendations that would make the least possible change in the *status quo*. If alternatives were offered by means of "split" recommendation, these rarely reflected the real policy choices available but simply the basic divergences of interest among the several departments involved.

[12] *Ibid.*, p. 7.

Under Kennedy, the initiation of new policy guidelines and other planning papers for ultimate Presidential approval devolves largely upon the Secretary of State who relies heavily upon his Assistant Secretaries in charge of regional (such as Far Eastern) and functional (such as International Organization) affairs. They, in turn, are expected to consult closely, continually, and in large measure informally with representatives of other relevant departments and agencies. But the responsibility for recommendations and for coordination devolves far more sharply on an individual official than was the case during the Eisenhower Administrations.

On some extremely sensitive, explosive, or specialized functional matters, such as policy regarding Berlin, Laos, disarmament, or atomic testing, the initiation of policy or the recommendation of policy guidelines to the President is performed in the Presidential office or by a designated agency—such as some branch of the Pentagon or Central Intelligence Agency —under close White House supervision.

In the first years of the Kennedy Administration some of the policy coordinating and forward planning functions once left to the Planning Board were handled in weekly informal luncheon meetings called by the State Department and attended by planning officers from the Pentagon, CIA, and occasionally the United States Information Agency and the Bureau of the Budget. But these meetings did not produce planning documents or serve in a formal sense as a subordinate level of the National Security Council.

Kennedy also relies on what has come to be called the "Bundy Group," after the President's Special Assistant for National Security Affairs, who with his small staff acts as a catalytic agent for the President, on national security policy, keeping him informed on the latest intelligence and the actions and reactions of the line departments.

The Kennedy Administration abolished, in an Executive Order of February 19, 1961, the Operations Coordinating Board established by the Eisenhower Administration in September 1953 to see that the national security policies of the

President and the NSC were carried out and that government actions and programs had the intended effect.

Prior to 1953, the State Department had been the principal agency for the coordination and surveillance of foreign military programs. But until the OCB was created, there was no interdepartmental group with a Presidential mandate to coordinate national security programs.

At Presidential direction, the OCB was to take those NSC policies assigned to it by the President and "supervise their implementation in coordinated fashion by the proper departments and agencies."[13] By subsequent Order (No. 10700, February 27, 1957) the OCB was placed organizationally within the NSC structure.

It was recognized that the President's initials on an NSC paper, making it official national policy, would not automatically produce speedy implementation at all levels. By the time successive Planning Board drafts reached the NSC for deliberation and approval some of the language was almost inevitably very general, vague, or ambiguous; sometimes deliberately so.

Major national policy must always be interpreted at the operational level, and can often be changed by the way in which it is applied. Bureaucrats at the operational level have interests, loyalties, and ambitions that sometimes go beyond or clash with the allegiance expected by a temporary White House occupant. Each administrator has individual ideas about policies, particularly those falling within his special competence. It was in an attempt to meet and overcome this fact of administrative life that the OCB was constituted with the Under Secretary of State as its chairman and top officials from the defense, intelligence, foreign aid and foreign information agencies as its members.

The basic operational device used by the OCB in the Eisenhower years was the interdepartmental committee. The committee member whose department had the primary responsibility for carrying out a given policy served as chairman,

[13] National Security Council, *Operations Coordination Board*, Descriptive Handbook by OCB's Executive Office, February 1958, p. 1.

but the OCB representative on the committee was the normal channel of information to and from the OCB and the NSC. No member of the committee, including its chairman, possessed decisive authority. The State Department theoretically supplied foreign policy guidance. But, as has been suggested, most policies have to be "negotiated" with the various influential agencies of government, not only when the policy is being formulated but in the equally important act of carrying it out.

Giving life to policy decisions may in many instances be the most significant step in the entire process. When the OCB came to prepare what it called the "Operation Plan" for a national policy it was in effect interpreting that policy and stipulating how it was to be applied. Yet it remained far from the public and Congressional eye, an agency of invisible government.[14]

In the opinion of the incoming Kennedy Administration the OCB, like the Planning Board, was an ineffective administrative device. It did not "match the style of operation and coordination" of the new administration.[15] While it was directed by Presidential Executive Order to "provide for the integrated implementation of national security policies" by the various departments and agencies, the new leadership considered that, unless government-wide unanimity existed on an issue, OCB lacked authority, and that as an interdepartmental committee, representing often competing missions and interests, it had been given a task beyond the capacity of committees, in which no one man had effective authority.

In the order abolishing the OCB Kennedy announced that it "had been used for work which we plan to do in other ways. . . . First, we will center responsibility for much of the Board's work in the Secretary of State. He expects to rely particularly on the Assistant Secretaries in charge of regional

[14] For a detailed description of OCB, see *ibid.*; see also "Organizational History of the National Security Council," Study for Senate Government Operations Subcommittee on National Security Policy Machinery, August 1960, pp. 37–48.
[15] Letter, Bundy to Jackson, *loc. cit.*, p. 1337.

bureaus, and they in turn will consult closely with other departments and agencies." The new system was based upon a dual concept: that the Department of State should have primacy in all foreign affairs matters, with the Secretary of State as a kind of first secretary, at least in the realm of policies toward other nations; and that the responsibility for coordinating and carrying out national security policies should be assigned to an identifiable single official instead of to elaborate formal machinery. The President implied that he was going to take over OCB's job of seeing that Presidential decisions were appropriately applied at the operating level, "by maintaining direct communication with the responsible agencies, so that everyone will know what I have decided, while I in turn keep fully informed of the actions taken to carry out decisions."

II

Perhaps the best way for an outsider to try to evaluate overall NSC performance is from the public record of how major national security crises have been handled since the Council was created, incomplete though this record is.

The main events of the period between 1947 and 1950 included the Russians' blockade of land access to Berlin; the collapse of Nationalist China on the mainland; the creation of the North Atlantic alliance and the planned build-up of American military power; the unprecedented question of the impact of nuclear power as a military instrument of national policy and its effect upon the organization, size, and interrelationship of armed forces.

In facing these great events the available record hints that NSC played a formal but often ineffective role. President Truman appears to have had an ambiguous attitude toward it. On the one hand, it was the great deliberative body, helping the President guide national security policies. On the other, the President seems to have continued the old process of using groups of *ad hoc* advisers—the Bureau of the Budget acting in the President's name, the State Department, and the Joint Chiefs of Staff—to help him make independent decisions on issues over which they claimed primary jurisdiction.

Korea was an important test of America's decision-making mechanism. The North Korean invasion in June 1950, described in Chapter VI, came as a complete surprise. The United States was tragically unprepared. Thus the NSC, given its purpose, may be said to have—like central intelligence—failed its first major test. The American political leadership (President and State Department) and its military advisers (Joint Chiefs of Staff) were indeed "coordinated" on the position that South Korea need not be included within the "defense perimeter," but this was a policy that ignored the realities of power—it represented a purpose without power; accordingly it was inadequate policy. The failure was not in formal coordination, but in the substance of policy itself.

In the decision to resist Communist aggression in Korea the NSC as an institution was virtually ignored. As one careful case study of the decision concludes, the fact that the United States decided in *ad hoc* decisional units to resist aggression in Korea suggests that "a multidimensional crisis decision which requires top-level authority necessitates the formation of a key group which can escape organizational formality and normal procedures."[16] The NSC did meet, late in the first week of the North Korean attack, but an analysis of the decision suggests in retrospect that it played a minor role.[17]

Shortly before the Korean crisis, the NSC had been involved in its own organizational crises. Within the Administration feeling was widespread that the national security mechanism was performing inadequately. Attendance at NSC meetings was thought to have become so large and unwieldy that it inhibited frank discussion by responsible decision makers. The absence of the President from most NSC meetings often resulted in a less sharply focused discussion and

16 Richard C. Snyder and Glenn D. Paige, "The United States Decision to Resist Aggression in Korea," *Administrative Science Quarterly*, December 1958, p. 373.
17 *Idem.*

deprived the Chief Executive of full and direct expressions of views. An additional criticism was that individuals on the NSC staff, on loan from the various agencies, were increasingly cut off from their departments and often by-passed by Council members who regarded them as departmental expatriates. Further, the growth of special-purpose committees to handle special policy problems was fragmenting the organization.

These and other shortcomings were discussed within the Administration. Plans were underway for improving the NSC when the Korean War started. The war itself had an impact on the Council's structure and procedures; President Truman began to preside regularly over its meetings; and in July 1950 he issued a directive reorganizing the NSC and its staff.[18] In August he appointed a "Senior Staff," later to be transformed into the Planning Board.

The record of the NSC's role in the conduct of the Korean War is even more obscure than its activities prior to the war. One thing is certain: United States policy and strategy during the war were marked by a lack of precision and clarity. With all the elaborate machinery for political-military coordination, most decisions on military action in Korea, subsequent to the decision to intervene, were left up to General MacArthur. MacArthur's objective, apparently, was the reunification of Korea. Meanwhile, the NSC and the President seemed unaware of the possible implications or complications of the equivocal policy. The JCS, or MacArthur independently in the field, rather than the NSC often appeared to be setting the policy guidelines.

The NSC did produce a war objectives paper, approved by President Truman on September 11, 1950, which left MacArthur's objectives contingent upon actions by the Chinese Communists and Russia. If Russia or Red China entered the war, United Nations forces were to stay south of the 38th parallel.[19] This was a fuzzy statement, of the kind the NSC

---

[18] For a fuller discussion, see "Organizational History of the National Security Council," pp. 15-23.

[19] Truman, *op. cit.*, p. 359.

is so often accused of producing. But since the ultimate responsibility is the President's the NSC cannot be held mainly culpable.

When UN troops crossed the parallel early in October, in the words of one analyst, "perhaps the one most critical decision of the Korean War had been taken. But it had been taken in the worst way, for confused reasons, on deficient intelligence and with an inadequate appreciation of the risks."[20]

A number of significant changes occurred in the Administration during this turbulent period. General Marshall replaced Johnson as Secretary of Defense in September. A new chief of the Central Intelligence Agency, General Walter B. Smith, was appointed.

General Marshall's testimony in the 1951 "MacArthur Hearings" tells how the decision-making system worked under the new leadership in late 1950 and 1951. Military directives were initiated in JCS. If these did not seem to involve high policy, they were approved by the Defense Secretary and brought to the President by the Chairman of the Joint Chiefs. With the President's approval, the directives were transmitted to military commanders in the field. On questions of high policy, the matter was negotiated between the Pentagon and State Department, and a policy paper drafted for NSC's senior staff to consider. A policy recommendation would then be submitted for Presidential approval.[21] Significantly, the policy mechanism seemed to work more smoothly under one set of leaders than another, raising the familiar issue of the relative importance of quality of leadership and quality of organization. At any rate the system was guided more purposefully in a time of national emergency than during a period of what was called peace.

Even so, when crisis decisions had to be made, the formal NSC procedure was disregarded. The NSC as a group could not assist President Truman in his difficult dealings with General MacArthur after the Chinese Communist overt interven-

[20] Millis *et al.*, *Arms and the State*, p. 278.
[21] *Hearings*, Senate, Committees on Armed Services and Foreign Relations, 1951, "Military Situation in the Far East," pp. 326-27.

tion in the Korean War in November 1950. Yet President Truman's *Memoirs* make clear his heavy reliance upon the NSC for formal advice during these tense days.[22] NSC was, however, often used merely to give official sanction to policies that had been negotiated in less formal fashion among State Department leaders, the Secretary of Defense, and the Joint Chiefs of Staff. The war confronted the President with problems that neither State nor Defense was competent to deal with alone. The NSC provided a convenient forum for debate in the Presidential presence and for the negotiation of consensus among the President's deputies. The President could always informally summon his Secretaries of State and Defense, the Joint Chiefs, and his most trusted policy advisers. But if their advice was to be well grounded, it had to be based upon detailed thought and staff work that, within limits, a coordinating mechanism can provide.[23] The Korean experience suggests that a crucial factor in the effective functioning of the Presidency, no matter how it is organized, is a spirit of mutual trust and cooperation among decision makers and, most important of all, the ability and willingness of the Chief Executive to provide leadership in the exercise of his power and to assume unequivocal responsibility for decisions.

An experienced White House newsman[24] characterized the new style in national policy making brought to Washington in 1953 when he observed, "I don't believe that Eisenhower has ever used the expression 'my administration' or 'my cabinet.' If so, he has done it seldom. He speaks of *the* Cabinet or *the* Administration." The style was not radically new, but it contrasted with President Truman's and strikingly resembled the military staff system. Responsibilities, functions, and "papers" flowed up and down the hierarchy in routine, prescribed channels. Staff duties were more precisely assigned:

[22] See Truman, *op. cit.*, pp. 378–79; Neustadt, *Presidential Power*, pp. 139–42 and *passim*.

[23] *Arms and the State*, pp. 387–88.

[24] Robert J. Donovan, *Eisenhower: The Inside Story*, New York, Harper, 1956, p. 65.

there was a Special Assistant for National Security Affairs, a Presidential Staff Secretariat (managed by a Regular Army officer), a Cabinet Secretariat, and an Assistant to the President, who during Sherman Adams' tenure operated as Chief of Staff to the President with much greater authority than any of Truman's deputies had had.[25]

The Eisenhower Administration was pledged to end the Korean War, to lower taxes, reduce government expenditures, and balance the budget, while simultaneously waging a more aggressive Cold War against the Communist bloc. One of the early products of the super-staffed NSC mechanism was the so-called "new look" in military strategy announced in a speech before the Council on Foreign Relations by Secretary of State John Foster Dulles on January 12, 1954. The heart of this policy—often termed "massive retaliation"—was to substitute atomic weapons for large numbers of men armed with conventional weapons. It was perhaps the most significant policy decision of the 1950s, but its essence dated back to the 1948 report of President Truman's Air Policy Commission, "Survival in the Air Age," which advocated a "new strategy" including deterrence of the enemy by "the prospect of a counterattack of the utmost violence." This required an Air Force capable of inflicting unacceptable damage upon the cities and industries of the Soviet Union, and a "counterforce" capacity to attack the enemy's strategic striking forces.

Eisenhower's "new look" strategy was heavily influenced by the desire to save money and incorporate nuclear weapons into strategic doctrines. And despite the proclamation that such policies would be fully debated within the governmental staff system, basic decisions appear to have been imposed upon the Pentagon by budget-minded civilians, led by the Secretary of the Treasury, with the sympathetic and detailed

[25] Louis W. Koenig, *The Invisible Presidency*, New York, Rinehart, 1960; Sherman Adams, *Firsthand Report*, New York, Harper, 1961. The most detailed study of selected high policy decisions during this period is Warner R. Schilling, Paul Y. Hammond, and Glenn H. Snyder, *Strategy, Politics, and Defense Budgets*, Columbia University Press, 1962.

support of the President, the Chairman of the Joint Chiefs of Staff, and Secretary of State.

Dulles stated publicly that in planning the new policies the President and his advisers "as represented by the National Security Council, had to take some basic policy decisions." Army and Navy chiefs dissented strongly from the policy adopted. But the "new look" was announced to the world as a "basic policy decision" of the NSC, the result of the paper NSC-162, worked up during the summer of 1953 and "adopted" on October 7, 1953.[26]

The policy was rather narrowly based on the notion that the only enemy to worry about was Russia, and the great threat, total war. Even though Secretary Dulles referred to retaliation "by means and at places of our own choosing" little attention was given to what many regarded as the more imminent threat: limited or ambiguous Communist aggression, to which a nuclear-weapon response would not be appropriate. The "new look" assumption was that general war or large-scale limited war would be waged with nuclear weapons; and that a large-scale "conventional" war was no longer a possibility. So it might be said that the NSC again failed to achieve its ideal goal: balancing foreign policy commitments with proper military force and force levels, with particular relevance to the potential enemy's capabilities. The record between 1954 and 1960 suggests in retrospect that even with the elaborate NSC machinery, the nation's foreign policy and military doctrine continued to be out of balance.

Within months after the declaration of the "new look," the nation was involved in another crisis: the deterioration of the French position in the Indo-China war. Though in one sense a French war, the United States was paying a large share of its cost (over one-third) and supplying large amounts of materiel and technical aid. Declared American policy seemed to suggest that Indo-China's freedom from Communist control was vital to United States interests. But when it came to a showdown, America failed to have the kind of

[26] Walter Millis, "The NSC," New York *Herald Tribune*, February 25, 1954.

force, or the will, to intervene unilaterally to prevent a French defeat by Viet-Minh (Communist) forces and the partition of Indo-China in July 1954. Granted there were additional complications with America's allies, with Congress, and with the political paradox of a situation in which the United States was torn between allegiance to France and the recognition that as a nation we must not be identified with colonialism, national policy, owner, and will were nevertheless out of balance.

Meantime Eisenhower was publicly proclaiming the "domino theory." Indo-China was the first domino. If it were pushed over by the Communists, Burma, Malaya, Thailand, and Indonesia might topple. Yet while the President was insisting on the importance of Indo-China to United States security, a truce was being made in Korea, spending for American armed forces was being reduced, and some American troops were being withdrawn from Asia.

As one observer of this period has written: "Superimposed on the whole picture of the development of American policy in 1954 is the impression one gets that the problem came before the President piece by piece and not altogether at the same pace as events on the battlefield."[27]

Within a few months of the domino theory proclamation France had agreed to a cease-fire and partition of Vietnam. Part of a domino, at least, had fallen, but without the immediate broader consequences predicted. The Southeast Asia Treaty Organization founded on September 8, 1954, grew out of this experience, but the United States continued, in the Eisenhower years, to cut back Army manpower and other "limited war" forces, seemingly ignoring relevant experience.

In the latter half of the 1950s, Russian and Chinese achievements in military technology and economic growth raised further doubts about the adequacy of America's decision-making machinery. The series of crises after Indo-China —Formosa and the Chinese offshore islands, Suez, Lebanon, access to Berlin, the feared "missile gap" and competition in

[27] Donovan, *op. cit.*, p. 262.

outer space, arms control, disarmament, weapons-testing problems, the Communist foothold in Cuba—were dealt with through the NSC, at least formally. But whether the system dealt with the really fundamental security issues and allowed innovative proposals to be adopted in good time remains a question. During the eight years of the Eisenhower Administration, guidelines for American diplomacy in general and in particular for disarmament negotiations, for domestic and international economic policy, for military manpower in the technological revolution, for a rationalized defense organization, and for proper organization and support for scientific research, were set in a restrictive, unimaginative way.

President Kennedy came into office aware of the NSC's weaknesses and committed to the idea that the President should exert strong personal leadership. Several years before his election, he commented on the NSC's shortcomings. "The massive paper work and the clearance procedure, the compulsion to achieve agreement among departments and agencies," he wrote, "often produce policy statements which are only a mongrelization of clashing views."[28] The capacity for leadership, the future President noted, along with "clear articulation of policy at the pinnacle" are "an essential dynamic of our system of government." He warned that the central policy-making mechanisms could become "mere vendors of compromise," and later declared, implicitly criticizing Eisenhower's use of the NSC, "It is the President alone who must make the major decisions of our foreign policy."[29]

In the early days of his Administration, Kennedy attempted to institute the concept of personal rather than collective responsibility, not only in his own office but in the major functional areas of government. As a student of Presidential power and an experienced politician if not administrator, he showed every intention of actively using the great potential powers of the Presidency, in sharp contrast to his predecessor.

[28] "A Democrat Looks at Foreign Policy," *Foreign Affairs*, October 1957, p. 57.
[29] Speech to National Press Club, Washington, D.C., January 14, 1960.

In Kennedy's first years, no change was made in the statutes regarding the NSC. The President reasserted the principle that his predecessors had stressed: that the NSC gave advice only; that *he* made the decisions; and that the NSC was no more than an institutional vehicle to be used according to the incumbent President's attitude toward his great office. Nonetheless, President Kennedy and his associates, including a number of academic intellectuals who were students of the Presidency and of national decision making, set about to develop new processes for using the NSC. In addition to the abolition of the Planning Board and OCB, two major changes became evident early in the new Administration.[30]

First, formal NSC meetings were held less frequently than in the Eisenhower years. "Much that used to flow routinely to the weekly meetings of the Council is now settled in other ways, by separate meetings with the President, by letters, by written memorandums, and at levels below that of the President,"[31] wrote the President's Special Assistant for National Security Affairs, McGeorge Bundy, in September 1961. The new concept was that meetings of the NSC were called only after the President had decided that a policy issue was ready for NSC deliberation. In other words, the NSC was only one of several instruments of discussion and counsel available to the President.

President Kennedy made it clear that he wanted unvarnished information from the heart of government, not information processed and packaged through hierarchical, interdepartmental committees. His practice of telephoning directly to a minor official for information or opinion was a widely publicized feature of the regime in 1961–62. The new operating concept was direct Presidential access to the foreign policy and defense domains. And Kennedy, unlike Eisenhower, did not appoint a single White House civilian chief of staff. In 1962 at least three aides seemed to be filling the role played

[30] These were outlined in the letter, Bundy to Jackson, *loc. cit.*, pp. 1336–38.
[31] Letter, Bundy to Jackson, *loc. cit.*

by Sherman Adams as Eisenhower's staff chief. Kennedy's apparent hope was to maintain open channels of communication within his Administration, making his office simultaneously time-consuming and difficult to fill but more responsible and powerful in policy making.

"The National Security Council is one instrument among many; it must never be made an end in itself," wrote Presidential Assistant McGeorge Bundy. The role of the NSC staff was to see that a careful record of decisions and responsibility was kept, either by the department with the primary responsibility or by the NSC Secretariat for the President.

Second, there has been a determination to erase the sharp distinction between planning and operation, a distinction "real enough at the extremes of the daily cable traffic and long-range assessment of future possibilities" but breaking down in "most of the business of decision and action."[32] President Kennedy has expected his national security staff members, fewer in number than in the previous Administration, to be both planners and operators, thereby enabling him to control planning, policy, and implementation more firmly and effectively, for the same deputies who assist him in making policy also oversee its application.

It is too early at this writing to judge the success of the new techniques of the Kennedy Administration. In April 1961, before the new techniques had been fully applied, decisions were made in the abortive Cuban invasion that can only be described as ill-advised, and that brought disastrous consequences.

This experience was undoubtedly very much in the President's mind in October 1962 when he assembled an "Executive Committee" of the NSC to aid him in decisions and actions on the existence of long-range Russian missiles in Cuba. In this case the President, in effect, reconstituted the NSC by including in the committee such non-statutory members as the Attorney General, the Secretary of the Treasury, and the UN Ambassador; excluding a statutory member, the Di-

[32] Letter, Bundy to Jackson, *loc. cit.*

rector of the Office of Emergency Planning; and apparently giving the Director of Central Intelligence and the JCS Chairman, by law merely advisers to the NSC, the same role as full members. In other words, in the emergency, President Kennedy, paying little attention to formal institutions, called upon trusted individuals who in his eyes occupied positions of pertinent responsibility to advise him as a "Crisis Cabinet."

This seems to indicate that the existence of statutory Presidential national security advisers and institutions has little predictable meaning in actual decision-making habits of a President. Since his is the sole responsibility, he must maintain the freedom to seek advice from any source he chooses.

III

The basic concepts of the NSC mechanism created in 1947 prompt important questions: Is it possible for the NSC to make a narrow delineation of "only those issues affecting national security"? What about health, education, highway, and welfare programs? Does not a breakdown in labor-management relations in a major private enterprise—steel, communications, or transport, for example—pose a major national security issue? The fact that with only five statutory members some twenty officials have been in regular NSC attendance in recent years suggests that problems of national security must, in practice, be broadly defined.

In today's complex world is it realistic to say that the NSC gives advice only? Does the President really have the power of decision? On how many decisional issues worked out through a vast, elaborately staffed interdepartmental mechanism and based upon intelligence reports and interpretations of information that even a superhuman President could seldom challenge effectively is the President going to "decide" contrary to the NSC "recommendation"? And on what kinds of national issues involving strategy, allocation of resources, and normally conflicting functions are the heads of various government departments or agencies going to perform as national statesmen rather than as spokesmen for a parochial departmental point of view?

Given the ponderous mechanism of national security decision making, is it wise for any President to commit himself to a procedure by which all important decisions are to be made within the NSC framework? Conversely, is it wise to leave great issues to more independent or even individual judgment? Obviously there may be times and issues when such a commitment will not be in the national interest. A President must try to maintain discretionary power to avoid potential strangulation of the Presidency by a routinized decision-making system. Unless he has that power, efficient, coherent, democratic government is endangered, as the Kennedy Administration is apparently fully aware.

Available evidence indicates that the NSC failed in the 1947–60 period to meet its own operational concepts. Rather than serving as a closely knit forum of Presidential advisers who engaged in cold and hard analysis and discussion of the most critical security problems facing the nation, the NSC, particularly in the 1953–60 period, became a highly institutionalized, bureaucratic staff system for generating policy recommendations and attempting to supervise their implementation. It concerned itself with harmonizing competing or conflicting departmental positions on major foreign policy issues and the development of policy papers stating in broad terms national policy toward various areas of the world. At the same time, it neglected such crucial national security problems as correlating foreign policy commitments with capabilities. Indeed, according to a 1960 Senate study, departments and agencies were said to "work actively and successfully to keep critical policy issues outside the NSC system," rather than submit their jealously guarded interests to an interdepartmental forum where the outcome would be uncertain.

The alleged advantage of the Eisenhower system was that, in the words of one of its former managers, Robert Cutler, the NSC procedure eliminated "insofar as is possible a most

serious threat to the rational and orderly conduct of government: *ex parte* decisions by the highest authority."[33] His successor, Gordon Gray, wrote that "President Eisenhower has
made it a practice not to determine, on the unilateral recommendation of one department head, national security matters
which are clearly of interest to more than one responsible
department."[34] But in the process innovations or urgently
needed new policies were vetoed or watered-down to a meaningless compromise before they ever reached the Presidential
desk. President Eisenhower seemed to prefer to have issues
fully threshed out before they came to him, so that his decision could be a simple "yes" or "no." Perhaps more *ex parte*
decisions were needed for effective democratic policy making.
National security policies in the making must not only march
up policy hill under the command of half-a-dozen leaders,
but, having reached the summit, march down again, whether,
as formerly, under the direction of a committee (the Operations Coordinating Board), or, more recently, that of a single
deputized agent of the President or Secretary of State.

In one sense, NSC has fulfilled its basic function. As an
advisory agency to the President, it has produced national
security policy papers on most major defense problems. These
papers, once approved by the President, represent national
policy. Duly recorded and, bearing at least TOP SECRET
classification, they are then stored in the proper vaults. Few
Americans, including members of Congress, ever see these
papers. As outsiders all we can know is that such papers exist.
But a State Department area chief once reportedly declared:
"If the decisions have to be made on a basis of the NSC
papers we see, God help us."[35]

Decisions in today's complex and fast-changing international setting can best be made by reliance on responsible
individuals, rather than upon overly compromised "position"
papers or elaborate institutions. The Kennedy Administra-

---

[33] Cutler, *loc. cit.,* p. 11.

[34] Gray, *loc. cit.,* p. 12.

[35] Quoted in Bernard K. Gordon, "The Top of Policy Hill," *Bulletin of the Atomic Scientists,* September 1960, p. 291.

tion's innovations in national security decision-making techniques can be applauded as offering better promise of both defense and democracy. But if their promise is to be fulfilled, the innovative spirit must be kept alive—a particularly great challenge within any huge bureaucratic system.

CHAPTER III

DEPARTMENT OF DEFENSE: UNITY OR CONFEDERATION?

I

To create and manage the military power required in pursuit of the objectives set by the President and the National Security Council is the particular responsibility of one NSC member—the Secretary of Defense. From General Pershing's massive walnut desk in the Pentagon, the Defense Secretary presides over an establishment employing 3,750,000 military and civilian persons situated all around the globe and spending each year an amount greater than the total national budgets of England, France, West Germany, and Italy combined.[1] He "presides over" but does not fully control this vast enterprise. Here, in the largest and by far the most expensive sector of American government, we are face to face with the issue of centralization versus decentralization—an issue of far-reaching impact on the problem of defense and democracy.

American armed services are engaged in world-wide activities, from the operation of diaper services overseas to radio broadcasting networks in foreign lands. At the end of 1962, more than one million American servicemen were on duty in forty-one foreign nations around the globe. Defense Department exchange-of-foreign-military-persons programs—in which foreign military personnel are exchanged with similar Americans for limited periods of training—are more extensive than those of civilian agencies. Pentagon officials, civilian

[1] More than $350 billion in taxpayers' money was spent by the Pentagon from 1954 to 1962. The 1963 bill adds up to more than $50 billion.

and military, make many more speeches and write several times as many articles on foreign policy subjects as officials of the Department of State. And, as one observer has commented, through its nation-wide links with battalions of individuals and organizations (such as veterans groups, large industrial complexes, mayors and other officials of towns adjoining military establishments), the Defense Department has "a built-in system of communication with the American people unequaled in scale by anything available to other Federal agencies."[2]

In his farewell address to the nation as President, Dwight D. Eisenhower voiced concern about the impact upon American democracy of such "an immense military establishment and a large arms industry . . . new in American experience," adding that "the total influence—economic, political, even spiritual—is felt in every city, every State house, every office of the Federal government." He recognized the "imperative need" for a mighty defense establishment, but noted its "grave implications" for the "very structure of our society."[3] Our concern in this chapter is not primarily with the structure of American society, but with the structure and procedures of the Department of Defense as the focal point for significant decisions about national defense requirements.

Pentagon organization does not present a simple picture. Edwin Weisl, a New York lawyer working as a special counsel for a Senate subcommittee investigating the defense program in 1958, aptly referred to the defense establishment as "this complex and difficult and sometimes un-understandable organization . . . this tremendous chart of bureau on top of bureau, committee on top of committee, office on top of office . . . the most complicated jigsaw puzzle that ever was invented."[4]

[2] Waldemar A. Neilsen, "Huge, Hidden Impact of the Pentagon," *The New York Times Magazine*, June 25, 1961, p. 9.

[3] Address to the Nation, January 17, 1961.

[4] Edwin Weisl, Chief Special Counsel, Senate Preparedness Investigating Subcommittee, quoted by John Osborne, "The Man and the Plan," *Life*, April 21, 1958, p. 118.

The Pentagon Building, like the organizational chart of the Department of Defense, is massive and complex though deceptively simple in basic design. It contains about 160,000 miles of telephone cable and has housed as many as 32,000 persons, from the Secretary of Defense down to the clerk in its jewelry shop. This city of workers is both the heart of a partially "unified" defense establishment and the world's largest business enterprise, spending more than $50 billion a year and with physical assets estimated in 1962 at $158 billion.

In theory, this military colossus serves as an instrument of national policy, which in turn, according to the American ideal, is based upon the consent of the governed. The armed forces, their organization and weapons systems, are, ideally, instruments of government to be used in pursuit of national purpose as defined in the consensus achieved through the political process. This basic idea underlies modern-day concepts of "civilian control" of the military: armed forces must always remain instruments of national policy.

As we have seen, modern technology and the geopolitical facts of life tend to dim the distinction between "purely military" and "purely political" factors in national policy making. But the meaning of civilian control need not be blurred, even in an age of radical changes in the nature of military professionalism. The guiding concept of civilian supremacy was once succinctly stated by a professional military officer turned President: "Basic decisions related to the military forces must be made by politically accountable civilian officials," said Eisenhower.[5] President Kennedy, reaffirming this principle, more recently declared: "Our arms must be subject to ultimate civilian control and command at all times, in war as well as peace."[6] Whether this condition has prevailed in the period since World War II—and grave doubts exist that it has—has been heavily influenced by the organi-

[5] Message to Congress, Reorganization Plan No. 6 of 1953, April 30, 1953.

[6] Special message to Congress on the defense budget, March 28, 1961.

zation for military defense, which in turn is conditioned by the American constitutional system.

The most significant and controversial features of defense organization in the United States are: (1) the existence of four huge military institutions, each with a distinct tradition, a sense of service identification, and a public following and friends in powerful sections of the industrial community and on Capitol Hill; (2) the revolution in technology that is not only changing the nature of military professionalism but is believed by many to be erasing the traditional organizational rationale for separating armed services according to mode of transport—land, sea, and air (in which traditional service, for example, does the long-range missile belong?); (3) the widespread belief that changes in the existing administrative structure are needed to accommodate the new technology; (4) the strong differences of opinion as to how best to alter the existing organization in order to promote simultaneously efficient fighting forces with the requisite *esprit de corps* and logical and purposeful allocation of resources and effective democratic decision making; and (5) the fact that while the President as Commander in Chief of the armed forces and Chief Executive has the initiative and final say in defense decisions, his authority and power are shared with Congress.

The question to be explored here is whether the organizational arrangements in the Department of Defense foster or impede the coherent resolution of the issues of purpose, strategy, and organization, and are in keeping with the pursuit of the ideals of security and democratic government. If not—that is, if politically responsible leaders cannot in reality make the decisions about military forces that rationally accommodate both the implications of technology and the requirements of self-government—this is indeed a serious indictment of the organizational structure. A corollary question is whether power, authority, and responsibility within the defense establishment are properly allocated, defined, and identifiable, or whether the defense establishment, reflecting the American distrust of concentration of government power relevant in an earlier age, is characterized by fragmented authority and ill-defined responsibility.

Hoping to "provide for the common defense," Pentagon activities proceed under a deliberately ambiguous working concept and structure. In 1947 Congress enacted legislation that partially "unified" the separate armed forces under the Secretary of Defense, and since then, as one veteran observer commented, "There have been only two modes of life in the Pentagon: preparation for the next reorganization and recovery from the last one."[7]

II

The concept of a highly centralized or "unified" defense establishment had the support in 1945–47 of President Truman, the War Department, and the many supporters of air power; and its promise of economy and efficiency had wide public appeal. Yet Congress blocked the enactment of proposals for a highly centralized defense system, fearing a loss of power by Congressional units—although it had itself "unified" naval and military affairs committees in the House and Senate in the Legislative Reorganization Act of 1946. The upshot was compromise legislation, strongly influenced by a carefully worked out plan commissioned by Secretary of the Navy Forrestal and developed under the aegis of Ferdinand Eberstadt, a civilian consultant.

The term "unification" was itself variously defined, as a summary of three of the most important organizational issues of 1944–47 and their resolution in the National Security Act of 1947 shows:

1. *A single war department versus three separate departments.* The Army advocated a single department, the Navy insisted upon confederation with the Defense Secretary as a relatively powerless coordinator, and the Air Force put its existence as a separate department first and a unified Department of Defense second. The final outcome was a National

[7] Col. William E. Depuy, *Army*, April 1961, p. 30.

Military Establishment and three separate departments. The office of Defense Secretary was created but with ambiguous powers.[8] These powers, over the years, have gradually increased, at the expense of the separate armed forces departments and the Congress. But the authority of the Defense Secretary *vis-à-vis* the separate services, the Joint Chiefs of Staff, and the Congress remains the most basic and controversial issue of defense organization.

2. A *single chief of staff*. The Army supported a single chief assisted by a general staff; the Navy opposed this as dangerous centralization and risky separation of authority and responsibility. The Navy argued, with powerful bipartisan support on Capitol Hill, that to separate the JCS planning role from the active leadership of the armed services would produce unrealistic plans and pose the threat of cutting off the final decision makers, such as the Secretary of Defense, the NSC, and the President, from important dissenting views and alternative choices. The Navy won the day when the concept was adopted of Joint (confederated) Chiefs of Staff, with a *joint* staff, both organized on the basis of equal representation of the Army, Air Force, and Navy (including the Marines). Each service chief wears two hats—that of head of his service and that of JCS member.

3. *Roles and missions of the Army and Air Force versus the Navy and Marine Corps*. The Army had hoped that in the postwar shaping of the military structure the Marine Corps would be strictly limited in size and function, and the corps' missions restricted virtually to the shore line. The Army lost this battle; the Marines were accorded full divisional strength and full participation in amphibious operations. The Air

---

[8] In addition various coordinating devices were established: a National Security Council, a Central Intelligence Agency, and a National Security Resources Board. In general the new structure followed the lines suggested by the Navy's Eberstadt Committee Report. A good, if somewhat pro-Navy account is found in Robert G. Albion and Robert H. Connery, *Forrestal and the Navy*, Columbia University Press, 1962, Ch. 11; the most complete general account is Hammond, *Organizing for Defense*; also useful is Stanley, *American Defense and National Security*.

Force, for its part, had hoped to take over from the Navy important aspects of anti-submarine warfare and the control of land-based aircraft, to protect shipping and for reconnaissance. The Air Force lost. The assignment of basic service functions has remained to date virtually unaltered since the 1947 Act, despite the incompatibility of traditionally assigned missions and new weapons. Attempts to re-evaluate the situation in keeping with modern technology continue to run into the active opposition of the supporters of the separate services, notably in Congress.

Much "unification" history and most of the basic organizational concepts are contained in the words—and between the lines—of the often-overlooked "Declaration of Policy," which is, in effect, the "Preamble" to the National Security Act of 1947.[9] This part of the statute expresses the "Intent of Congress," with deliberate and significant ambiguity as follows:

> In enacting this legislation, it is the intent of Congress to provide a comprehensive program for the future security of the United States; to provide for the establishment of integrated policies and procedures for the departments, agencies, and functions of the Government relating to the national security; to provide three military departments, separately administered, for the operation and administration of the Army, the Navy (including naval aviation and the United States Marine Corps), and the Air Force, with their assigned combat and service components; to provide for their authoritative coordination and unified direction under civilian control of the Secretary of Defense but not to merge them; to provide for the effective strategic direction of the armed forces and for their operation under unified control and for their integration into an efficient team of land, naval, and air forces but not to establish a single Chief of Staff over the armed forces nor an armed forces general staff (but this is not to be interpreted as applying to the Joint Chiefs of Staff or Joint Staff).[10]

[9] Public Law 253, 80th Congress, July 27, 1947, 61 *Stat.* 495.
[10] National Security Act of 1947, as amended.

Here we have a document that calls simultaneously for "integration" *and* "separation"; for "unified direction" *but not* merger; strategic "integration" but *not a unified* staff by which this can be accomplished. This hodgepodge emerged from sharply varying approaches to defense organization, the Presidency, the National Security Council, the Cabinet, the Secretary of Defense, and the place of military advice in decision making, and from the aggressive attitude of Congress toward its role in defense policy making.

The 1947 Act was a compromise between those, like President Truman, Secretary of War Robert Patterson, General Marshall, General Eisenhower, and most Army and Air leaders, who, initially at least, had favored a centralized civil and military setup and those, like Navy Secretary Forrestal, his adviser Ferdinand Eberstadt, most Navy leaders, and some influential members of Congress—notably Democratic Rep. Carl Vinson, Georgia, and Senator David Walsh, Massachusetts—who feared a "monolithic" organization that would not only merge, but submerge the Navy—particularly naval aviation and possibly the Marine Corps, and chip away at Congressional influence. The Navy raised the further objection that a centralized structure would be unwieldy and inefficient.

Walt W. Rostow observes of the 1944–47 unification controversy: "It was a struggle of bureaucratic politics and of men—not of military ideas."[11] Underlying the organizational debate was a major strategic issue of the time: What can airpower do? But though there were some discussions of the potentialities and limitations of strategic airpower, little attention was given to the main issues: national purpose, strategic doctrine and military requirements of the postwar decade. More often the debate centered on the issues of which service was to perform which function with how much money. One fundamental issue was summarized by Admiral Richmond Kelly Turner, testifying before the Senate Naval Affairs Committee in 1946:

[11] *The United States in the World Arena*, New York, Harper, 1960, p. 175.

Frankly, I believe the Navy as a whole objects to the so-called unification because under any system the Navy will be a numerical minority and the Army, and the Air Force, a military majority . . . [which] will always be in a better political position than the Navy. Because the Navy has had and should retain in the future its position as the first line of military security for the United States, I believe the Navy will never willingly agree to a consolidation of national military forces in any manner that will silence the Navy's voice in military affairs or materially restrict its present responsibilities.

In sum, the 1947 unification compromise was characterized by administrative federalism, distrust of effective concentration of power, a busy Congressional hand in details of defense requirements and organization, and a general disregard for an accelerating technology and for questions of national purpose and the reality of possible enemies who might have to be engaged or, at best, deterred.

James V. Forrestal, who effectively fought the proposals to establish a strong Secretary of Defense, became the first Secretary of Defense. He was not long in office before he realized that his authority was much too limited to allow him to function effectively as administrator of a sprawling defense establishment in which the main elements were competing fiercely for a larger share of limited resources. His first annual report called for a strengthening of his authority and much greater centralization than he had been willing, as Secretary of the Navy, to admit was advisable. Upon retiring as Defense Secretary, Forrestal wrote to the chairman of the Senate Armed Services Committee, Millard Tydings, pointing to weaknesses in the unification statute that he had not foreseen. "I am . . . convinced that a failure to endow [the Secretary] with sufficient authority to control effectively the conduct of our military affairs will force upon us far greater security risks than will be the case if singleness of control and responsibility are achieved."[12] Forrestal's recommendations,

[12] Quoted in Murray Green, "Today's First Line of Defense," *Air Force and Space Digest*, July 1961, p. 60.

along with those of the (Hoover) Commission on Organization of the Executive Branch of Government—and its 1948 force report—prompted a further defense reorganization in 1949.

III

Since 1947 the trend of defense organization, on both the civil and military sides (OSD and JCS), has continued toward greater centralization. The 1949 and 1953 amendments produced some thirty-odd "Mr. Secretaries" and a huge secretariat which has numbered as high as twenty-five hundred persons in the Pentagon superstructure. The importance and power of the Chairman of the JCS have also increased. But the "states' rights" of the separate services have remained, as has their power of "interposition" in the strategic planning process.

In the 1949 amendments the Army-Navy-Air Force Departments lost their cabinet rank and became "military" departments with the Secretary of Defense speaking for all three in the National Security Council. At the same time the word "general" was omitted from the phrase giving the Secretary of Defense "direction, authority and control" over the Service Departments; and the "reserved powers" clause for the separate Departments, limiting the power of the Defense Secretary to specified authority, was eliminated. But transfer, reassignment, abolition, or consolidation of combat functions (roles and missions) was prohibited, and Congress had to be kept fully informed of any other consolidation of functions.

Two further legislative enactments of importance occurred in 1952. One created a Director of Installations and a Defense Supply Management Agency within the Department of Defense. The Director was charged with coordinating military public works planning and construction; the Agency, with developing a single catalog system and programs of interservice supply standardization. The other established a floor under the authorized personnel strength of the Marine Corps, and provided for the participation of the Marine Commandant in meetings of the Joint Chiefs of Staff when matters of concern to the Marine Corps were to be discussed.

The next major change came in 1953, following the Korean War and the 1952 Presidential election. There was considerable dissatisfaction in many quarters about the defense-organization performance during the Korean War. A rapid turnover in the Secretaryship had occurred during this period, with Louis Johnson succeeded by General George C. Marshall who was in turn followed by Robert A. Lovett. After the election of 1952 the outgoing Mr. Lovett submitted to President Truman a detailed letter criticizing Pentagon organization and recommending more authority for the Secretary and improvements in the strategic planning process. Experience had convinced him that the existing defense structure "would require drastic reorganization to fight a war." Among other things, Lovett had found it "extremely difficult for the Joint Chiefs of Staff to maintain a broad non-service point of view. Since they wear two hats . . . it is difficult for them to detach themselves from the hopes and ambitions of their own service. . . ."[13]

General Eisenhower was an early advocate of defense centralization and unification. As President he appointed a seven-man committee, headed by Nelson A. Rockefeller, to study defense organization and to make recommendations. The Rockefeller Committee's Report, submitted in April 1953, resulted in transmittal to Congress of Reorganization Plan No. 6. Some of the proposed changes were described to Congress as "terrifying" by Ferdinand Eberstadt, and organizations such as the Navy League continued to warn of the dangers to our form of government of increasing centralization within the defense establishment. Concepts of federalism, free enterprise, and competitive capitalism were equated with the organizational requirements of the military establishment. Congress made an unsuccessful attempt to reject the plan, but it went into effect on June 30, 1953.

Under the 1953 reorganization, service autonomy was re-

[13] Letter, Lovett to Truman, November 18, 1952.

duced still further by making the Chairman of the Joint
Chiefs of Staff responsible for managing the Joint Staff and
selecting its membership; eliminating various boards and
agencies with equal service representation; and tripling the
number of Assistant Secretaries,[14] bringing the total to ten,
including the General Counsel. Assistant Secretaries of Defense soon became "staff executives" in charge of major functions: legislative and public affairs, international security
affairs, manpower, research and development, financial management, supply and logistics, properties and installation,
health and medical services, applications engineering and
General Counsel.[15]

Between 1953 and 1958 the controversy was nurtured and
sustained by accelerating technological developments, which
continued to challenge existing defense concepts and to ag-
gravate both the normal competition among the services for
defense dollars and the conflict over assignment of "missions."
Proposals for further centralization of authority in the Office
of the Secretary of Defense and for a more unified strategic
planning system remained at the heart of the problem, entwined with the debate over the kinds and levels of forces
needed for deterrence of general war and for limited war.
Critics of the defense structure as reorganized in 1953, including Senator Stuart Symington, many Air Force generals,
some Army leaders and a number of academic observers, continued to decry the loose federalism that they claimed still
characterized the relationship of the Defense Secretary to the
armed services and of the services to one another.

In late 1957 and 1958 the rising cost of weapons systems,
and public shock at the discovery of Russian progress in technological development, particularly Russian exploits in space,

[14] The main effect in most cases was to change the title of existing
statutory positions. For example the Chairman, Research and Development Board became Assistant Secretary, Research and Development.

[15] The legislative and public affairs functions were separated into
two secretariats in 1957, and research and development and applications engineering were combined into "Research and Engineering."

intensified the criticisms.[16] Simultaneously interservice rivalries were aggravated by inflation and by ceilings on the total defense funds available.

IV

Following a White House-Pentagon study,[17] President Eisenhower early in 1958 moved on three fronts: he ordered important organizational changes that did not require legislation; he submitted to Congress personally drafted legislation for Pentagon reorganization; and he issued statements, including personal letters to several hundred influential friends around the country, designed to engender support for his proposals and to counter expected opposition to his reform measures, particularly on Capitol Hill and in naval circles.

In brief outline, the Administration's 1958 reorganization program called for increasing the authority of the Secretary

[16] In addition to the continuing advocacy of Department of Defense reorganization by such groups as the Air Force Association, a number of influential studies and reports were published in the wake of Russian sputniks which sharply criticized existing defense organization. These included: Rockefeller Brothers Fund, *International Security, The Military Aspect*, Special Studies Report 2, Garden City, New York, Doubleday Headline Books, January 1958; Kintner and associates, *Forging a New Sword*; and, presumably, the secret report of the Gaither Committee in late 1957. Henry A. Kissinger's *Nuclear Weapons and Foreign Policy*, New York, Harper, 1957, was also highly critical of existing defense organization. Important ideas circulating within the RAND Corporation during this period can be found in A. C. Enthoven and H. S. Rowen, "Analysis of Defense Organization," RAND Paper P-1640, 1959.

[17] Instructed by President Eisenhower to reorganize the Pentagon, as one of his first major tasks as new Secretary of Defense, Secretary Neil H. McElroy appointed a Special Assistant for this purpose. The assistant was Charles A. Coolidge, Boston lawyer and former Assistant Secretary of Defense. Consultants used were JCS Chairman Nathan Twining; former JCS Chairmen General Omar Bradley and Admiral Arthur Radford; William C. Foster, former Deputy Secretary of Defense; Nelson Rockefeller, then Chairman of President's Advisory Committee on Government Organization; and General Alfred M. Gruenther.

of Defense in strategic planning, in administration of the defense establishment, and in military operation; for greater military unification of strategic and tactical planning; and for using the unified field commands as operational instruments for implementing President Eisenhower's oft-stated view that "separate ground, sea and air warfare is gone forever."

The Administration-drafted legislative proposals submitted to Congress were quickly answered by the counterproposals contained in a Congressionally drafted bill introduced by a bipartisan group of opponents of centralization. Some parts of the "opposition" bill were patently tongue-in-cheek proposals designed for bargaining purposes, to deter the Administration from insisting on what many influential Congressmen regarded as too much centralization in the Pentagon. The Congressional bill, in part, called for the return of the Secretaries of the Army, Navy, and Air Force to membership on the National Security Council; limited the number of Assistant Secretaries of Defense to four; placed a ceiling of six hundred on the number of civilians employed in the Office of the Secretary of Defense, reducing the existing number by two-thirds; and curtailed drastically the authority of the Assistant Secretary of Defense, Comptroller, limiting sharply his supervision over the programs and requirements of the separate armed services. These proposals, submitted in the names of veteran Representatives Carl Vinson, Democrat, Georgia, and Paul Kilday, Democrat, Texas, were apparently designed to scare the Pentagon bureaucracy away from any scheme that either significantly reduced Congressional influence in military affairs or seriously impaired the independence of the separate services.

The "opposition" bill reflected a set of principles in sharp contrast to those espoused by the White House. Many influential legislators believed that defense decisions should be an amalgam of the divergent views of the several military departments and not the doctrine of one service or individual. They also felt that the President and Congress should share responsibility for defense.

As in 1947, the case was settled "out of court," by compromise. Significant steps, nonetheless, were taken in direction of unification. The 1958 reforms in their long-range effect represented the greatest advance toward unification since 1947. The changes may be grouped in the following categories: Authority of the Secretary of Defense; Joint Chiefs of Staff and Joint Staff; Roles and Missions of the separate Armed Service Departments; and Lines of Command. Note, however, that there is an inter-relationship among them. If the Secretary of Defense gains greater authority, it is likely to be at the expense of the separate services and the Congress.

The Secretary of Defense. Secretarial authority was appreciably strengthened by the 1958 reform, although the Presidential desire to give the Secretary "greater flexibility in money matters" ran into a stone wall on Capitol Hill. The Departments of Army, Navy, and Air Force were no longer required by law to be "separately administered" but simply "separately organized," and, after the 1958 legislation, came under the clearly stated "direction, authority, and control" of the Defense Secretary.

The service Secretaries became responsible to the Secretary of Defense for the "efficient operation" of their departments. Orders to the departments would be issued through the service Secretaries or the Defense Secretary's various deputies—including Assistant Secretaries of Defense—but their authority in this regard had to be, at Congressional insistence, specifically delegated in writing by the Secretary of Defense.

The Secretary could propose to reassign, transfer, consolidate or abolish major combat functions—in effect, service roles and missions—subject, through specified procedure, to Congressional veto. And he could reassign at his discretion noncombat functions, such as supply.

The Joint Chiefs of Staff, as a corporate body, became "directly responsible" to the Secretary of Defense; and it was to be the Secretary who made the nominations to the President for the promotion of all officers above the rank of Brigadier General, with "suggestions" from the service Secretaries and "advice" from the Joint Chiefs of Staff. The President let it be known that such promotions would be based in part upon the officers' ability to cooperate with the other services.

The Director of Defense Research and Engineering was by statute designated the Defense Secretary's principal adviser on scientific and technical matters. He was to supervise all research and engineering in the Department of Defense and to control, assign or reassign any research and engineering activities the Secretary thought required central management. The Secretary in turn could assign a new weapons system, regardless of which service might have developed it, to any of the three armed services for production, procurement, and operational control.

The Joint Chiefs of Staff. The maximum size of the Joint Staff, a strategic planning group serving the JCS and composed of officers on assignment from the Army, Navy, Air Force, and Marine Corps, was raised from 210 to 400. And the Chairman of the Joint Chiefs of Staff, instead of the JCS as a group, was to select the Director of the Joint Staff, in consultation with the JCS and with the approval of the Secretary of Defense.

The enlarged Joint Staff was also reorganized. A "J-Staff" system replaced the old interservice committees, the "J" implying more truly integrated thinking. Of most significance was the creation of J-3, which became a new, integrated operations division of the Joint Staff and an essential addition now that the JCS assumed strategic direction of the unified field commands for the Defense Secretary, replacing the designated service departments that had been previously responsible for the Army in Europe, the Navy in the Far East, etc.

Other J-Staff directorates, containing integrated units with roughly equal representation from the three services and the Marine Corps were: Personnel (J-1); Intelligence (J-2); Logistics (J-4); Plans and Policy (J-5); and Communications-Electronic (J-6). Additional functional units established were a Joint Military Assistance Affairs Directorate, a Joint Program Office, and a Joint Advanced Study Group. The new operational concept required these units to produce "agreed" rather than "split" position papers for the Joint Chiefs of Staff.

On the negative side, Congress stipulated that the new Joint Staff "shall not operate or be organized as an over-all Armed Forces General Staff and shall have no [independent] executive authority," and placed a three-year limit on Joint Staff service.

With the approval of the Service Secretary and with the understanding that responsibility was not being delegated, the Chiefs of the armed services were authorized by statute to turn over to their Vice-chiefs such duties as were deemed necessary to permit the Chiefs to give primary attention to their JCS role.

Roles and Missions of the Service Departments. The 1958 statute specifically provided for the continued existence of separate Departments of the Army, Air Force, and Navy, the latter explicitly "including naval aviation and the United States Marine Corps." Although the authority of the Secretary of Defense in the "unified direction" of the departments was increased, Congress reiterated its intention "not to merge these departments and services." The Departments were to remain "separately organized," and the authority of the Secretary to reassign major combat functions was, as noted above, subject to veto by Congress. Assignment of roles and missions remained as ambiguous as ever, except for the effect of a strengthened unified command system—explained below—on the independence and command functions of the service Chiefs.

Two additional provisions of the 1958 legislation might be noted. One was the right of the service Secretaries and service Chiefs to make recommendations on their own initiative to Congress. President Eisenhower voiced strong objections to this, which, he said, "endorses the idea of disunity" and suggests "that Congress hopes for disobedience and interservice rivalries."[18] Congress nonetheless insisted. Congress also

18 Text of President's statement in *The New York Times*, May 29, 1958, p. 8. For pro and con comments, see *Air Force*, May 1958, p. 39, and *Navy*, October 1958, p. 46. For Congressional reaction,

granted, over Presidential objection, statutory existence to the
National Guard Bureau and its Chief, eliminating the possibility of any transfer, consolidation, reassignment, or abolition of the Guard's functions, which are strongly supported
in Congress on behalf of state and local constituencies.

Lines of Command. Prior to 1958, the establishment of
unified commands had been authorized, but the reality of the
commander's control over elements on assignment from the
several armed services within his domain remained in doubt.
In the 1958 reorganization, commanders of unified (e.g., Pacific Command) and specified (e.g., Strategic Air Command)
commands were given the authority to exercise "full operational control" over all forces assigned to them, and the possibility that a service chief might withdraw assigned forces or
portions thereof was removed.

Lines of command were also clarified. They were to run
from the Commander in Chief (the President) through
the Secretary of Defense—via the JCS—to the unified or specified commanders. The service Secretaries and service Chiefs
were removed from the chain of command except insofar as
the latter, in their role as JCS members rather than as service Chiefs, were involved in issuing strategic directives in the
name of the Secretary of Defense. For example, the Secretary
and the Chief of Staff of the Air Force were no longer the
"bosses" of the Air Force general in charge of the Strategic
Air Command; only the Secretary of Defense was. But since
the individual services retained the authority to organize,
train, and equip forces for the operational unified commands
and to administer and support the forces so assigned, considerable ambiguity was left.

The 1958 reform necessitated numerous adjustments in
the procedures and interagency relationships of a huge bureaucracy. Extensive procedural changes were required in the command structure, the staffing and operation of the Joint Staff,
the roles of the military departments, the JCS and Research
and Engineering Secretariat, and the staff role of the Assistant

see House *Report* No. 1765, 85th Congress, 2d Session, May 22,
1958.

Secretaries of Defense, to name but a few. Thomas S. Gates, Jr., a former Secretary of the Navy who succeeded Neil McElroy as Defense Secretary late in 1959, instituted a number of important operational changes. In December he began to sit regularly with the Joint Chiefs of Staff so that each service view could be presented and debated in his presence and he could resolve basic differences among the chiefs on strategy and force levels. The practice has been continued in the Kennedy Administration by Gates' successor, Robert S. McNamara. Secretary Gates also took an important step toward unification by establishing a Joint Strategic Target Agency, which had become particularly urgent as the Navy entered the strategic bombing field with its Polaris nuclear submarines. A Joint Strategic Targets List was established in August 1960 as part of a Single Integrated Operational Plan, and a Joint Navy-Air Force planning staff was created—a somewhat makeshift arrangement designed to mitigate, in the event of major warfare, the absence of true unification in the defense system.

V

The platform of the victorious Democratic Party in the 1960 Presidential election contained a commitment to a "complete examination of the organization of our armed forces." On September 14, 1960, Senator John F. Kennedy commissioned a special committee to survey the problems of defense organization and to recommend to him "what changes should be made in the organization and administration of our defense agencies to eliminate or at least to diminish the present crippling effect of these problems upon our defense power."[19] Senator Stuart Symington was appointed to head this committee. Among other members were Clark M. Clifford, Thomas K. Finletter, and Roswell L. Gilpatric, all of whom, like Symington, had extensive experience with defense organizational problems.

[19] Press release by Senator Kennedy, St. Louis, Missouri, September 14, 1960.

The Symington Committee reported to the President-elect in December 1960. Its concise report was based upon the premise that the existing Pentagon organization was "patterned primarily on a design conceived in the light of lessons learned in World War II, which are now largely obsolete." The report argued that no really fundamental change had occurred in defense organization after 1947, while, "the whole state of the art in military science has been revolutionized."

The prime objective in the recommendations made by the Symington Committee was "the clarification and strengthening of the authority of the Secretary of Defense over the entire U. S. military establishment." Additional objectives were to shorten the time required to bring new weapons from conception to utilization, to improve the strategic planning process so that strategy and plans are not merely positions compromised among the several services, and to realign the defense organization in keeping with contemporary military functions to be performed. "No longer can this nation afford the luxury of letting each service strive to develop in itself the capability of fighting any future war by itself," stated the report.

Among the report's specific proposals were these: eliminate the existing department structure of the Army, Navy, and Air Force, while preserving the military services as separate organic units; do away with the service Secretaries, while vesting directly in the Secretary of Defense the administration of the services; create two new Under Secretaries of Defense, one for Weapons Systems and one for Administration, and consolidate under them the existing functions performed by Assistant Secretaries of Defense and the Departmental secretariats; reconstitute the JCS, making the Chairman the principal military adviser to the President and the Secretary of Defense and transforming the JCS into a Joint Staff under a single chief; establish three major unified commands—Strategic Command, Tactical Command, and Defense Command—and various minor commands; establish a unified budget process within the Office of the Secretary of Defense, to whom Congress would appropriate all defense funds, some of which (e.g., for research and development) would be placed on a multiyear basis.

No attempt was made during the first two years of the Kennedy Administration to implement these recommendations by major new legislation. Opposition to the most fundamental changes were quickly made known on Capitol Hill by influential legislators, who kept a watchful and suspicious eye upon a new Secretary of Defense who seemed determined to force greater unification upon the Pentagon, if not by requests to Congress for statutory changes, than by vigor in exercising the considerable administrative power already at his disposal. There was a widespread impression that many of the objectives of the Symington report could be accomplished by Executive Order and administrative action, but to do this the Defense Secretary would have to surmount or circumvent the opposition of many powerful skeptics on Capitol Hill and many seasoned in-fighters within his own Pentagon domain.

Secretary McNamara set about to make full use of existing authority. First he assembled an unusually sophisticated team of deputies. As Deputy Secretary, he chose Roswell L. Gilpatric, a former Air Force Under Secretary, who himself had been seriously considered by President Kennedy for appointment as Defense Secretary. An able New York lawyer, he had helped to prepare the Rockefeller Report of 1958, as well as serving on the Symington task force. Among McNamara's Assistant Secretaries were Paul H. Nitze (as head of International Security Affairs, known as the Pentagon's "little State Department"), a widely respected expert on strategy and foreign policy with extensive State Department experience; Charles J. Hitch (as Comptroller), a leading economist, member of the RAND Corporation and one of the foremost scholars of defense budgeting and the economics of national defense; and Harold Brown (Director of Research and Engineering), a first-line physicist from the Livermore Laboratory of the University of California.

Each of these deputies, in turn, assembled his own team of brilliant and knowledgeable specialists in strategy and foreign policy. Perhaps never before had so much civilian talent, sophisticated in military strategy, been assembled under a Defense Secretary, himself known for exceptional intellect combined with the ability to make difficult decisions with dispatch. If knowledge and analytical ability convey power, then the new Secretary was prepared to consolidate his position as chief of the vast and complex Pentagon.

Secretary McNamara, bolstered by the information contained in scores of task force reports and studies he had commissioned, used existing statutory authority to institute the following changes in 1961–62: (1) merger of the Army's various technical services, like ordnance, signal, finance, quartermaster, into a Materiel and Logistics Command; (2) a speed-up of the consolidated handling of all-service common use goods, like purchases of food, gasoline, spare parts, blankets, in a unified Defense Supply Agency; (3) creation of a Defense Intelligence Agency, combining in large measure the formerly separate intelligence units in Washington but not in the field commands of each of the armed services; (4) tightening of the Defense Secretary's control over the press releases and public speeches in the armed services; and (5) the strengthening of the Secretary's line of authority to the major military commands, bringing North American Air Defense, Strategic Air Command, and others under his effective control.

In addition, McNamara unified the Strategic Army Corps and the Tactical Air Forces into an operational Strike Command; placed the conception of all new weapons systems under the jurisdiction of the Director of Research and Engineering, thereby consolidating the control once held by separate services; assigned to the Air Force prime responsibility for the military aspects of outer space; and—of major long-range importance—began to revise the entire budgetary approach within the Pentagon. (The budgetary reforms will be discussed in greater detail in Chapters IV and V.)

Vigorous new assertion of civilian authority caused considerable apprehension among, and some friction with, military professionals. Early in 1962, for example, Hanson W. Baldwin, *The New York Times* military analyst, noted "the uneasiness that many military men have felt increasingly in the last year since . . . McNamara started a quiet revolution in the Pentagon's organization and methods." Later a similar fear of "creeping unification" was stated more bluntly on Capitol Hill. In August 1962, the Chairman of the House Armed Services Committee, Carl Vinson, endorsed a subcommittee report accusing McNamara of overcentralizing military authority in his own office and of jeopardizing the independence of the Army, Navy, Air Force, and Marine Corps. In Vinson's view, this could lead to "disastrous" erosion of military responsibility and readiness.[20]

Main points in a broader criticism voiced by the military journals but generally muffled by the widespread praise accorded McNamara were these: that the Secretary was thinking too much in terms of machines and mathematical calculations rather than of men; that he was relying too heavily upon academic theorists and their techniques of abstract calculations of probabilities rather than upon human judgment based upon "common sense" and experience; that inadequate attention was paid to the advice of military professionals and too much to the ideas of brilliant young slide-rule analysts; and that an inordinate centralization of the decision-making process was taking place in the offices of the Defense Secretary and his band of bright young brain trusters. On this latter point, Secretary of the Army Elvis T. Stahr, Jr., retiring after eighteen months of service with McNamara, added that "more and more, the decisions once made by the service Secretaries and the military chiefs, as individuals, are made by the Secretary of Defense and his staff." He said, in a *New York Times* interview published July 8, 1962, that the Defense Department is far too big to be run by a few people at the top and suggested that Secretary McNamara's techniques constituted "overreaching" in personal control. Essentially

[20] For Baldwin's comment, see "An Uneasy Military-I," *The New York Times*, January 18, 1962; the Armed Services subcommittee's views and Vinson's endorsement of them are found in House, Committee on Armed Services, *Report* No. 69 of Special Subcommittee on Defense Agencies, 87th Congress, 2d Session, August 13, 1962.

the complaints added up to an allegation that Secretary Mc-Namara was imposing a kind of backdoor unification, without advice and consent from Congress or from the professional military leaders representing the separate armed services.

VI

But with all the changes, evidence supports the argument that the defense organization existing in 1962 was predicated on popular and Congressional distrust of the concentration of decision-making power. In the years since World War II the existing defense organization has produced a formidable array of military power. But its adequacy in terms of foreign policy objectives and commitments has remained in question. This may be because the armed services have been preoccupied with organizational and jurisdictional issues, at the expense of meeting the true requirements for the common defense. An offhand comment made in 1956 by the Air Force Chief of Staff is suggestive. Said General Nathan Twining: ". . . the Navy and Army are watching me like a hawk. Every time I make a move, they are making sure what I am doing and vice versa." General Twining conceded that there are advantages to this: "no one can really get off the beam," and he acknowledged the danger of a "real bad mistake" if a single military dynasty were created. Apparently as an afterthought he added, "But that [competition] can . . . lead to lack of development, too, and that is dangerous for the country."[21]

Since World War II, interservice rivalry has been the prime characteristic of the defense establishment. More time and energy has probably been expended at the policy-making levels of the three armed services on who's going to do what with how much money than on appraising the external threat to the nation. The familiar interservice controversies of the 1950s were often irrelevant to the central question of the

[21] Senate Armed Services Subcommittee on the Air Force, *Hearings*, "Study of Airpower," 1956, p. 1505.

principal military functions to be performed, i.e.: strategic deterrence, deterrence of less than all-out aggression, control of the seas, continental defense.

The organizational atmosphere in which the military system operates has been so fraught with debate that during his term as Secretary of Defense Charles E. Wilson ruefully commented that "in the [armed] services we at least ought to treat each other like allies." With all of the reorganizations since World War II, and with all of the administrative vigor and decisiveness exercised by an exceptionally able new Secretary in 1961–62, the defense structure continues to resemble an alliance of semi-independent, sovereign units, often engaged in bitter jurisdictional warfare.

A fact of recent history should be noted here: Every major investigation and report on Department of Defense organization since World War II has recommended a more unified structure and greater concentration of authority in the Office of the Secretary of Defense.[22] Even the important Eberstadt Report in 1945, which opposed the degree of centralization advocated by many persons, recommended greater unification. Yet the opponents of unification continue to make their voices heard.

Serious problems remain in the defense structure. In proposing or implementing further defense reform, extreme care must be taken not to sacrifice any required capability for deterrence and defense. Effective armed forces are those capable of deterring war or applying military force with discretion at any moment. This inevitably places limits on how rapidly any radical reorganization scheme can be put into effect. It

[22] A vast literature exists on defense organization and reorganization proposals. Very useful bibliographies are those printed by the Senate Committee on Government Operations (Jackson Subcommittee): "Organizing for National Security—A Bibliography," December 15, 1959; and "Administration of National Security," December 28, 1962. See also "Recent Writing in Military Politics—Foci and Corpora," in *Changing Patterns of Military Politics*, ed. Samuel P. Huntington, New York, The Free Press of Glencoe, 1962, pp. 235–66.

also underlines the need for long-range organizational planning and the importance of laying the foundation *now* for what is likely to be needed *later*.

To postpone needed reorganization is to permit the Department of Defense to lag behind technology at great future peril to national security. Concern about "lead-time" in weapons—that is, the time between the drawing board and the production line—has overshadowed the equally serious problem of organizational "lead-time." There is urgent need to identify remaining defects in the defense organization structure, to study remedies, and to plan for smooth transition to the inevitable next step. Above all, attention must be given to the education, training, and indoctrination of the junior members of the defense establishment—civilian and military—who will assume posts of leadership in the future, to make them aware of the nature of the technological revolution under way. And finally, serious attention must be given to the solution of the chronic problem of the short-term service of civilians in the upper levels of the Defense Secretariat.

Some identifiable risks are inherent in complete defense unification, because of the massive size and extensive scope of the Defense Department. Logical rearrangements of decision-making and leadership roles at the top will not guarantee effective operational units at the lower echelons. Three basic operational prerequisites for any defense organization can be listed: First, unification must be compatible with the efficiency value of decentralization. A central technique, perhaps a basic prerequisite, of democratic government is to guarantee competition among ideas and interests. Our system of government and our way of decision making is distinct from that of totalitarianism largely in this regard, and the system is not likely to endure in the absence of opportunities for responsible dissent in policy making, which will come about only through a degree of decentralization of authority. But the danger of too much administrative pluralism is paralysis or stalemate as we enter an era in which proper decisions made *in time* may spell the difference between survival or surrender.

Morale and *esprit de corps*, too, must not be the victims of overcentralization, for they are vital ingredients of military strength.

Second, greater unification must try to avoid, in former Secretary of Defense Wilson's blunt phrase, the risk of "concentration of stupidity." Greater unification must not stifle the expression of diverse opinions or of alternate recommendations for national security.

Third, in concentrating responsibility at the top, the risk of generating irresponsibility at the lower operating levels must be avoided. Given these prerequisites, where is further reform needed? What direction should further changes take?

The Joint Chiefs of Staff. Given the complex nature of strategic planning and the enormous size of the armed services, the dual role of service Chief of Staff and membership on the JCS seems impossible to fulfill effectively. A service Chief now is authorized to delegate duties to his Vice Chief. But, in practice, Congressional committees, Service Secretaries, and various public groups want to see and hear the Chief; to deal with the No. 1 man. The Service Chief as a member of the JCS is inevitably torn between the loyalty expected by his service and the objective, unified outlook required by the national interest.

An example of how this works has been given by General Thomas D. White, who as Air Force Chief of Staff was a member of the JCS for the four years ending in June 1961. Each service chief annually certifies to his department Secretary and the Defense Secretary that the budget he submits represents the minimum required for his service to perform its mission. Shortly thereafter the Defense Secretary refers the budgets of all the armed services to the JCS for their recommendations. At this stage each service chief must judge his own budget in the context of all other service requirements and against an over-all dollar-target ceiling. "Since the combined service requirements always exceed the tentative dollar limitation," writes General White, each service chief faces a dilemma as he "must either renounce as false or padded his earlier declaration, or lose face with his own Secretary, his staff, and his service as a whole. . . ."[23]

One authoritative critic of this system stated that "at the Joint Chiefs of Staff level, we have probably the least effective military organization to haunt the United States since the fiasco of the Civil War. . . . This means, in effect, that our present military operations are governed by a committee with widely divergent views. There is no example in history of military command being successfully exercised under those circumstances."[24]

To remedy this, the role of member of the JCS should be separated from that of chief of service. Membership on a reconstituted JCS, perhaps limited to four years, might normally follow the tour as service Chief of Staff. But while serving on the JCS, the officer would not be identified with or return to his service.

Unified Commands. Unified commanders are said under the system of 1962 to have "full operational control" of forces assigned to them. Yet the selection, basic training, equipment and supply of these forces continues to be administered by the existing departments, which maintain firm control over the development of service doctrine and personnel administration. Unified commanders have responsibility for *joint* training of assigned forces, but the system is beset by an artificial separation of policy and administration that promises serious trouble. Perhaps these problems cannot be solved without a radical redesignation of military forces and missions on something other than the present largely *geographical* basis for existing commands.

A long-range goal might be a gradual transition into a functional rearrangement of forces, based upon the principal missions to be performed. Meanwhile there should be a speed-up of the integration of the technical forms and procedures

[23] "The Impossible Role of the Joint Chiefs," *Newsweek*, June 11, 1962, p. 28.

[24] Major General John B. Medaris, *Countdown for Decision*, New York, Putnam, 1960, pp. 58–59.

among the military services, including nomenclature, stock numbers and specifications for all standard items such as food, clothing, and transportation. Procurement, supply, and service of common-use items should be completely integrated. Uniform systems of paper work should be developed. And the question should be asked whether the present arrangement of three separate undergraduate service academies, which perpetuate outmoded concepts and instill interservice rivalry, represent the best undergraduate educational base for future leaders of "unified" armed forces. Perhaps long-range planning for a radical revision of military education and realignment of educational institutions for the military functions of the future—strategic striking power, limited war, sea communications, air defense, logistics, reserves, and civil defense—should begin at once.

Defense Secretariat. The eventual establishment of regrouped military specialists will have to coincide with a rearrangement of the civilian hierarchy of the defense establishment. A principal goal must be to provide the Defense Secretary with full authority and with objective information and advice about defense requirements, particularly about the major military functions to be performed. The separate Service Departments and their Secretariats will have to be abolished, and Deputy Secretaries of Defense for each of the major military missions created in their place. And, ideally, the career civil service, its prestige and rewards, will be extended upward so that eventually only the very top positions will be filled by political appointees.

None of these changes can be effected suddenly. But, to recall the theme of this book, the greatest threat to America's defense and democracy is a failure to recognize that an accelerating technology in a totally new world environment demands the closest possible attention to organizational requirements ten, fifteen, or more years hence. History suggests that basic changes in defense structures come about either as a result of military disaster or, more rarely, imaginative leadership supported by public opinion. In the nuclear age, military disasters are no longer tolerable. This puts a premium on innovative leadership supported by an enlightened public.

The Department of Defense is but one part of the structure where leadership and innovation are required. Let us turn next to an equally important and closely related policy instrument, the defense budget.

CHAPTER IV

THE DEFENSE BUDGET PROCESS

I

A common saying in the Pentagon for years has been that "the only person in the United States who can force a decision is the Government Printer." The rigid pre-Christmas printing deadlines required in order that the President meet the legal obligation to submit his annual budget to Congress in January force many of the most important defense decisions.

The defense budget is at the heart of national security; in one sense it is the most important foreign policy document in any year. It states the choices made after appraising the nature of the international situation, determining specific foreign policy objectives and priorities for attaining them, and evaluating alternative means by which these objectives may be realized. The budget is at once an expression of current defense policy, a reflection of decisions and commitments made long before, and the detailed framework within which the defense administration must move toward attainment of national objectives. It should, assuming an entirely rational and efficient budget process, represent national strategy in concrete terms. But the American defense budget process, which involves decisions on some three to four thousand separate items, has in the past fallen far short of this ideal. The testimony of an experienced witness, General Maxwell D. Taylor, might be cited:

> . . . we never build our forces or buy our forces in a budget sense in terms of military functions such as atomic retaliation, limited war capability, antisubmarine warfare, con-

tinental air defense. . . . I doubt personally that anyone knows exactly what we are buying with our budget.[1]

The central questions to be considered in this and the following chapter are: From what procedures are defense budgets derived? What have been the prevailing attitudes about how much the national economy can afford for the common defense? What can be done to improve the budget process?

Years ago a prominent leader in the government economy-and-efficiency movement declared that the "growing hostility to doing business in the dark, to 'boss rule,' to 'invisible government,' became the soil in which the 'budget idea' finally took root and grew."[2]

The Budget and Accounting Act of 1921, which created the U. S. budget system, may properly be described as one of the most significant reformations in government practices in the history of the American Republic. Before it was enacted each government agency had prepared its own requests for funds, which the Treasury Department then presented to Congress. Under the 1921 Act only the President may submit an Executive Branch request to Congress for funds. The Act also established the Bureau of the Budget, to receive all the government units' requests for funds, analyze and review them, and submit them to the President; and it required the

[1] Testimony to Senate Armed Services, Preparedness Investigating Subcommittee, *Hearings*, "Missiles, Space and Other Major Defense Matters," 86th Congress, 2d Session, February 4, 1960, p. 199.

[2] Frederick A. Cleveland, "Evolution of the Budget Idea in the United States," *The Annals*, November 1915, p. 22. Standard works on the budget process include: Jesse Burkhead, *Government Budgeting*, New York, Wiley, 1956; Frederick C. Mosher, *Program Budgeting: Theory and Practice*, Chicago, Public Administration Service, 1954; Arthur Smithies, *The Budgetary Process in the United States*, New York, McGraw-Hill, 1955. For a theory of budgeting, see Paul Appleby, "The Role of the Budget Division," *Public Administration Review*, XVII, 1957, pp. 156–58. For background on the development of the U. S. budget system see Fritz Morstein Marx, "The Bureau of the Budget: Its Evolution and Present Role," *American Political Science Review*, XXXIX, 1945, pp. 653–84, 869–98.

President to submit a complete budget to Congress annually, containing his spending proposals and the source of the anticipated funds to support his program.

As an adjunct of the Treasury Department, the Budget Bureau's role in its first two decades of existence was primarily to reduce or hold down Federal expenditures under the slogan of "management improvement." This concept changed with the Reorganization Act of 1939, which followed the Report of the President's Committee on Administrative Management and called for a substantial bolstering of the White House staff to assist the President more effectively in his enormous and multifarious tasks as Chief Executive. The Budget Bureau was moved from the Treasury into the newly created Executive Office of the President where it became a Presidential instrument, not only for management improvement, narrowly interpreted, but for the review and coordination of all proposed government programs and expenditures— a role extending far beyond that of budgeting.

Under the post-1939 philosophy of Presidential management the Budget Bureau grew in size, and its organization began to assume its present form. The Bureau's major divisions, established in 1940 and reorganized in 1952, reflect its areas of concern: Military, Commerce and Finance, International, Labor and Welfare, Resources and Civil Works. There are also four "offices": Budget Review, Legislative Reference, Management and Organization, and Statistical Standards. Since 1940 the Bureau has not grown appreciably (as of 1962 it had about three hundred permanent professional staff members) nor have its basic functions changed. But as the size of the Federal government and its budget have grown, particularly in the Cold War years, the Bureau has stressed its more traditional functions—legislative clearance (reviewing legislative proposals and coordinating agency views on pending legislation for the President) and statistical services (coordination and improvement of the government's statistical activities, techniques, and publications)—while its program planning and coordinating role has been shared with such other agencies in the Executive Office of the President as the National

Security Council, the Council of Economic Advisers, the Office of Emergency Planning, and the greatly enlarged planning and programing offices of the various departments and bureaus, particularly the Defense Department.

There have been certain statutory changes. The Budget and Accounting Procedures Act of 1950 embodied the recommendation of the 1949 Hoover Commission that the so-called "program" or "performance" budget be adopted. The Hoover Commission defined a "program budget" as one "based on functions, activities and projects . . . which would focus attention upon the general character and relative importance of the work to be done, or upon the service to be rendered, rather than the things to be acquired, such as personal service, supplies and equipment. . . ." In the military field, however, this concept was never fully realized in the decade that followed, although the Budget Bureau was somewhat reorganized to fulfill the recommendation.

The General Appropriations Act of 1950 clarified the Bureau's responsibilities over monies appropriated by Congress to the various Federal departments, and prescribed procedures for setting up apportionments and reserves. This meant that even after a department had received a Congressional appropriation, the Bureau had the power to apportion it over the budget year, controlling the flow of monies assigned to the various departments and thus strengthening Presidential authority over the details of policy implementation. A continuing Presidential hand on the purse strings throughout the year better enables him to enforce his will.

One of the major divisions in the Bureau is the Military, with a staff of about forty, which works closely with the budget branch (Comptroller) of the Department of Defense. This collaboration, which has no counterpart in other government departments, has been dictated by the immense size of Department of Defense operations, the complex nature of some military functions, and the comparatively small staff of the Budget Bureau's Military Division. Perhaps the staff remains small because the Pentagon, in effect, has its own defense budget bureau. The size of the task involved in preparing an annual defense budget is suggested by a 1959 Pentagon estimate of the annual cost of defense budget preparation: $30,000,000.

The Budget Bureau's Military Division has two principal jobs: budget preparation and the distribution of appropriations made by Congress. But it also performs collateral tasks, including the review of legislative proposals dealing with military matters or the improvement of organization and management in the Department of Defense. The sum total of its activities have made it the bogeyman of the military strategists and the proponents of greater emphasis on particular weapons systems. To them, the Military Division views its central task as holding down military expenditures rather than meeting military "requirements." It is a unit of government that can say "No" with great authority, as it speaks for the President, and an instrument of enormous potential for effecting civilian control of the military. Under both Eisenhower and Kennedy, the Budget Director has been a frequent participant in the meetings of the National Security Council. Those who attack the Budget Bureau or its Military Division for their restraining influence on higher department or agency budgets are in reality attacking the President and his policies. The Budget Bureau is a convenient, safer target.

II

Under the American constitutional system, fiscal authority is shared by the executive and the legislative branches. The President relies upon the budget to direct the many administrative agencies under his domain. But because every penny of public money must come from the legislature, Congress looks to the budget as the prime instrument for the exercise of legislative power in government. Budgets are, in fact, multipurpose instruments of democracy: ideally they provide choice and power within the executive branch, between the executive and legislative branches, and, through the representative concept, between the people and the government.

In matters of national defense, choice is exercised in three

major categories. First, the nation must decide how much is
to be allocated for the combined functions of government.
Second, a choice must be made between defense and non-
defense uses of national resources, and the total amount to
be allocated for defense must be determined. Third, there
must be a decision as to the best assignment of resources
within this amount.

These choices cannot be made as separate "steps" in a
process, or necessarily in the order described. Each must be
arrived at within the context of the values and aspirations of
the society, as determined by the American political processes; the state of the economy; and careful assessments of
technological trends, the international power balance, and
national resources. The choices are, of course, interrelated,
but the order in which they are made is crucially important.
The total size or "ceiling" of any annual budget should not
be considered separately from that budget's composition.

The requirements of, say, deterring a potential enemy by
military means or of successfully pursuing a political objective such as maintaining unity among our Western European
allies, cannot be calculated with absolute precision. Yet in
considering alternatives one must rely upon the methods of
economics, broadly defined, to determine the most efficient
use of resources in any given situation. National security requirements in the contemporary world are virtually limitless,
while the resources that can be devoted to defense will always
be, to some degree, limited. "Since it is the shortage of resources," Bernard Brodie has written, "measured by dollars,
which obliges us to make hard choices, the dollar becomes
the instrument by which we measure the wisdom of our
choice."[3]

But budget problems are problems of economics only in its
broadest sense; the dollar cannot be the sole standard of
measurement. A given number of dollars will not guarantee,
for example, the neutrality of Laos, the independence of
Vietnam, or the freedom of West Berlin. And yet dollars,

[3] Bernard Brodie, *Strategy in the Missile Age*, Princeton University
Press, 1959, p. 380.

grouped in budget categories, are the standard instrument for allocating resources, suggesting that the best choices will come from the most precisely meaningful budget categories.[4] For example, a traditional budget category, "operation and maintenance" has much less meaning to the budget decision maker than, say, "strategic retaliatory forces."

In recent years defense policy makers have struggled with hundreds of possible programs in the annually recurring crisis of the budget: Shall the United States concentrate on trying to match the U.S.S.R. with existing weapons systems, or try to anticipate technology by investing more heavily in future systems? (A most difficult question in 1959–60 was whether to buy large numbers of liquid-fuel intercontinental missiles or to wait for the development of solid-fuel rockets.) Shall the United States concentrate on attaining the alleged psychological advantage of being first with a nuclear-powered aircraft, or on producing such a plane at a later date but with real military capability, or not produce it at all? Shall we rely on a large, modernized ground army, or on perfecting the development of invulnerable nuclear-missile deterrent power? What proportion of resources should be allocated to active air defense and what to passive civil defense, such as home fallout shelters? In the missile age what proportion of the national resources should be allocated to manned aircraft—such as a two thousand miles-per-hour plane? Shall we step up our plans to send a man to the moon at the expense of producing more sophisticated military rockets? How much money shall we give to research and development, military air transport, naval fleet modernization, and hundreds of other items included on the always ready "shopping list" in the files of the armed services?

These are not either-or questions. Accepting one program does not mean completely abandoning another. But there must always be a ceiling on the total resources allocated for a balanced program of military defense. And no matter how

[4] For enlightening details, see Charles J. Hitch and Roland N. McKean, *The Economics of Defense in the Nuclear Age*, Harvard University Press, 1960.

high the defense budget goes in periods of international tension, there will always be more ways proposed to spend money than there will be available funds. Increasing the defense budget for any given fiscal year by 50 or even 100 per cent would still not eliminate difficult choices, or the need for a system that makes it possible to base such choices upon reasonably accurate knowledge of what more money can buy or estimates of the consequences of spending less money for any given program.

III

The choice of means to attain national objectives is called strategy making at one level and budget making at another. The commitment of national resources, for which the budget is the principal instrument, is a crucial step in national security policy making. A nation may have a sharply defined national purpose, an invincible will, the best possible intelligence estimates, brilliant strategies, and energetic leadership, but these mean little until they have been transformed into concrete programs setting priorities and allocating resources for specified functions. The budget process is the anvil on which policies, strategies, and programs are forged, by committing resources to the attainment of specific objectives. Let us examine the steps in this complex process that were the pattern of the Eisenhower years, but that have come under major reform in the Kennedy Administration.[5]

Formulation of the annual defense budget under Eisenhower followed this chronology:

[5] It is impossible to set forth a standard chronology for the defense budget process for two reasons: for each year 1946–62 it has been different and the Kennedy Administration for 1963 instituted major and radically new procedures still under development at this writing. This chronology and the accompanying discussion relate to the pre-Kennedy era and the dynamic period which came with a new Administration. Some of the material in this section has been derived from Marshall Wood, W. Barton Leach, and H. H. Ransom, "The Budgetary Process and Defense Policy," Harvard Defense Policy Seminar Serial No. 122, November 18, 1957 (Mimeographed).

Fiscal Year 1961—Beginning July 1, 1960

Jul 58–Oct 58 — Joint Chiefs of Staff development of objectives, force-levels, and war plans, based upon broadly stated Presidential (NSC) policies and Defense Secretariat guidance on major military functions and missions.

Nov 58–Jan 59 — Development of war plans, programs, and requirements within the separate Army, Navy, Air Force, and Marine Corps.

Feb 59–May 59 — Program revision takes place, meanwhile, to reflect Presidential decision on the previous year's budget request.

Feb 59–Jul 59 — Development of Budget estimates in the field by each of the services and the separate commands.

Jun 59–Sep 59 — Review within each military department (and incorporation of revision as necessary).

Sep 59–Nov 59 — Department of Defense and Bureau of the Budget review.

Dec 59 — Final composition of President's annual budget.

Jan 60–Jun 60 — Congressional consideration of President's budget for FY 1961.

Jul 60–Jun 61 — Apportionment and obligations of funds (may continue for several additional years in case of continuing appropriations).

Under this system, each budget cycle spanned about two years up to the time the funds were appropriated, and from one to three or more additional years to spend the appropriated monies. About six months of the first two years were spent making programs; six months translating the programs into budget estimates; six months in Executive review; and six months in Congressional review—a dangerously slow process in a fast-moving, dynamic world.

Inevitably, there is considerable interaction between the overlapping cycles for successive fiscal years. Three budgets are constantly being administered: last year's, this year's, and next year's. Executive and Congressional decisions on the previous year's budgets may invalidate the size of the programs for the following year by making their attainment impossible within the time available. Major decisions are made at the completion of the Executive and Congressional reviews, and these decisions show up in the following as well as the current cycle.

There is also, necessarily, some interdependence within each cycle. Objectives, the actual personnel strength of military units, and programs have to be revised if their cost, as developed in the budget estimate, seems excessive. These internal feedbacks have been largely accomplished within the review periods, but rather unsatisfactorily because there are no adequate procedures for making consistent revisions in all parts of the program within the short time available.

Theoretically, the budget process should start with policy guidance by the President and the National Security Council. To allow time for subsequent operations, this guidance is needed about two years before the start of the budget year and up to five or more years before the completion of the actions controlled by the budget. Since the guidance should define the tasks the military forces must be prepared to perform, both in deterring war or fighting, if necessary, this involves a forecast of international conditions for several years ahead, as well as tentative judgments about United States reaction to those conditions in the light of foreign policy objectives.

At the starting point in any given budget cycle, Congressional action on the budget, initiated two years earlier, has just been completed, and Executive review of the preceding fiscal year's budget is about to begin. At this stage of the cycle, guidance from the highest political authority—the White House and the National Security Council—was not always provided in the past. In its absence the task of providing initial guidance falls to the Joint Chiefs of Staff, who have often been unable to agree among themselves. Thus the task has usually been defaulted to the individual military departments.

In translating their requirements into budgets, the services have generally proceeded under guidelines, or ceilings, set by the Defense Secretary interpreting Presidential policy, as the first step in a complex bargaining process. Fearful of eliminating a sizable budgetary claim for their particular service, military leaders have often clung to unrewarding weapons systems. Most of their effort has been devoted to waging war with the budgeteers in order to keep up or to increase the over-all budget levels for their service.[6]

Military budgets, in theory, derive from military requirements. Military requirements, in turn, supposedly fulfill national policy objectives and international commitments, assigned functions or "missions," and approved strategic plans based upon assumptions and estimates about the nature of the threat and of a potential enemy's capabilities and intentions and about the utility, capability, and purpose of given weapons systems. Requirements are translated into programs. And programs, finally, are assigned dollar costs and converted into budgets.

Much of the political discussion of the nation's military needs centers around the assumed existence of specific requirements. In the great defense debates over the past decade it was often asserted by this or that group that a given program was "required" for national security. This may have been stated in terms of a given number of Army divisions, missile sites, or nuclear-powered missile-firing submarines, or in a certain fixed amount to be devoted to research and development or to the operation and maintenance of military

[6] A good discussion is found in Brodie, *op. cit.*, pp. 358–98, and in Henry Rowen, "National Security and the American Economy in the 1960's," Study Paper No. 18, Joint Economic Committee, 86th Congress, 2d Session, January 30, 1960, pp. 63–72.

forces. But the advent of atomic weapons, missiles, and other devices of the space age has made the question of how much security will result from any given combination of the instruments of warfare more speculative than ever before. And these uncertainties must be superimposed on the inherent unpredictability of the enemy's capabilities and intentions.

During the Eisenhower years, broad national objectives, such as containment of Russia or the capability to retaliate "massively," were recommended to the President by the National Security Council. After an annual review, the President approved a paper labeled "Basic National Security Policy," which for planning purposes was promulgated in twenty-five typewritten pages to those agencies having a national security function. This document included no statement of the finances required for implementing policy. And though it ultimately had a great impact on defense budgets, its creation cannot be said to have had a direct relationship to the budget process.

In drafting this annual statement the NSC secretariat consulted the armed services, the Office of the Secretary of Defense, and the Joint Chiefs of Staff who, somewhat independently, continued to work on various categories (short-range, long-range) of strategic plans. Major debates among the armed services on military strategy ensued in the process of bringing the paper to a final draft, which should have served as the capstone for national strategic doctrine and for strategic planning by the various units. As General Taylor, who observed the process as Army Chief of Staff, has noted, this was a false hope:

> The end product . . . has thus far [1960] been a document so broad in nature and so general in language as to provide limited guidance in practical application. In the course of its development, the sharp issues in national defense which confront our leaders have been blurred in conference and in negotiation. The final test thus permits many different interpretations. . . . the partisans of the importance of air power or of limited war, as well as the

defenders of other shades of military opinion, are able to find language supporting their divergent points of view.[7]

In the Truman and Eisenhower years, the Budget Bureau often seemed to be setting a ceiling on the total size of the defense budget without precise knowledge of the size of the budget requests simultaneously under preparation by the military departments. Strictly speaking, the Bureau did not set a ceiling on the defense budget total. While the procedure varied, in most years the President and his Budget Director reached an agreement with the Secretary of Defense on a "target" total. Within this total, the ceilings for each military service were established by the Secretary of Defense under his own authority, although the President, to be sure, did not remain aloof from the interservice competition for funds. If the Presidentially approved totals turned out to be substantially at variance with the military departments' objectives and force levels, major downward adjustments in the programs and budget estimates had to be made in an unreasonably short time.

Aware of the inefficiency of this procedure, the Eisenhower Administration in its last years began to send alternative budgetary targets to the military services long enough in advance (usually July) to permit them to prepare and review estimates at both the ceiling levels and the higher levels they usually desired. The Budget Bureau, with some participation by the Defense Comptroller, also prepared long-range forecasts of the defense budget on alternative bases, with the knowledge of the military services' objectives and proposed level of forces. So, while ceilings were finally set, they were not necessarily arrived at blindly.

At the point when "ceilings" or "targets," however derived, were received by each of the armed services, their respective missions and functions had to be redefined with reference to the plan. The requirements lists of the separate departments were also influenced by the suggestions (plans and require-

[7] General Maxwell D. Taylor, *The Uncertain Trumpet*, New York, Harper, 1959, pp. 82–83.

ments) submitted by unified (e.g., Far Eastern) or specified (e.g., Strategic Air) commands, whose requests were reviewed by the Joint Chiefs of Staff. These commands were established by the President through the Secretary of Defense, who specified their force structure; and forces once assigned to them could not be taken away by unilateral service action. For example, the Air Force had to supply the Strategic Air Command with men and materiel and could not withdraw personnel from SAC without the concurrence of the President and the Secretary of Defense. If Congress did not appropriate sufficient funds for the requirements of each of the armed services, adjustments had to be worked out in the Joint Chiefs of Staff and the Office of the Secretary of Defense.[8]

Military budgets are derived by "pricing" military requirements, which are determined from functions, "missions," or foreign commitments established in the strategic planning process. It is the strategic plan that provides the constitutional framework of the defense budget, and strategic planning goes forward under the direction of the President and the management of the Secretary of Defense. The actual plans are drawn by the Joint Staff serving the Joint Chiefs of Staff. Three separate plans are made annually. These are:

(1) *The Joint Long-Range Strategic Estimate* (JLRSE). This provides a strategic appraisal for a time period eight to twelve years in the future. Because it usually demands no immediate budgetary decisions, it usually has not provoked interservice disputes. Its greatest impact has been upon research and development budgets which, compared, say, to procurement, have constituted a relatively small portion of our defense budgets. And since needs for years so far in the future are speculative, the armed services have managed to

---

[8] For details on how military requirements are determined see Charles H. Donnelly, "Determination of Military Requirements," in *Hearings*, "Military Procurement," Senate Armed Services Subcommittee, 86th Congress, 1st Session, July 1959, Appendix I, pp. 495–503.

speculate in harmony. Phrased in sweeping generalities, JLRSE is commonly called an "intelligence plan."

(2) *The Joint Strategic Capabilities Plan* (JSCP). This is an estimate of short-term objectives, designed to guide the use of military resources on hand or quickly available on call (such as organized reserves or procurement items available "on the shelf") in the event of an emergency. In essence it is a war mobilization plan, commonly called the "fighting plan," to deal with contingencies requiring varying degrees of mobilization, deployment, or commitment of forces in limited warfare, or for expansion of forces in any kind of warfare. It is the basis for the nation's war plan "if war comes tomorrow."

(3) *The Joint Strategic Objectives Plan* (JSOP). This is the most important, and certainly the most controversial, of the military plans, dealing with a period four to seven years ahead—the period most affected by the defense budget of any given year. It sets the size of various types of forces and gives guidance for programs to procure the weapons and equipment needed to support the defense establishment and to mobilize the manpower, equipment, and supplies to implement a war plan. It is the central requirements plan.

JSOP is supposed to be the military-planning response to the NSC's annual "Basic National Security Policy" paper. But in recent years, it has proved to be the most difficult plan for the Joint Staff to work out. The Chiefs have been unable to agree on the best combination of military forces that could be supported by the money the Defense Secretary has considered feasible for planning.[9]

The three strategic plans, revised annually and subject to the approval of the Secretary of Defense,[10] provide the basis

[9] Taylor, *op. cit.*, pp. 86–87. In August 1962, General Taylor was appointed Chairman of the JCS by President Kennedy, whom he had served as special White House military adviser for over a year.

[10] A new Secretary of Defense in the Kennedy Administration, Robert S. McNamara, began in 1961 to institute new procedures for programing and budgeting. The apparent purpose is to provide clear "guidelines" for development of some three hundred major weapons

for the armed services to determine, on their own, what will be required to meet their assignments under various contingencies. If the Joint Chiefs of Staff cannot agree on a plan, important issues, such as the amount of airlift to be provided for ground forces, must be resolved by the Secretary of Defense on the basis of "split papers" from the JCS containing dissenting views. The guidance the Defense Secretary finally gives to the military department is in the form of decisions on the total size of the forces that the services may maintain; these determine the kinds and numbers of combat forces and suggest the strategy to be used in developing war and mobilization plans, which, in turn, prescribe the requirements for supply and "support" of military forces.

From figures on the size of forces ("force levels") and policy objectives developed by its own central planning staff, each service prepares its war plan, spelling out how the projected forces would be used in war so as to ascertain the size and composition of the supporting forces, the reserve forces, and the reserve stocks of materiel needed for combat.

Ratios of combat to support forces vary widely, depending upon the character of the contemplated operations. A large part of the support forces that would be necessary in wartime are not needed to support peacetime operations, and are included in the peacetime force only to meet anticipated wartime requirements. Similarly, judgments about the probable character of a future war may greatly alter the ratio between forces-in-being and civilian components—the Reserve and the National Guard. The fact that there has been no experience in atomic warfare aggravates the difficulty inherent in defining future requirements.

Once the combat forces and supply requirements are determined, there must be a program—a schedule of the actions necessary to proceed from the current status to the status fixed by the projected force-level and war plans.

Developing the program, which must describe the rate at which every function and activity will proceed from its cur-

systems for five-year periods. The new approach is described below in more detail.

rent status to its projected future status by monthly or quarterly periods over a span of two-and-a-half to four years, involves the active participation of every staff office and field command and takes three or four months. In the Air Force, for instance, the program for 1960 contained about six thousand pages of documents stating the manpower and materiel requirements for each unit, and many times more pages of secondary and supplementary programs prepared by the field commands.

A Presidential decision may alter budget-planning assumptions for the following fiscal year and necessitate substantial changes in the program under preparation. For example, President Kennedy in late 1962 cancelled the Air Force's "Skybolt" (air-to-ground nuclear-tipped missile) program, causing major changes in Air Force budgetary plans. Such decisions are not uncommon, and may be expected in the future. The timing of the decision and the extent of the modification decreed determines the way in which changes are incorporated into the program. If the changes are not major, revision of the program may be deferred to a later stage in the cycle, perhaps by running a second program cycle concurrently with the preparation of the budget estimate. In this case, the results of the second cycle could be used as a basis for adjustments in the budget estimates during the later departmental review.

Under recent procedures, about sixteen months before the beginning of the budget (fiscal) year, the Defense Department Comptroller issued a "Call for Estimates" letter to the service departments. This provided technical direction on the timing and format of budget submissions, and sometimes contained more or less detailed statements implying ceilings on total expenditures and on the forces and equipment that each service was expected to develop and maintain, all based on the President's decisions on the budget request prepared the *previous* year. At the time the military department received the estimates call, however, its program was already completed and its budget preparation process well under way.

Various expedients were used to incorporate the call. When possible, attempts were made to revise the detailed departmental programs to make them compatible with higher policy guidance. Otherwise preparation of the budget estimate continued without interruption, and the "Guidance" (usually cutbacks) was incorporated as far as possible during the departmental review. Neither expedient was satisfactory.

The next step was the translation of the program into estimates of the need for and expenditure of the funds that program required. This operation proceeded in several different ways, depending upon the appropriation category. The traditional major categories have been:

1. Military personnel (pay and allowances).
2. Operation and maintenance.
3. Procurement of major equipment.
4. Research, development, test, and evaluation.
5. Military construction.

As we have seen, when the objectives and force-levels were first decided, neither the President nor the Congress had finished considering the budget estimate of the preceding year. Under the system prior to the 1964 budget year the initial departmental budget estimates were completed by late summer, the very time when the President, the National Security Council, and the Budget Bureau were first able to turn their attention to guidance.

Either during departmental budget preparation or immediately thereafter, an NSC-Presidential decision was made on force levels for the coming budget year, followed or accompanied by a Budget Bureau-Presidential decision on the maximum budget the Defense Department would be permitted to request.

The President must submit his budget to Congress in January within the first fifteen days of each session. This allows about six months for its resolution within the lengthy legislative appropriations process. By Christmas—in order to allow the Government Printer time to print it—the President must have completed the executive budget formation process, prescribing funds to be spent largely in the government's fiscal year beginning the following July 1. Because of unforeseen contingencies, subsequent requests for "supplemental" appropriations are common.

Budgeting for national security can never be a neat and simple process when officials from the President on down have to struggle to keep in mind simultaneously at least three different problems: spending money already appropriated, planning the budget for the fiscal year immediately ahead, and setting budgetary guidelines for the fiscal year after the one immediately ahead. An Army budget chief once described the process as follows:

> Most of the time the preparation of the Army Budget resembles a three-ring circus. For example, in the spring we're funding the current budget; we're defending next year's budget; and we're formulating the budget for the succeeding year. Add to this the post-mortem on last year's financial performance and it is bigger than the Biggest Show on Earth.[11]

The Kennedy Administration came to office determined to reform the system so that it would become a more effective instrument for rational choice. In 1961 Budget Director David E. Bell, Secretary of Defense Robert S. McNamara, and Defense Comptroller Assistant Secretary Charles J. Hitch outlined a new system in testimony to a Senate subcommittee.

Beginning with the fiscal year 1963, a projection of requirements and tentative approved programs with dollar costs attached, extending five or more years into the future, would be available at all times. As Secretary McNamara told a Congressional subcommittee:

> We propose to maintain that plan or budget up to date with monthly revisions to it so that at any particular time when a budget for a special period, such as the fiscal year,

[11] Lieutenant General William S. Lawton, Army Comptroller, prepared address, Harvard Defense Policy Seminar, November 12, 1958.

is required, it can be abstracted from the continually modified and continually adjusted military program.[12]

The stated purpose was to make the budget more useful as an instrument for forward planning and for illuminating alternative programs and measuring program performance. Toward this end, the Administration began budgetary reform along three major fronts.

First was a new system—initially called "program packaging" and later called simply "programs"—to supplement, and perhaps ultimately to substitute for, the traditional budget forms by cutting across the traditional armed forces and expenditure categories. The new categories will be "Strategic Retaliatory Forces," "Continental Air and Missile Defense Forces," "Sealift and Airlift," "Reserve Forces," "Research and Development." A further category, "General Purpose Forces," covers Army, Air Force, Navy and Marine Corps units with conventional war missions short of all-out nuclear war, while funds for armed services "housekeeping"—food, clothing, and shelter—are under "General Support."

Second was the establishment of "country development programing," to relate U. S. foreign aid programs—both military and economic—more closely to a foreign nation's self-help development programs and to aid coming from sources other than the United States. Hopefully this will produce more coherent foreign-aid programs, from the point of view of both the nation aided and United States national interest.

Third was the creation in the Budget Bureau of "coordinated forward budgets" covering future needs in such interrelated fields as foreign aid, intelligence, and American propaganda overseas and, especially, research and development, an activity dispersed among many different departments and agencies. These provide central information about the government's total programs in these areas, making it easier for the individual agencies or departments to plan their own

[12] Senate Government Operations Subcommittee on National Security Policy Machinery, *Hearings and Report*, "The Bureau of the Budget and the Budgetary Process," October 16, 1961, p. 5.

budgets and for the President and the Congress to recognize, on the basis of the over-all picture, which policies and programs seem best.

IV

Each of the thousands of units within the national security establishment presumably has a specific purpose—a "mission," in military parlance. The requirements for each must generally be calculated in annual fiscal year terms, both because Congress insists upon annual reviews and because the Constitution prohibits appropriation of money for the Army for use beyond a term of two years (Article I, Section 8). So, in a general sense, defense budget making involves an arithmetic compilation of what each subdivision of the defense establishment considers to be its annual needs. In a practical sense, because of a number of intricate and incalculable factors, this compilation occurs within the context of implicit or explicit ceilings or guidelines. Consequently, defense budgeting rests finally on judgment of the relative importance of various programs, the setting of priorities, and attempts to achieve a "balanced program."

In determining security requirements, the United States is handicapped in two important ways. First, because of national values, objectives, and tradition, America's Cold War strategy will inevitably be defensive. It is one thing to calculate the requirements for aggressive national strategy designed to attain specific objectives within a given time schedule. It is quite another to calculate what is needed to deter a potential opponent from action by making his objective appear to be attainable only at an unacceptable cost. It is impossible to measure the effect of alternative United States programs upon his perceptions of the situation or upon his original intentions.

The second complicating factor is the profound disagreement over the effects of the new technology upon military means. This controversy takes place, as we saw in the previous chapter, within an organizational framework that inhibits the development of a unified strategy. Military requirements are currently calculated not only with a particular external enemy in mind, but with the survival of separate military institutions as well. Even after the introduction of the new budgetary forms described above, Secretary McNamara, in 1962, continued to criticize the military services' lack of unified planning and their parochial views on possible future warfare.[13]

The separate services make dogmatic statements of what is "required" to carry out a given military mission without taking into account the fact that both we and our potential enemies usually have a wide range of objectives and means that continually interact in the dynamics of international politics. Most narrow statements of military requirements overlook, or oversimplify, the great uncertainties inherent in strategic planning.

Military requirements and defense budgets ought to be derived from a rational process of strategic planning that, though inevitably and properly characterized by disputes among those advocating competing strategies, would proceed somewhat as follows: National policy objectives reflecting the most accurate possible assessment of the threat to national security and the values and goals of American society would be set at the Presidential level. Next would come an assessment by the President, aided by the great staff resources at his command, of the means available for pursuing these. Then would be formulated, first, a *national* strategy, based upon the considerations above, and, following that, a *military* strategy, from which military requirements could be ascertained. Such a military strategy would have no inherent *raison d'être*; it would be rather a plan to seek those foreign policy objectives that military power can aid in attaining. Finally, the defense budget would be determined after scrupulous examination by the President, the Secretary of Defense and the JCS of the requirements military professionals set forth as necessary to implement a given strategy. A final determination would, of course, be the result of an ultimate

[13] Jackson Committee, *Hearings*, p. 769.

Presidential weighing of each proposed use of resources for defense, support of health, education, and welfare, roads, conservation, and so on.[14]

While budgets must be based upon policy objectives and existing strategy, they must also provide the resources to support prospective strategies that may have to be chosen in future years. For example, in 1962 defense officials were discussing whether to develop medium-range ballistic missiles for possible deployment to Europe. Under existing NATO strategy and United States policy, such weapons are not required. However, since it would take about five years to develop and produce them, there had to be a decision as to whether or not to proceed with the development so that decision makers five years later, in the international situation then existing, could adopt a strategy including such weapons.

V

A number of the major critics of the budgetary system as it existed prior to 1961 were recruited into positions of authority in the Kennedy Administration and instituted reforms to meet many of the defects. The total budget process has been speeded up, and presumably can be further accelerated by modern systems of data processing. Budget categories have been revised, enabling them to reveal more accurately—at least in dollar figures—the costs of identifiable military functions. Certainly the category "continental air defense" is more revealing than "operation and maintenance."

Long-range program planning now goes forward simultaneously with budget estimates extending over a number of future years. Prior to 1961 the optimum program was difficult to determine because estimates of its costs in future years were often not available. Within the Budget Bureau, it is true, some long-range cost projections were made prior to 1962. But until the Kennedy Administration's reforms, such forward estimates were not systematically consolidated by

[14] For astute criticism of how the system worked, see Kissinger, *Nuclear Weapons and Foreign Policy*, p. 411.

the central officials of the Defense Department or used effectively in the budget process.

Within the limitations of economics and intelligence systems as predictive sciences, the budget process has been adjusted since 1961 so that responsible choice makers can in fact choose more efficiently. Still needed are more logical categories and systems that distinguish among not just major military functions but "capital" expenditures and routine operating costs.[15] Along these lines one of the systematic breakdowns applied to all programs beginning in 1962 is a three-way division into research and development, investment, and operating costs. This can help inform decision makers as to what, specifically, the nation is buying, and also provide significant knowledge about the impact of the defense budget on the nation's economy.

More fundamental change in the Executive and Legislative branches is still required. In the Executive, need for greater defense unification has been discussed in previous pages. In Congress, the traditional item-by-item review of categories of expenditure, which have little relevance to strategic choice, must be abandoned.

As usual, Congress speaks with many conflicting voices regarding reforms. Congressman George Mahon of the House Defense Appropriations Subcommittee has since 1958 pressed the Defense Department for more revealing budgetary analyses on a mission basis. Congress generally is coming around to accept the notion that there must be at least a dual system of budget preparation—the old-fashioned item-by-item presentation and another that is more revealing in terms of major military functions to be performed. Although it presents the greatest obstacle to basic innovations that would permit more meaningful evaluation and choice of programs fulfilling defense requirements, Congress is certainly not entirely resistant to change.

Budgets, as instruments in the American political process,

[15] For detailed reform proposals see: Hitch and McKean, *op. cit.*, pp. 44–65; 233–39; Smithies, *op. cit.*, pp. 257–77; and Mosher, *op. cit.*, pp. 230–49.

serve many purposes and meet many needs. For example, they must be produced in a form acceptable to Congress. But Congress has normally been inclined to view executive-branch requirements for a system allowing coherent planning and budgeting as incompatible with its own requirements for influence in final budgetary choices.[16] A more coherent, efficient budget process within the Executive branch may be possible only at the expense of the influence and power of Congress in choice making—unless Congress institutes its own internal reform. That is to say, if budgets are drawn up in still broader categories, indicating what money will buy in terms of major strategic forces—such as limited war, all-out nuclear war, or air defense—rather than under separate headings of "Army," "Navy," and "Air Force," and under them item-by-item categories, Congress will be dealing with the unfamiliar. It may seem to members of the legislature that they are also dealing with the unmanageable, in terms of ability to change items in the budget. A fact of political life under the American system is that, if it so desires, Congress can be a roadblock to full benefits from the Executive's budgetary reforms. But Congress need not sacrifice its significant role. More unification of authority and power within Congress would permit it to maintain major influence in budgeting, and also permit Executive budget reform.

With all the Kennedy Administration reforms of 1961–62 the defense budget cannot be evaluated or considered apart from the total American body politic, of which budgets are vital organs. Budgets stem from, and must be considered in, the context of Presidential leadership, the central intelligence function, Department of Defense organization, the free flow of information, Congressional habits, organization, and per-

[16] For views in interesting contrast on these and related issues see Bernard K. Gordon, "The Military Budget: Congressional Phase," *The Journal of Politics*, November 1961, pp. 689–710; Raymond H. Dawson, "Congressional Innovation and Intervention in Defense Policy: Legislative Authorization of Weapons Systems," *American Political Science Review*, March 1962, pp. 42–57; and Edward L. Katzenbach, "BuBud's Defense Policy," *The Reporter*, June 23, 1960, pp. 25–27.

formance, and the state of public opinion. A serious weakness in any of these debilitates the budget process. Any given budget for any fiscal year, if it be efficiently determined in the democratic sense, must be directed by the best possible political leadership interacting with an alert and knowledgeable public opinion. Without such leadership within the right organizational environment it is unlikely that defense budgets can be shaped by that other vital ingredient—a coherent, unified national strategy.

Budgets are merely instruments of governance, and their further sharpening—still required—will not solve all the problems. Only a truly innovating Presidential leadership exercised both outside of and to the greatest possible extent within Congress can promote defense and democracy in the years ahead.

CHAPTER V

THE DEFENSE BUDGET
AND NATIONAL CHOICE

I

The preceding chapter emphasized the structure and process of defense budgeting. This chapter will illustrate the various approaches to the economics of national defense that have been characteristic of national decision makers since World War II. The term "economics" here refers simply to the concept of the most efficient use of the limited resources available in a given situation.

In any year, the most mysterious part of the President's budget is that enormous portion of it—well over half the total —designed to provide for the common defense. The United States has spent more than $500,000,000,000 for military power since World War II. Outside of the government, defense is perhaps the least debatable part of the budget, although, paradoxically, over it hangs the largest question mark.

What is the best way to construct a defense budget? There are two principal alternatives. In grossly oversimplified example, they are either to decide that the nation needs a one-million-man army and then calculate the costs and construct a budget; or to say, "Here is nine billion dollars, how much of an Army can you buy for this amount?" This is your "ceiling."

The Washington world of defense decision makers can be divided, at the risk of further oversimplification, into two camps: the "requirements-firsters" and the "budget-firsters." And within both groups there are, of course, special interests, as, for example, vast industrial complexes with a huge stake

in particular approaches to defense and with strong views on
how the money should be spent, whatever the amount.

"Requirements-firsters" tend to give more weight to intelligence estimates of enemy capabilities and intentions than is
normally advisable, particularly to those intelligence forecasts
that make the threat most advantageous, in budgetary battles, to the service or speciality of the particular military
planner. Greater predictability than prudence dictates also
is often accorded estimates of the performance, total costs and
time-of-availability of new and developing weapons systems.

Examples of attitudes that produce statements of military
requirements can be cited. General Thomas S. Power as Strategic Air Command Chief, said in 1960: "As a field commander I think it is incumbent upon me to try to protect an
unfavorable set of conditions or, you might say, the worst condition. . . . we work on the premise of the worst set of conditions rather than the best set of conditions."[1] The costs of
basing military requirements on the worst contingency, when
all the competing elements are totaled, are bound to run high.

A more general statement was made by General Maxwell
D. Taylor, former Army chief and more recently JCS chairman, who complained in 1960 that United States military
forces were not based upon requirements. He said: ". . . we
must obviously have a strong atomic deterrent force properly
guarded against surprise attack. . . . we should budget in
terms of that force. We have never determined first how big a
force, how many missiles, how many planes, how many bombs
on target are really necessary to set as a goal for these forces."[2]

Although his broad point of view is valid, General Taylor's
apparent assumption, like General Power's, is that these requirements can be precisely calculated. This assumes an unrealistic competence on the part of the military—or anyone
else, for that matter—for outcomes always depend upon count-
less variables, particularly since the nuclear revolution.

[1] Senate Armed Services Preparedness Investigating Subcommittee,
Hearings, "Missiles, Space and Other Major Defense Matters," 86th
Congress, 2d Session, February 2, 1960, pp. 15–16.
[2] *Ibid.*, p. 188.

Admiral Arleigh Burke's testimony as Chief of Naval Operations represents another kind of approach to military requirements. He was asked about General Power's assertion in 1960 that United States retaliatory capability could be destroyed by an enemy launching three hundred ballistic missiles, half long-range and half intermediate-range. Having access to the same intelligence reports as General Power, he nonetheless disagreed: "First, Russia couldn't have 150 ICBMs; and second, I don't think if she did have them she could destroy our total retaliatory capability."[3]

These brief illustrations suggest the speculative context in which defense planning must proceed. Those who argue that national strategic planning must be based strictly upon the narrowly conceived "requirements" for the common defense would have difficulty reconciling this with the fact that a consensus has never been attained from the various professional experts as to what these over-all requirements are. In fact, as Samuel P. Huntington has poignantly asserted, "no absolute requirements exist which, if met, will make the country secure and which, if unmet, will leave it insecure."[4]

Military leaders, whatever their contrasting views, share the common experience of having to confront the budget-firsters, usually civilians occupying positions of political power and responsibility. Civilian budget-firsters adhere to the vague concept once expressed by Calvin Coolidge: "Dollars are the first line of defense in America." They fear the consequences of additional defense spending and often can be heard warning of inflation or, indeed, of national bankruptcy. Extremists among the budget-firsters can even be found minimizing the external Communist threat, once they are aware of the huge monetary cost of trying to meet it. Some of them prefer to stress internal Communist dangers, taking the line that the Kremlin "doesn't want war. We are endangered, rather, by Communists and their sympathizers (big-spenders) in our midst."

Budget-firsters habitually cite the existence of large-scale

[3] *Hearings, loc. cit.*, p. 315.
[4] *The Common Defense*, p. 250.

mismanagement and waste in the defense establishment. Representative Jamie Whitten's (Democrat, Mississippi) criticisms typify those made by foes of high-level defense spending:

> . . . there is a tremendous waste not only of dollars but of manpower. We in this country are committed to what appears to me to be a most unsound approach to meeting our military needs. . . . as long as Russia maintains her Iron Curtain she can open the curtain slightly just a few inches, at any time, show us a little sample, and claim that it is representative of the overall, and immediately our policy calls for us not only to protect ourselves against what we saw behind that slight opening in the curtain, but to follow a policy of protecting ourselves from every conceivable thing which we think Russia could possibly have. . . . they could lead us into spending ourselves into bankruptcy, which really means destroying our ability to support a real war. . . . I believe the most essential part of our defense is the strong economy we must maintain.[5]

Many legislators similarly question the budgetary claims of the great military bureaucracies.

Budget-firsters are convinced that intelligence estimates of the military power of potential enemies are vastly exaggerated; that the defense establishment is rife with waste and mismanagement; and that there are, in fact, strict—and low—limits on what the economy can afford for defense. It is this attitude that produces a common 3 or 5 per cent across-the-board cut in defense expenditures in Congress, and even deeper cuts in foreign aid requests. To the budget-firsters, this has seemed to be the only way to keep matters under some control. Certainly, evidence of mismanagement and waste can always be produced. But across-the-board percentage cuts in defense budgets are a poor way to counter this, for they represent blind choices.

Budget-firsters tend to rule out tax rises or controls by as-

[5] *Congressional Record*, May 3, 1960, pp. 8605–06.

suming that the danger to national survival is not great. Often they are oblivious to the diplomatic danger done to the national interest by apparent relative military weakness. They ignore the fact that, as one analyst has understated it, "a war is likely to be more wasteful than inefficiency in the Pentagon."[6] The fact that the nation was able to survive a policy of budgetary folly preceding the first and second World Wars and the Korean War does not prove that we shall be so fortunate in the future.[7] The changing face of warfare makes it even more dangerous to proceed from costs to requirements, even granting the fact that requirements must now be stated in imprecise terms. The new Administration in 1961 was determined to invert the process and to determine requirements first. But as of 1962 this still remained a challenge. In the last analysis the nation's requirements can be derived only from a clearly defined national purpose.

Arbitrary budget ceilings are encouraged by the lack of a unified doctrine—itself the outgrowth of separate services with jealously guarded jurisdictions and often overlapping functions—and a system that seems to offer only a very fuzzy choice of alternatives. A White House or Budget Bureau staff not sufficiently large or experienced to make an appraisal of defense needs in relation to all other factors that must be considered lends further support to the budget-firsters. And so, even more importantly, does a Secretary of Defense not adequately staffed to be able to judge objectively or with an inappropriate concept of his role. The Secretary of Defense should properly be an advocate of the nation's defense needs, and not of a Presidential party line on expenditure ceilings. Admittedly, a Defense Secretary will often face the dilemma resulting from his need to fight for fulfilling military requirements and his obligations as a member of the Presidential

[6] Henry Rowen, "National Security and the American Economy in the 1960's," Congressional Joint Economic Committee, Study Paper No. 18, 86th Congress, 2d Session, January 30, 1960, p. 65.

[7] For a concise history, see George C. Reinhardt and William R. Kintner, *The Haphazard Years*, Garden City, New York, Doubleday, 1960.

team. But a Presidential "yes man" in the Pentagon will in
the end serve neither the President nor the defense establishment well. The Budget Bureau serves the President in one
way. Serving him in another way, the Defense Secretary
should concern himself with determining, in the most precise
manner possible, military requirements. The rule should be an
"arm's length" relationship between the White House and
the Pentagon budgeteers, not the collaboration characteristic
of the Eisenhower years.

The budgeteer's operating philosophy was acutely summed
up by William F. Schaub, speaking in 1959 as Chief of the
Military Division of the Bureau of the Budget: "The object
of the Bureau of the Budget is to see that the least possible
amount of money is spent unjustifiably and that what we do
spend goes to produce the most effective results."[8] This remark overlooks the fact that the criteria for the effectiveness
of, say, deterrent military forces, are hard to come by, and
expresses no concern for a higher objective—national security
—to be sought even at the risk of spending "too much" money.
But apparently the staff of the Budget Bureau "by the very
nature of their operation," as W. J. McNeil (himself a budgeteer) once stated, "does think, as Gertrude Stein might have
said, that the budget ceiling is a budget ceiling is a budget
ceiling."[9]

The Director of the Bureau of the Budget, and the Comptroller (Assistant Secretary of Defense) in the Pentagon, in
their perennial role of whipping boy for the various interests
demanding more of this or that element of military power,
are not alone in approaching military planning from the
standpoint of ceilings or "guidelines." Perhaps inevitably, the
same also applies to the separate services as they build their
final departmental budgets.

A good example of this can be found in the testimony of
the Chief of Naval Operations to the House subcommittee
on defense appropriations in 1959. Admiral Arleigh Burke
was explaining the Navy budget process, which, he said, pro-

---

[8] Quoted in the *Register and Defense Times*, December 26, 1959.
[9] Jackson Committee, *Hearings*, July 1961, Part VII, p. 1072.

ceeded from a basic program objectives document. Program objectives, he stated, are the basis for Navy planning. "They should cost out in the neighborhood of the funds which the Navy can assume to be within reason of attainment. If the program objectives did not have a dollar value, the objectives in all areas could be limitless. . . ."[10] Clearly, ceilings exist, and must exist, in some form in the planning process. The basic issue is how, when, and on what assumptions these ceilings are to be derived and promulgated.

II

In the years of the Eisenhower Administration, bitter and constant criticism buffeted the Administration's alleged ceiling-first approach to defense budgets. In a steady stream of Congressional investigations, such as those by Senator Stuart Symington's "Study of Airpower" hearings and subsequent, post-sputnik public inquiries into the adequacy of the missile and space programs by Senator Lyndon Johnson's Senate Armed Services Preparedness Investigating Subcommittee, much publicity and pressure were generated by the requirements-firsters. It was argued, with some validity, that conservative domestic economic theories dominated the Eisenhower Administration to the detriment of the establishment of adequate military power and support for the space exploration programs. Basic assumptions in these criticisms were twofold: that it was always entirely clear what were the requirements for defense, and that this procedure was somehow different from the way defense expenditures had been planned by the pre-Eisenhower (Democratic) administrations.

In this respect it is interesting to recall some of the post-World War II history of defense budgeting and expenditures. The separate services commonly establish initial force levels and requirements greater than Administration leaders believe the economy can (or the taxpayer will agree to) "afford"

[10] House Appropriations Subcommittee on Department of Defense Appropriations, *Hearings*, "DOD Appropriations for 1960," p. 664.

within a given period of expenditure. When this happens, either force levels may be cut down, or the period for which they (and basic maintenance and modernization programs) are to be provided may be extended over a long period—commonly called the "stretch out." Either the cutback or the stretch out may increase the risks of war or diplomatic failure. But if one has to choose, as the armed services often do, the stretch out may be the lesser risk. Generally, it is easier to speed up a stretched-out military force than to build a new one suddenly.

In 1946, President Truman assembled his military chiefs and announced to them that in the budget for the following year, $6 billion was required for interest on the national debt. Of the remainder of the total budget, not more than one-third could be used for defense.[11] At this stage the fact that the requirements of foreign policy or military strategy might impose imperative demands of their own was not recognized.

From all the evidence, President Truman adhered to the ceilings approach stubbornly in drawing up the 1948, 1949, and 1950 budgets. With the Bureau of the Budget taking the leadership in defense-budget details, ceilings of $11 billion for 1948, $12 billion for 1949, and $15 billion for 1950 were set. To level off defense spending at $15 billion in 1950, the Director of the Bureau of the Budget proposed a reduction of air groups to 55, postponement of significant parts of the Navy shipbuilding program, and sharp reductions in material support for the Army. The President endorsed this ceiling, although it was some $3 billion below the "minimum figures" the Joint Chiefs of Staff and Secretary of Defense James V. Forrestal were advocating.

The Defense Secretary, though he often voiced the need to balance "military necessities with national solvency," recorded in his diary at the time: "Is the world situation such as to warrant appropriations on this order at the present time?"[12] Believing the answer to be "No," Forrestal carried his fight

[11] This approach to the defense budget is described in *The Forrestal Diaries*, p. 160.

[12] *Ibid.*, p. 430.

for a higher defense budget to the White House to assure himself that the Budget Bureau was not making independent decisions. At a meeting with the President, Forrestal was also confronted by the Secretary of State, George C. Marshall. The President asked Marshall to explain to Forrestal basic assumptions behind the level of defense expenditures. Forrestal recorded in his diary: "Marshall said the policy of this country was based upon the assumption that there would not be a war and that we should not plunge into war preparations which would bring about the very thing we were taking these steps to prevent."[13]

In this instance, as in many others preceding and following it, it was easy to place limits on military budgets by assuming that the best, not the worst, would happen. Forrestal's successor, Louis Johnson, slashed one third of the initial $16 billion military request for fiscal year 1950. He was motivated by a belief that, as he put it, "Stalin doesn't look to a clash of arms, . . . he expects America to spend itself into bankruptcy."[14]

The Korean War was an unexpected disruption of peace expectations. The Defense Department had to begin to shape its budgets not only for the heavy expenditures involved in fighting that unforeseen "police action," but also for an expanded military mobilization base for a war that would possibly be more general and more serious. But even in this situation the "ceilings first" approach prevailed. Secretary of Defense Robert Lovett, testifying before Congress on the defense budget for fiscal year 1953, made it clear that in order to reach the state of readiness the armed services considered essential, a much higher expenditure was necessary than the Bureau of the Budget and the President were willing to allow. Consequently there would have to be a stretch out and a much later target date for the achievement of the required state of readiness. Secretary Lovett told Congress:

The decision to build toward these goals rather than attempt to reach them in fiscal year 1953 or 1954 was made

[13] *The Forrestal Diaries*, p. 432.
[14] "MacArthur Hearings," p. 2627.

after careful consideration of the economic, material, fiscal and military implications involved. The reduction of our initial request to the Bureau of the Budget was in line with these considerations and with an expenditure limitation as directed by the President.[15]

Committed to balancing the budget, the new Eisenhower Administration in 1953 continued to make strict budgetary ceilings the basis for defense planning. In his first State of the Union message, President Eisenhower spoke of the need "to achieve adequate military strength within the limits of endurable strain on our economy." But, as has been shown, this was not an extraordinary approach to the problem. It fits the model of the "three constraints" often invoked in determining the magnitude of the military effort in any given period: absolute requirements that will guarantee security; absolute limits on "what the nation's economy can accommodate"; and absolute limits on "what the taxpayer will support." As Samuel P. Huntington notes, "all three are artificial constructs invoked by the participants in the policy-making process."[16] The pre-sputnik goal of the Eisenhower Administration was to reduce the defense budget to a $35 billion level. There is a consistency in the difference between what the armed services requested and what the President allowed in the first four years of the Eisenhower Administration:

Fiscal Year	Requests by Services (in millions)	President's Budget
1954	$41,286	$36,039
1955	$35,901	$30,950
1956	$37,397	$32,860
1957	$41,129	$35,389

In explaining the $5 billion reduction in the fiscal year 1954 budget request—which had already been submitted to

[15] House Subcommittee on Defense Appropriations, Hearings, "Department of Defense Appropriations for 1952," 82nd Congress, 1st Session, 1951, p. 14.
[16] The Common Defense, p. 250; see also Schilling et al., Strategy, Politics and Defense Budgets.

Congress by the outgoing Truman Administration—Secretary of Defense Charles E. Wilson noted that procurement, construction, and training programs were not well coordinated and that there had been slippages in such programs as aircraft production. These and other considerations provided the excuse for eliminating about $5 billion from the various programs, and bringing the total figure down close to the preconceived $35 billion ceiling.

The Symington Senate Armed Services Subcommittee hearings on the Air Force "Study of Airpower" in 1956 reveal interesting details about the budgetary process in the first three years of the Eisenhower Administration. The subcommittee was under the leadership and control of the requirements-firsters in Congress, who had allied with the various armed services and other interest groups urging larger defense expenditures. The following exchange occurred between the subcommittee's counsel and the Defense Secretary: *Mr. [Fowler] Hamilton:* Now, sir, the committee has received testimony . . . that your objective was to keep Defense expenditures in the order of $35 billion. . . . *Mr. [Charles E.] Wilson:* I wouldn't say it was, quite. . . . I have no arbitrary figure that I work to, though I wouldn't quarrel too much with someone who said that that [$35 billion] was an average of what it looked like to him.[17]

Later Secretary Wilson was questioned about reports that the defense budget for fiscal year 1958 had come to a preliminary estimate of $48 billion. He replied:

> I don't think our country is faced with anything like a $48 billion defense program. There is nothing changed in the world suddenly. And any such requirement would require some controls and partial mobilization. . . . It [$48 billion] is the summation of all the hopes and fears of the military department, and they cannot finance that, and that is why the civilians are on the job. . . . I don't quite sub-

[17] Senate Armed Services Subcommittee on the Air Force, *Hearings,* "Study of Airpower," 84th Congress, 2d Session, June 29, 1956, p. 1663.

scribe to the fact that just because we have a prosperous country we should spend more and more money on the military machine. . . . we have got to spend what we need for the security of our country, and if we have to have higher or lower taxes or if we have to give up some other things we would like to have, why we will have to do it.

On the other side I don't think the military services should just grow on their own to be bigger and better, you know, like the average businessman every year he wants to have his business bigger and better.[18]

The questions Mr. Wilson did not face were: Who decides how much the nation needs for security and on what basis is it to be decided? He implied that the concept of civilian control of the military answers all such questions. But he did not make clear the assumptions upon which budgetary decisions were to be based.

III

Much of the defense budget debate has centered upon the choice of alternative strategic concepts. For example, the "minimum deterrent" or "finite" concept holds that, regardless of the military power any enemy may possess, the only basic requirement for deterrence is to maintain a force sufficient to inflict unacceptable losses upon that would-be aggressor in any contingency. If America possesses this capability, the potential enemy will be deterred from an initial attack. Thus the capability of destroying a finite number of major cities provides adequate deterrence. Such deterrence is assured when the potential enemy knows that you can and will, under provocation, destroy his homeland centers of political, industrial, and military control. Proponents of this concept usually argue that no such war will occur because in modern all-out nuclear war, there is no such thing as "victory" for either side.

Another strategic concept underlies the "counterforce" ar-

[18] *Ibid.*, pp. 1671–72.

gument. This suggests that, in addition to a vengeance or retaliatory—"second strike"—capability, the United States must have the ability to strike first and destroy the enemy's military capacity to do us unacceptable harm. Most promoters of this concept do not advocate the initiation of a "preventive" or "preemptive" general war,[19] but argue that the capability of destroying the enemy's major strategic instruments—missile sites and air bases, and not simply cities and populations—is requisite to deterrence.

Still a third concept is based upon the argument that both of the above doctrines are liable to miscalculation. There is too great a danger of underestimating the forces demanded for either finite or counterforce deterrence. Accordingly the safest course is to maintain at least equality, and at best superiority, in the face of enemy forces in all major categories. This third alternative might be labeled the fully "credible deterrent." It calls in effect for an arms race with Soviet Russia to maintain a wide spectrum of countervailing military power. This must include the capability of deterring or dealing effectively with local or limited wars and meeting the realities of warfare on still another level, that of "counterinsurgency," which includes guerrilla warfare, subversion, or insurrection in any part of the world.

How are such major arguments to be resolved? How much

---

[19] The main distinction between preventive and preemptive war involves time. A preventive strike against an adversary might occur weeks, months, or even years before you are certain he will strike you. A preemptive strike is against an enemy you judge will attack you within hours or a few days. A veritable five-foot shelf of publications on modern military strategy now exists. For broad coverage see: Brodie, *Strategy in the Missile Age;* Huntington, *The Common Defense;* Herman Kahn, *On Thermonuclear War,* Princeton University Press, 1960; William W. Kaufmann et al., *Military Policy and National Security,* Princeton University Press, 1956; Henry Kissinger, *The Necessity for Choice,* New York, Harper, 1961, Doubleday Anchor, 1962; Robert E. Osgood, *Limited War,* University of Chicago Press, 1957; and Rowen, *op. cit.,* to name but a few. For a useful bibliography, see Richard Brody, "Deterrence Strategies: An Annotated Bibliography," *Journal of Conflict Resolution,* Vol. 4, December 1960, pp. 443–57.

is enough for national security? Can the risks and costs of alternative strategies or types of military instruments be meaningfully calculated? Because there has been no consensus in response to such questions, decision makers have habitually relied upon compromises. This has led at least one Budget Director to suggest the axiom: "Effective budgeting is the uniform distribution of dissatisfaction."

IV

How much can the United States afford for defense? Budget-first exhortations by civilian political leaders or Secretaries of the Treasury are understandable, even if the economic assumptions underlying them have sometimes seemed primitive. It is more surprising to find that military chiefs have been concerned about the burden of military spending on the economy. Apparently the question as to how the economy affects military strategy has been basic to the disagreement between "strategic deterrence" (airpower and missile) economizers and Army leaders who have argued for years that the nation needs more conventional ground forces.

It is beyond the bounds of military professionalism for the military leader to have official judgments about strictly economic or political matters.[20] Yet consider the statements of some military leaders in the post-World War II debates on the adequacy of the defense budget. First, General Omar Bradley in March 1950:

> I had to go along with a $13 billion budget. I do not recommend a larger one at this time for various reasons. . . . if we had come here and recommended to you a $30 billion or $40 billion budget for defense, I think we would be doing a disservice. . . .[21]

[20] In this section I am indebted to a Harvard Defense Policy Seminar background paper compiled by Donald B. Keesing, November 1956.

[21] Senate Appropriations Committee, *Hearings*, "DOD Appropriations for 1951," 81st Congress, 2d Session, 1950, p. 73.

And again,

> This fiscal year '51 budget does not pretend to fill all the holes. But we hope that this budget and succeeding ones will give sufficient emphasis to these points of vulnerability so that the effectiveness of our forces is maximum and the risk to our security is minimum within a few years. If we did not take this view and make the assumption the appropriation request which we would have to recommend would be out of all proportion to that which we believe this country could afford at this time.

Quoting this later in his article "A Soldier's Farewell" in *The Saturday Evening Post*, General Bradley acknowledged that he had made a "special mistake":

> It was that last sentence which I now regard as outside the responsibility of the nation's military advisers. We have no way of knowing what this country *will* afford or its economy *can* afford. Only the economic advisers and the civilian advisers, including Congress, can make that estimate and that decision, and certainly our military recommendations on forces we need should not be curbed in any way by economic assumptions.[22]

Note also the assumptions of Admiral Arthur Radford, Bradley's successor and Chairman of the JCS in March 1954:

> . . . The Soviet leaders would be quite content to await the inevitable were we to embark on a program of maintaining force-in-being in such numbers as to insure our eventual economic collapse. . . . It is for just such reasons that we of the military view the economy of this country as a factor of military importance. . . .[23]

Comments by two other high-ranking military figures further illustrate the inclusion of economic assumptions in United States defense plans:

[22] *Saturday Evening Post*, August 22, 1953, pp. 63–64.
[23] Senate Appropriations Committee, *Hearings*, 83rd Congress, 2d Session, March 1954, p. 80.

General Twining, Chief of Staff of the Air Force, remarked in 1956:

> We cannot afford to keep in our Armed Forces conventional forces for the old type of warfare plus those for atomic warfare. . . .[24]

And General Curtis LeMay, Commander of SAC, declared in 1956:

> I assure you that while it is not our job in the military to determine how much money we can spend for defense or any other purpose in the Government, we think about it and I know we can lose the country through bankruptcy as well as we can lose it to an outside enemy.[25]

In recent years the more enlightened military officials have apparently learned to abstain from stating publicly their economic assumptions.

Democracies are not fond of tax increases, and national politics since World War II furnish few exceptions to the rule. It is only with trepidation that a party in power raises taxes except in a time of well-recognized emergency. Translated into budget level alternatives, the politics of taxation mean that the only politically desirable increase in government spending is one that generates so much new income that it automatically results in a revenue increase big enough to pay for the increase in expenditures.

During the spring of 1951 even the Congressional Joint Committee on the Economic Report supported, in a vote of 11 to 3, a statement on the defense budget that started out by saying the committee felt "that the defense budget should be cut to the revenue cloth." The majority went on to explain that, "In a long period of armed alert ahead, lavish military expenditures might readily wreck the economy if not limited to ceiling levels." The minority that disagreed countered, "In our judgment the revenue garment should be cut to the de-

[24] "Study of Airpower," pp. 1526–27.
[25] Testimony before Senate Subcommittee on Department of Defense Appropriations for FY 1957, *Hearings*, pp. 1249–50.

fense cloth. . . . Freedom is more important than opulence
and without freedom opulence will disappear."[26] This exchange suggests that most "economic" issues concerning defense become, ultimately, political questions.

Testifying to Congress in 1954, Professor Alvin H. Hansen
of Harvard cautiously stated the position of many professional economists:

> From the standpoint of national security I have no compe-
> tence whatever to judge whether or not these proposed
> reductions in military expenditures are justified. I do want
> to say emphatically that from the standpoint of economics,
> the economy is quite able to carry the current and even
> larger outlays for national security and for foreign aid pro-
> grams.[27]

Most economists tended to agree in the 1950s that, so long
as taxation and other manipulative devices were used to hold
down inflation, the nation could have spent many billions
more and still maintained an economy in which disposable
personal incomes were high and rising. Indeed, the hope seems
to persist among some economic analysts that in the long run
a larger military budget may stimulate what amounts to a
better use of resources, and employment and production will
grow faster than they would without such added revenues. Of
course, the government could instead build roads or schools
or engage in other public works and welfare programs to
stimulate the economy with widely beneficial results. The
opinion that defense spending can boost the economy at small
net cost stems from the generally accepted view that insufficient private civilian demand can diminish both national income and employment, whereas government demand can insure, up to a point, an increase in both.

Economists disagree as to how much private "demand"
would actually exist in the absence or diminishment of government defense spending. But it is widely asserted that Cold

[26] Senate *Report* No. 210, 82nd Congress, p. 15.
[27] Statement in *Hearings*, Congressional Joint Committee on Economic Report, February 1954.

War levels of government spending have helped to keep the economy going. Military procurement of hardware in particular has strongly benefited heavy and engineering industries, although the case for the argument that, because of this, defense spending beyond current levels would be "free" or beneficial is weak. Still it is quite possible that even though the Federal Government spends for defense beyond the recent years' level of about 10 per cent of the Gross National Product, economic benefits will be derived that will make defense procurement less "expensive" than it appears.

Few economists take seriously the idea prevalent in the Eisenhower years that the nation has been near any discernible economic limits, although problems of inflation and later foreign balance of payments and outflow of gold from the United States certainly were and are cause for concern. It seems more reasonable to suppose, however, that the arguments over the limits of economic strain involve ultimately political rather than economic judgments. This raises the question: How can members of Congress and leaders of public opinion be made to understand better the diplomatic and military consequences of fearing high defense expenditures more than potential external threats to the common defense?

Budget-firsters, to bolster their argument that "nobody really knows," can cite conflicting opinions among professional military advisers as to what is required, but they either ignore the fact that inflationary pressure can be offset by proper Federal fiscal management, or they fear such management as much as an external Communist threat. They also ignore the fact that, while extra expenditures in defense areas may not bring significant additional security, in such areas as foreign aid, overseas information, and other non-military foreign programs, expenditures may mean the difference between disaster (or diplomatic defeat) and survival (or diplomatic success). Budget-firsters do not see what is often the real issue in any given annual defense budget: the need to balance extra effort (and perhaps some sacrifice) against added, even crucial, margins of security in the long run.

The defense budget for 1962 was about 9 per cent of the

Gross National Product. At the height of defense expenditures in World War II, this figure was close to 50 per cent. In 1953 the figure, reflecting Korean War expenditures, was about 15 per cent.

Most economists have argued that if the 1962 defense budget had been increased by 50 per cent, bringing it to over $70 billion, it would not have caused sharp reductions in consumption or capital investment. Many studies have been published showing the very light impact a $10 or $15, or even $20 billion addition to defense spending would have on the nation's economy.[28]

V

The defense budget system in existence and the prevailing economic mythology since World War II reflect both the compromises made in the basic defense organizational structure and failures of political leadership. This structure and the nature of the compromise have been discussed in Chapter III. Suffice it to say here that one consequence of the budget system and the prevailing attitudes has been an inefficient allocation of resources for national security. Each of the armed services, in the process of bargaining among themselves and with the Secretary of Defense, the Bureau of the Budget, and the President, has concentrated more attention on higher budgets and the preservation of jurisdiction for individual armed services than upon efficient allocation of resources within the services. This has indubitably produced enormous waste.

A great difficulty with the defense budget system has been Congress, with its complex authorization and budget review procedures. Congressional appropriations committees tend to

[28] See, particularly, Gerhard Colm, "Can We Afford Additional Programs for National Security," Washington, D.C., National Planning Association, 1953; Manuel Helzner, "Impact of More Defense Dollars," *Harvard Business Review*, March–April 1960; Hitch and McKean, *The Economics of Defense in the Nuclear Age*, Part I; and Rowen, *op. cit.*, Part II.

look upon budgetary reform with great suspicion, as a threat to their power. Consequently, Congress effectively destroyed President Eisenhower's proposal during the 1958 defense reorganization to appropriate money to the Defense Secretary for use at his discretion, within limits, and has set up similar roadblocks in the Kennedy Administration.

The new Administration in 1961 hoped to steer a rational course between the extremes of "ceilings-first" and "requirements-first." President Kennedy came to the White House with a record of speeches and statements highly critical of the Eisenhower Administration's approach to the common defense, and he assembled in his Administration numerous critics of the previous regime, who had produced virtually a "five-foot shelf" of books on strategy, defense budgeting, and related subjects. In his Inaugural Address the President seemed to be casting aside the budget-first approach: ". . . we shall pay any price, bear any burden, meet any hardship, . . . to assure the survival and the success of liberty." The defense budget was increased steadily in the first Kennedy years.

Mention was made in the previous chapter of the reforms imposed by Kennedy's Secretary of Defense, Robert S. McNamara, to make the defense budget a more useful instrument for national policy and for tighter civilian control of the defense establishment. Before McNamara took over the Secretaryship, a looseness and ambiguity of executive control permitted the separate armed services to prepare, defend, and propagandize their own separate budgets. The Defense Secretary would provide policy "guidelines" for the services to follow, and when the budget was prepared he would appear before Congress as sponsor of the total amount requested and its division into various proportions among the services. Each service, represented by its civilian Secretary and Chief of Staff, would then go to Capitol Hill to defend its particular share of the budget, and it was not uncommon for the services, while vowing loyalty to the President and the Secretary of Defense, to make clear their "personal opinion" that too heavy a cut had been made here or there in their particular budget.

In other words the debate over requirements was allowed to continue beyond the point of coherent choice.

Secretary McNamara radically modified this procedure by replacing the separate budgets of the services, insofar as they pertained to major military functions, with interservice budget categories. And the requirements of these categories were projected over a five-year period so that Congress could not only see the initial research and development costs for the various weapons systems but also have a clearer notion of their cumulative costs after they had become operational in the field.

There are still separate service presentations to the Congressional appropriations committees on personnel, procurement, operation and maintenance, and so on. But these pertain mainly to support and logistics functions for the broader military missions referred to above.

With Secretary McNamara's reforms, the budget was, in the first two years of the Kennedy Administration, an important instrument of change in the direction of a more meaningful approach to the requirements of defense, at the expense of the identity of traditionally separate services. As such, it represents the "requirements-first" approach.

Although important reforms were under way, the budget, as of 1962, nonetheless confronted the President, a top agency official, or a Congressman with the necessity of, as a Senate report describes it, running "an obstacle course of obscure funding concepts, archaic appropriations categories, and fiscal jargon in using the budget to help make policy and program decisions."[29] Despite improvements effected since that description the budget submitted to Congress in January still resembles in broad format the first budget President Harding submitted under the budgetary reforms of forty years ago.

Within the statutory limits, each President decides how he will use the budget—as a device for keeping the lid on expenditures, or as his "lengthened shadow" in fiscal policy and ex-

[29] Senate, Government Operations Subcommittee on National Policy Machinery, "The Bureau of the Budget and the Budgetary Process," 87th Congress, 1st Session, October 16, 1961, p. 4.

ecutive leadership. As stated at the outset, the defense budget is at the heart of the politics of choice in the realm of national security. Thus budgetary decisions reflect national psychology, the level of public information and opinion, the attitudes and effectiveness of the current leadership, and, ultimately, the basic constitutional structure.

There are few intellectual challenges greater than establishing criteria for measuring the effectiveness of given defense programs. Perhaps "How much is enough?" is not the right question to ask. The more pertinent and realistic question may be, as one analyst has put it, "How much is needed for defense more than it is needed for other purposes?"[30]

The basic purpose of budgetary reform should be twofold: to enable the nation's leaders to decide more accurately what resources are needed for the common defense, and to enable those responsible for national security to make better informed decisions in assigning the resources Congress allocates for national defense.

[30] Hitch and McKean, *op. cit.*, p. 48.

CHAPTER VI

SECRET INTELLIGENCE:
USE AND ABUSE

I

In the growth of invisible government power since World War II, no instrument, except possibly the budget, has been more significant in defense policy making or more mysterious in the public mind than America's relatively new central intelligence apparatus.

Prior to World War II, the President and his principal policy-making associates received bits and pieces of foreign information from many sources, principally State Department officers in foreign countries, but also military attachés, friends, and associates, or the press. The postwar idea of national security "unification" included the concept of a Central Intelligence Agency to coordinate the many separate information-gathering activities and provide the best possible intelligence reports for the President and the National Security Council. Without eliminating the separate departmental intelligence units, the central agency was to perform such functions as producing a unified "national intelligence estimate" and daily monitoring millions of words of foreign radio broadcasts.[1]

[1] What has come to be known in Washington as the intelligence community comprises those government agencies represented on the U. S. Intelligence Board, of which the CIA Director—in his second role as "Director of Central Intelligence"—is chairman. Represented on the Board are the heads of Intelligence of the Army, Navy, Air Force, State Department, Atomic Energy Commission, and representatives of the Secretary of Defense, the National Security Agency, and Federal Bureau of Investigation. For further organizational de-

The Central Intelligence Agency, as leader of the intelligence community, has multiple functions: to warn of impending crises and dangers and prevent future Pearl Harbors; to provide a base of foreign information, usually concerned with identifiable, measurable physical elements, ranging from daily intelligence digests to encyclopedic surveys of foreign nations to guide national decision making; to prepare short- or long-range estimates of political trends and the intentions of leaders of foreign states for policy planning, which often involves interpreting what the more humble intelligence professional calls the "unknowables"; and, finally, to engage in secret operational activities overseas, including counterintelligence, clandestine political action, and paramilitary adventures. This last category will be discussed in the following chapter.

Some national security decisions are irretrievable, in the sense that time lost on a wrong decision usually cannot be regained. Information is a vitally important ingredient, though the best possible intelligence does not, of course, guarantee the right decision.

The Soviet emplacement of long-range missiles in Cuba in October 1962, bringing the great powers to the brink of war, is a two-sided illustration of the crucial importance of accurate intelligence. Distorted and inaccurate information in the Kremlin apparently led Soviet decision makers to believe that the United States would allow the missiles, once discovered, to remain emplaced. On the other hand, it was very late before American leaders, who assumed that the Kremlin would not dare such a maneuver, possessed firm, positive information that the missiles were, in fact, in Cuba. A few weeks of cloudy weather and the United States might have confronted a possibly disastrous strategic imbalance as the consequence of intelligence failure.

Perhaps nothing is more important to world peace today than to close the gap between the distorted image and reality in both the White House and the Kremlin. If this is so, intel-

tails, see Harry Howe Ransom, *Central Intelligence and National Security*, Harvard University Press, 1958.

ligence agencies assume a role of first importance to defense and democracy.

National security policy planning at all levels of government looks to the intelligence estimate for an appraisal of the external situation now; probable future economic, political, and military trends; and forecasts of the most likely development in foreign attitudes, interests, and policies. Whether the planning is in the State Department, the Joint Chiefs of Staff, or one of the armed services, some form of intelligence estimate is indispensable.

Intelligence in all its forms—daily digests, national estimates, and encyclopedic country surveys—has become a standard commodity in Washington's policy councils. The President begins each work day in the White House with a perusal of daily digests prepared by the CIA. The Secretary of State receives a daily briefing from his intelligence chief. In preparing the annual defense budget, the Secretary of Defense and his associates lean heavily upon intelligence estimates. Each meeting of the National Security Council hears oral reports from the Director of Central Intelligence, analyzing important current events or submitting a national intelligence estimate of the policy proposals under consideration.

Intelligence is the cornerstone of policy building, yet the intelligence system remains peculiarly immune to public inspection. However, these organizational features of the system at least are clear:

A *Central Intelligence Agency*, which has, although actual figures have never been disclosed, an estimated 15,000 employees and an annual expenditure of perhaps $750,000,000, and which presides, as integrator and coordinator—as well as being a major producer of intelligence reports—over the government-wide intelligence community.

A *National Security Agency*, which had a "domestic" budget in 1961 of $116,000,000, and which with its affiliates spent perhaps three times that amount overseas. Details of its functions have been kept even more secret than those of CIA, but its activities and organization were unexpectedly disclosed for the first time, in apparently authentic detail, when two of its employees defected to Moscow in June 1960, and subsequently issued a detailed statement on NSA operations.[2] NSA is known to be engaged principally in "communications intelligence," that is, the making and breaking of codes, the intercepting of secret messages of foreign governments, the development of techniques for the secret transmission of information, and the use of electronics for acquiring, communicating, and protecting all forms of information.

A *Defense Intelligence Agency*, established under the Secretary of Defense in October 1961, to unify the intelligence efforts of the Department of Defense by combining many of the formerly separate activities of each of the armed services. The Army, for example, had a separate intelligence budget exceeding $100,000,000 a year. Ultimately the DIA will furnish all Department of Defense current operations intelligence, determine all Defense intelligence requirements, and produce all military intelligence estimates for the Joint Chiefs of Staff, United States military commands around the world, and the Secretary of Defense. The intelligence staffs of the armed services, now much diminished in size, continue to supply particular service intelligence requirements. The size of the DIA as of 1962 was secret, but an eventual staff of several thousands of specialists seems a reasonable estimate. The Director of DIA, of three-star military rank, represents the Defense Department on the United States Intelligence Board, the board of directors of the intelligence community.

The Department of State. Since its establishment in 1789 the State Department has supplied political, economic, and cultural information on foreign countries to national policy makers. Under the central intelligence concept, State has been assigned the task of collecting this information from nations outside of the Iron or Bamboo Curtains. State's Bureau of Intelligence and Research now regards itself as largely a research and analysis arm of the Secretary of State's office. Given the primacy of the Secretary in foreign policy making, this bureau is of great potential importance, although its an-

[2] For text of their statement see *The New York Times*, September 7, 1960.

nual budget of several million dollars is a small fraction of
that of other intelligence units.

Miscellaneous. Intelligence units include the intelligence
sections of the Atomic Energy Commission, the Federal Bureau of Investigation, and a number of other government
departments and agencies, such as the Department of Commerce and Post Office Department. In a broader sense, significant information is also supplied by the Library of Congress,
the National Aeronautics and Space Administration, the National Science Foundation, and a number of government-
affiliated research organizations.

The sources of foreign data utilized in the intelligence
process can be divided into three major categories:

I. Information from research and analysis of overt sources.
This includes data from analysis of the foreign press, radio,
and official announcements; interviews with refugees; reports
of accredited foreign service officers, military attachés, and
American businessmen and tourists in foreign countries; trans-
lations of foreign technical journals, and a wide range of
published materials. In this area by far the greatest amount
of money and effort go toward the jigsaw-puzzle task of making a meaningful mosaic out of a mass of data.

II. Communications and electronics intelligence, which in
recent years has utilized air-borne, infra-red and other detect-
ing devices, such as probing by receiver-equipped reconnaissance aircraft along Soviet borders to obtain data on the nature and deployment of Russian radar complexes; long-range
radar to track missile tests in the Soviet Union; analysis of
atmospheric particles to detect nuclear tests; high altitude,
long-range aerial photography by U-2 aircraft, for example, of
industrial complexes and military bases; high-flying surveillance balloons equipped to detect nuclear reactors and tell-
tale electric power lines; and eavesdropping on communications of foreign governments by intercepting and breaking
coded secret messages. Increasing use is undoubtedly being
made of reconnaissance "spy" satellites in orbit around the
earth. Although little authentic information has been revealed, it can be assumed that spying from space is in the

process of creating a revolution in certain types of intelligence work.

III. Espionage by secret agents, including defectors from Iron Curtain nations, and by other clandestine devices. This branch of intelligence is under the exclusive jurisdiction of the CIA. But, contrary to the popular notion, it accounts for only a small percentage of the total intelligence effort. And while agent espionage remains the most romantic and dangerous intelligence work, it produces an even smaller percentage of significant data for reports and forecasts.[3] Nevertheless the right spy in the right place at the right time can be an invaluable source of information.

When the new central intelligence system was established in 1947, hopes were high that, with the collation of the information from all these sources, national policies and programs would be informed by an all-seeing intelligence, future surprises in world affairs would be eliminated, and foreign policy and strategic planning would be based upon the best attainable knowledge of the outside world. Unhappily the system has failed in many important instances, notably in Korea in 1950, in Berlin in 1961 when the wall was built, at the Bay of Pigs in Cuba in 1961, and partially, at least, in the Cuban missile crisis of October 1962. At the same time, it has grown in size and importance until it must now be recognized as a major feature of the government. This raises important questions about its potentialities and limitations, which can be at least partially answered by tracing the events of the Korean War and the more recent 1959–61 "missile gap" and comparative economic growth-rate debates. Although no claim is made that the following analysis is based upon the entire range of information that was available to intelligence analysts and policy makers, circumstances produced a reasonably full disclosure of the essential facts about how central intelligence operates.

---

[3] For a fuller discussion, see Harry Howe Ransom, "How Intelligent Is Intelligence," *The New York Times Magazine*, May 22, 1960, pp. 26, 80–83.

II

In the dawn hours of June 25, 1950, North Korean infantry and armored forces attacked in strength across the 38th Parallel.[4] Simultaneously North Korean air forces attacked Kimpo Airfield near Seoul. Although they had been preceded by many weeks of Communist probing along the border, the attacks came as a surprise to Washington, American Far East Command Headquarters in Tokyo, and South Korea itself. A year earlier the last American combat team had been withdrawn, and it is an "iffy" question whether or not this encouraged the attack. It seems likely that the Communists misread the withdrawal of troops to mean that the United States had no intention of defending the area. In any case,

---

[4] There is a voluminous and growing literature on the Korean War. The testimony in the "MacArthur Hearings," 1951 is invaluable. Among other useful sources: Roy Appleman, *The United States Army in the Korean War*, Washington, D.C., Department of the Army, 1961; Leland M. Goodrich, *Korea, A Study of U. S. Policy in the United Nations*, New York, Council on Foreign Relations, 1956; Trumbull Higgins, *Korea and the Fall of MacArthur*, Oxford University Press, 1960; William W. Kaufmann, "Policy Objectives and Military Action in the Korean War," RAND Paper, June 26, 1956; Robert Leckie, *Conflict, The History of the Korean War*, New York, Putnam, 1962; Martin Lichterman, "Korea, Problems in Limited War," *National Security in the Nuclear Age*, eds., Gordon Turner and Richard Challener, New York, Praeger, 1960, pp. 31–56; S. L. A. Marshall, *The River and the Gauntlet*, New York, Morrow, 1953; Lynn Montross and Captain Nicholas Canzona, *U. S. Marine Operations in Korea*, Washington, D.C., Historical Branch, U. S. Marines, HQ., 1954–57, Vols. I–III; Robert G. North, *Moscow and Chinese Communists*, Stanford University Press, 1953; Rutherford M. Poats, *Decision in Korea*, New York, McBride, 1954; Richard Rovere and Arthur M. Schlesinger, Jr., *The General and the President*, New York, Farrar, Straus, 1951; John W. Spanier, *The Truman-MacArthur Controversy and the Korean War*, Harvard University Press, 1959; Allen S. Whiting, *China Crosses the Yalu*, New York, Macmillan, 1960; Major General Courtney Whitney, *MacArthur, His Rendezvous with Destiny*, New York, Knopf, 1956; Major General Charles Willoughby and John Chamberlain, *MacArthur, 1941–1951*, New York, McGraw-Hill, 1954.

Republic of Korea forces were quickly overrun. By the end of the following week the United States, acting through the United Nations, was involved in an entirely new and un-planned-for military and political situation.

By June 30, sea, air, and ground forces, inadequate though they were, had been committed to the defense of the Republic of Korea. By the end of November, the Chinese Communists had intervened on a major scale. Although this was also preceded by mass movements of Communist troops, and pointed warnings from Peking to Washington, it was as much of a surprise in Washington and Korea as the original invasion. On the surface it appeared that the three-year-old central intelligence system had failed in 1950, just as a far more haphazard intelligence system had failed in the case of Pearl Harbor a decade earlier.

In the controversy over the conduct of the Korean War the public got a rare look at the intelligence performance, particularly during the "MacArthur Hearings" in the Senate in 1951 when the management of the war was publicly debated.[5]

In his memoirs, President Truman states that in the spring of 1948 he and his advisers discussed Korea as one of the places for a possible Communist military attack.[6] But from the high policy level in Washington, Korea seemed to be only one of a half-dozen places where the Communists might strike. And until the actual attack, on the basis of intelligence information now seen to have been patently inadequate, American officials assumed that the Kremlin was not ready to incur the risks of a major military action. American strategy —derived from a "containment" policy—was concentrated on resisting possible air attack in Western Europe and against a defense perimeter in the Pacific that at best left the defense of Korea ambiguous.

The Joint Chiefs of Staff, having considered Korea's stra-

[5] U. S. Senate, Committees on Armed Services and Foreign Relations, *Hearings*, "Military Situation in the Far East," 82d Congress, 1st Session, May–August 1951. Some 3600 pages of censored testimony were published. Hereafter referred to as "MacArthur Hearings."

[6] *Memoirs*, Vol. 2, p. 331.

tegic value in 1947, had recommended withdrawal of American forces. Yet the 1947 report of General Albert Wedemeyer, based upon a study expedition to China and Korea commissioned by the President, stated that North Korea was developing a well-trained aggressive army, clearly superior to the defensive constabulary maintained in South Korea by the United States and the United Nations.

The Wedemeyer Report was not made public until 1951, and, according to testimony during the MacArthur Hearings, was not even given to the Director of Central Intelligence.[7] Its public release in September 1947 would not necessarily have changed either American intelligence estimates or United States policy, based, as it was, on budget cutting, total war concepts, and dependence upon strategic atomic striking power. Officials are prone to see only what they prefer to see unless the warning signal is unmistakably clear, which it can rarely be. But the failure to circulate Wedemeyer's report indicated the lack of an adequate information system within Washington policy councils in late 1947.[8]

As is usually the case after the fact, intelligence officials at a lower level pointed to sheaves of reports containing warnings of coming events. General Douglas MacArthur's intelligence chief, Major General Charles A. Willoughby, pointed out that in the six months immediately before the North Korean attack, a total of 417 special intelligence reports were filed from Tokyo to Washington. "All of them," he claims, "were of increasing urgency and covered every facet of the North Korean Communist threat. . . ."[9] Indeed in his book, *MacArthur, 1941–1951*, Willoughby cites reports indicating a possible North Korean attack in June 1950.[10] But, like most intelligence reports, they contained hedges and qualifications, leaving the ultimate decision maker to judge the risks. Secretary of State Dean Acheson later testified:

[7] "MacArthur Hearings," p. 1989.
[8] See "MacArthur Hearings," p. 3582; also General A. C. Wedemeyer, *Wedemeyer Reports!*, New York, Holt, 1958, pp. 459–79.
[9] Willoughby and Chamberlain, *op. cit.*, p. 351.
[10] See *Ibid.*, pp. 351–52.

Intelligence was available to the [State] Department prior to the 25th of June, made available by the Far East Command, the CIA, the Department of the Army, and by the State Department representatives here and overseas, and [it] shows that all these agencies were in agreement that the possibility for an attack on the Korean Republic existed at that time, but *all were in agreement that its launching in the summer of 1950 did not appear imminent.*[11] (Italics added.)

General Willoughby specifies in his book that Washington was advised as early as March 10, 1950 of a possible attack in June. But he does not include the "Comment" attached to one report (contained in the joint weekly intelligence cable) from Commander in Chief, Far East:

Comment: The People's Army will be prepared to invade South Korea by fall and possibly by spring of this year indicated in the current report of armed-force expansion and major troop movements at critical thirty-eighth parallel areas. Even if future reports bear out the present indication, it is believed civil war will not necessarily be precipitated; so that intentions in Korea are believed closely related to Communist program in Southeast Asia. Seems likely that Communist overt military measures in Korea will be held in abeyance, at least until further observations made by Soviets of results of their program in such places as Indochina, Burma, and Thailand. If the Soviets are satisfied they are winning the struggle for these places they probably will be content to wait a while longer and let South Korea ripen for future harvest. If checked or defeated in their operations in these countries in Asia they may divert large share of their effort to South Korea, which could result in a People's Army Invasion of South Korea.[12]

[11] "MacArthur Hearings," pp. 1990–91. For a provocative view of Korean conflict origins, see D. F. Fleming, *The Cold War and Its Origins*, Garden City, New York, Doubleday, 1961.
[12] *Ibid.*, p. 1991.

Fifteen days after this report, Willoughby stated on March 25, 1950, his conclusion that:

> It is believed that there will be no civil war in Korea this spring or summer. The most probable course of North Korean action this spring or summer is furtherance of its attempt to overthrow the South Korean Government by the creation of chaotic conditions in the Republic through guerrilla activities and psychological warfare.[13]

This sharply contradicts Willoughby's claims that Washington was "fully informed" by intelligence agencies. He later stated in his book that "In spite of all the warnings from G-2 Tokyo, the visit of [John Foster] Dulles, and the fact that the American Embassy in Seoul was well equipped as a listening post, the invasion of South Korea came as a jolt to Washington."[14] It is clear that it came as a jolt to MacArthur's Far East Command as well. Whatever warnings were given were, in typical intelligence fashion, equivocal.

Korea was, in fact, outside the jurisdictional boundaries of MacArthur's Far East Command after the withdrawal of U. S. troops in July 1949. Willoughby, in his book, calls it "a jealously guarded State Department conclave."[15] Actually, the Navy had taken over the general administrative responsibility and the State Department the intelligence responsibility. But MacArthur's G-2 maintained a small surveillance unit there, the "Korean Liaison Office." The fact that the military command felt it necessary to maintain an intelligence system outside of its jurisdiction underlines the duplication that has plagued American intelligence as well as military operations since World War II.

During the American occupation of Korea after World War II the United States maintained an intelligence network in North Korea to supply information on Chinese Communist movements during the period when the Communists were

[13] "MacArthur Hearings," pp. 1991–92.
[14] Willoughby and Chamberlain, op. cit., p. 354.
[15] Ibid.

using Korea as a sanctuary in their battles with the Chinese Nationalists. These intelligence activities are described in *The River and the Gauntlet* by S. L. A. Marshall, a military analyst and historian who later was intimately involved in Korean War operations.[16] By 1949 when the American occupation ended, lack of American interest and support had sharply curtailed such activities.

During the crucial period, 1948–50, intelligence organization in the field, as in Washington, was weak. Serious jurisdictional squabbles allegedly existed between MacArthur and the infant CIA. Testifying in the MacArthur Hearings, the General described as "tommyrot" reports that his command hampered activities of CIA agents within and adjacent to his area. However, in an interview with a journalist in 1961, General Willoughby implied that such reports were not the "pure bunkum" that General MacArthur had also called them. The Army was apparently irked by the fact that in 1950 the CIA, fleeing mainland China, after applying for Army housing and logistics support in Japan, instead "moved in with the Navy at Yokusuka [at the entrance to Tokyo Bay]. We didn't consider this a very friendly thing after all we'd done. CIA was where we couldn't reach them, and that was bad because one thing that General MacArthur insisted on was that anyone in his theater of operations had to be under his direct control."

Recounting these events years later, General Willoughby further observed that the CIA operated its own radio communications with Washington from Yokusuka. "That's why we never let OSS operate in our theater [reference to the CIA's predecessor, the Office of Strategic Services during World War II]; no telling what they're sending back. Of course, we knew what CIA was sending. My cryptography boys merely broke their code."[17] Obviously something less than community spirit prevailed among the various govern-

---

[16] *The River and the Gauntlet*, p. 3.
[17] Quoted in Andrew Tully, *CIA: The Inside Story*, New York, Morrow, 1962, p. 189.

ment agencies in the field charged with keeping Washington informed.

Washington, too, was having organizational problems. Although the CIA had been in operation for over two years when the Korean War began, full coordination of intelligence was still only a hope. An effective system for a government-wide "National Intelligence Estimate" had not been developed. Decision makers continued to receive conflicting reports from various competing intelligence units.

Louis Johnson, Defense Secretary when the Korean War began, later told Congress:

> I got the intelligence, CIA flashes, and the CIA reports the minute they came in. . . . But each of the Secretaries, the three services, and the Joint Chiefs were likewise charged with the responsibility to call to my attention anything they thought of importance in the intelligence. . . . Then there were these meetings all the time with the Joint Chiefs and with the Secretaries. . . .[18]

Johnson further commented: "There was disposition in the military services at one time not to cooperate with the CIA. . . . When I left, it [coordination] still needed improvement." Interestingly, the 1952 Republican Party platform pledged "close coordination of our intelligence services."

In retrospect the North Korean surprise attack was not so much a failure of intelligence as a poor use of it. There were no positive, unequivocal predictions of an attack in June 1950, but Intelligence did supply a copious amount of information that might have alerted policy makers to existing dangers and risks, had they been willing, as they were not, to plan for the worst rather than hope for the best.

As Harry Truman later put it: "The North Koreans were capable of . . . attack at any time, but there was no information to give any clue as to whether an attack was certain or when it was likely to come."[19] But, as Mr. Truman did not

[18] "MacArthur Hearings," p. 2629.
[19] *Memoirs*, Vol. 2, p. 331.

observe, such certainty would be expecting too much from
Intelligence.

The reports of the United Nations Commission on Korea
gave perhaps the only kind of forewarning that normally can
be expected. For example, on September 29, 1949:

> There is much military posturing on both sides of the par-
> allel. This holds a serious danger of provoking open mili-
> tary conflict. . . . the North Korean regime has recently
> concluded a treaty with the U.S.S.R. . . . an agreement
> for military aid has been concluded between North Korea
> and the Chinese Communist forces in Manchuria. Border
> raids from the North are frequently reported and are said
> to be increasing in intensity.[20]

Underscoring the "unknowable" factor of intelligence forecasts—enemy intentions—MacArthur, during the Hearings,
aptly said:

> . . . there is a pretty definite limit to which intelligence
> can be gathered.
>
> The difficulties of first ascertaining the facts, and then
> of making conclusions from those facts, I don't think the
> normal public quite understands.
>
> It is not as though you had captured an enemy order
> and there it was all laid out there. Even if you know troops
> are being concentrated in a certain area, it doesn't follow
> that you make the correct conclusion whether they are
> there for defensive purposes, aggressive purposes; whether
> they are put there as a blind or as a bluff or caution or not.
>
> I don't think the criticisms of the Intelligence Service
> are well taken. I believe that the Intelligence Service col-
> lected about as much of the facts as it was possible to
> collect from an area that is behind the iron curtain.
>
> It is not easy to get in there and find out.
>
> Now, the assessment of all those things does not funda-
> mentally and primarily rest with a local command. About

[20] UNCK Report, September 29, 1949. General Assembly Official
Records, 4th Session, Supplement 9, p. 33.

all the local command could do is to tell you what is going on on its immediate front.

There has to be an evaluation made in the highest governmental level of all the information that flows in from the chancelleries of the world to make the predictions.

I don't see how it would have been humanly possible for any men or group of men to predict such an attack as that, any more than you could predict such an attack as took place in Pearl Harbor.

There is nothing, no means or methods, except the accidental spy methods—if you can get somebody to betray the enemy's higher circles, that can get such information as that. It is guarded with a secrecy that you cannot overestimate. Not even, probably, the commanding officers of the units, military units, concerned knew what was going on until they got the order to march.[21]

After the event, intelligence officials are apt to point to certain sections of reports issued before the event and say, "See this prediction? This *should* have warned you!" The commanding general or policy maker, on the other hand, points out the ambiguities in the intelligence estimates, which left him finally to make his own predictions from a range of possibilities. If the decision maker chooses the alternative that events prove to be the wrong one, he may blame the intelligence system for failure. Such blame is sometimes deserved; sometimes not. Whatever the case, rigid rules of secrecy put intelligence officials in a poor position to defend themselves.

The surprise in Washington at the full-scale Chinese Communist intervention in the Korean War in late November 1950 derived from the same ingredients that made the June attack a surprise, plus some new elements. The Chinese capability for major intervention was known in detail, and there were strong indications of Chinese intentions. But the United States clung to the hope that the Chinese were unwilling to

[21] "MacArthur Hearings," pp. 239–40.

risk what we were willing to risk, even after the last week in October, when the Chinese were known to have intervened on a limited scale. In the abstract such a hope was more than plausible. From the evidence available it is possible to support the hypothesis that the Chinese intervention was a belated reaction to United States-United Nations behavior, a last resort decided on reluctantly in response to the aggressive moves northward toward the Chinese border by MacArthur's forces.

Washington was also handicapped in predicting Chinese moves by the fact that the June 1950 attack had completely destroyed the meager native Korean intelligence resources. The training of new agents was a slow process, and such important intelligence techniques as aerial photo interpretation were unavailable in Korea.

Both the Eighth Army in Korea and top policy makers in Washington were aware of the possibility of Chinese intervention. Eighth Army Intelligence viewed it from the start as a major contingency, but took a more conservative and hopeful tone upon finding that it terrified the South Koreans and created serious morale problems in the field. This apparently had a misleading impact in Washington.

An important source of information about Chinese intentions was Peking, where crucial decisions were being made. There, even before American troops had crossed the 38th Parallel, Premier Chou En-lai made an open declaration that his people would not tolerate an American "imperialist" invasion of neighboring territory.

On September 15, MacArthur's forces had made a successful amphibious landing at Inchon, South Korea, in the rear of the Communist North Korean forces. Simultaneously a UN counteroffensive began at the Pusan perimeter. Three days later, General MacArthur accused Communist China of giving "substantial if not decisive military assistance," to North Korea by assigning Chinese troops to Korea prior to the June invasion. A few days later Peking officially admitted the MacArthur charge and announced that Red China "will always stand on the side of the Korean people."[22] Mac-Arthur's authorization from Washington to operate north of the 38th Parallel, which divided North and South Korea, was contingent upon the fact that neither Communist China nor Russia had intervened in the war. Once MacArthur seemed to be successful north of the 38th—after Inchon—he was further authorized to continue, even in the event of Chinese Communist intervention, as long as his progress seemed to offer "a reasonable chance of success."

The United States, having no official contact with Peking, was partially dependent upon what was regarded as a doubtful source, the Indian Ambassador to Red China, K. M. Panikkar. As early as September 25, according to the Ambassador's *mémoire*, General Nieh Jung-chen, acting Chief of Staff, pointedly told Panikkar that the Chinese did not intend to let the Americans come up to the Yalu. Panikkar writes, "This was the first indication that I had that the Chinese proposed to intervene in the war."[23] In the discussion, General Nieh made it clear that China was willing to risk even atomic bombardment: ". . . at all costs American aggression has to be stopped. The Americans can bomb us, they can destroy our industries, but they cannot defeat us on land." Certainly such messages were intended for United Nations leaders and American officials in Washington. In a speech on September 30, Chou En-lai declared: "The Chinese people absolutely will not tolerate foreign aggression, nor will they supinely tolerate seeing their neighbors being savagely invaded by the imperialists."[24] About October 2, Panikkar received similar information in a dramatic midnight meeting with Chou En-lai. Panikkar records: "I asked him whether China intended to intervene, if only the South Koreans crossed the 38th parallel. He was emphatic: 'The South Koreans did not matter but American intrusion into North Korea [on a large scale,

22 Quoted in Whiting, *op. cit.*, p. 93.
23 K. M. Panikkar, *In Two Chinas*, London, Allen & Unwin, 1955, p. 108.
24 *People's China*, October 16, 1950, p. 9, quoted in Whiting, *op. cit.*, p. 108.

implicitly] would encounter Chinese resistance.' "[25] Panikkar reported this to the British Minister in Peking.

These "messages" were rapidly transmitted to Washington and to General MacArthur. One of MacArthur's biographers asserts, however, that, until the mid-October Wake Island Conference, the General received no intimation from the State or Defense Departments or the CIA that Red Chinese intervention was "under serious consideration."[26] At the time of Chou's statement to Panikkar, an important resolution was pending in the Political and Security Committee of the UN General Assembly, recommending that UN forces take all appropriate steps to insure stability throughout Korea. In other words, UN authorization for crossing the 38th Parallel and, in effect, reuniting the country was proposed. President Truman later recalled that Chou's expressed intention to intervene was regarded as "a bold attempt to blackmail the United Nations by threats of intervention in Korea."[27] Probably this *was* one of its purposes. And in Mr. Truman's view the Indian Ambassador to Peking "had in the past played the game of the Chinese Communists." Parenthetically, it can be observed that the constraints of publicity, particularly criticism by Republicans and a hostile press, did not allow the President to appear to be giving in to a bluff.

Even though a large-scale troop movement into Manchuria was apparent, the intelligence consensus was that full-scale intervention was only a possibility. Similarly bellicose statements had previously been made from Peking with no follow-up. The UN resolution was adopted on October 7.

President Truman, however, lists the possibility of intervention as one of the reasons for his trip to Wake Island in mid-October for a personal conference with General MacArthur.[28] Mr. Truman records that in both private and group conferences with MacArthur, the General assured him there was very little chance of a major Chinese intervention. If

---

[25] *Op. cit.*, p. 110.
[26] See Major General Whitney, *op. cit.*, p. 392.
[27] *Memoirs*, Vol. 2, p. 362.
[28] *Ibid.*, p. 363.

they were "foolish" enough to intervene, MacArthur argued, they would be "slaughtered."

While the General and the President were meeting at Wake Island, a handful of Chinese "volunteers" captured in North Korea were being interrogated by field intelligence. Within two weeks after the Wake Island meeting, close to 100,000 Chinese soldiers were in Korea, although this fact was unknown to the UN Command. A large-scale Chinese troop movement of some five armies had gone undetected. American field intelligence clearly was not functioning well.

Red China's intentions remained an enigma in Korea, Tokyo, and Washington. Among the most hotly debated questions was: Are the few indications of the presence of Chinese troops in Korea simply a piecemeal commitment to reinforce North Korean elements, or is full-scale intervention about to begin? As always, theories abounded in Washington. Some quarters attempted to differentiate between "innately Chinese" and standard Communist behavior. Others theorized about basic conflicts in Peking-Moscow relations and concluded that Peking would not fight Moscow's war. Most of the answers were apparently based on American-preferred Chinese Communist strategies. United States strategy at this stage called for the occupation of all of Korea *if* the Russians and Chinese did not intervene on a major scale.

Secretary Acheson explicitly detailed for Senators in the MacArthur Hearings the reasons Washington felt the Peking government would not intervene on a grand scale: (1) an enormous number of Chinese troops would be required; (2) the Communists' hold on the mainland population might be weakened by war; (3) no real advantage to China was seen in major intervention; (4) China's world prestige would be weakened by such an aggressive move. In retrospect it is clear that only on the first point was the assessment correct.

From hindsight S. L. A. Marshall has written:

In the conduct of military operations, great illusions are born out of a poverty of information coupled with a wealth of confidence that the enemy in any case is unequal to the task of promoting a decisive change of events. This illusion was nearly complete.[29]

In Washington and in MacArthur's headquarters the illusion and the confidence were widespread. And they were perhaps bolstered by a CIA memorandum dated October 20 reporting that the Chinese would enter North Korea *at most* for the limited purpose of protecting the power plants along the Yalu River.[30]

On November 6, the CIA reported to President Truman that there might be as many as 200,000 Chinese troops in Manchuria and that the Chinese Communists were not only marshaling major forces but staking their prestige in Asia.[31] On November 7, however, MacArthur's message to the President reaffirmed the General's earlier belief that the Chinese did not plan full-scale intervention, even though he had advised the UN on November 5 of the existence of "Chinese Communist military units" in Korea, and a number of UN-Chinese skirmishes had occurred within the preceding ten days.

On November 9, the National Security Council met to consider the Joint Chiefs of Staff recommendations that MacArthur's relatively free-wheeling directives should not be changed, that the problem of Chinese Communist intervention be "solved" if possible by diplomatic means, and that the United States should recognize the increased danger of a general war; and apparently agreed in essence. As long as MacArthur's operations in North Korea seemed to promise success and hopes could be sustained that the Chinese Communists would be deterred from full-scale intervention, neither the Administration nor the Joint Chiefs were willing to curb activities, provided that they were limited to areas south of the Yalu. Following up these conclusions, President Truman attempted to reassure the Communist Chinese, by public declaration, that the United States had no intention of

29 *The River and the Gauntlet*, p. 14.
30 Whitney, *op. cit.*, pp. 401–02.
31 Truman, *Memoirs*, Vol. 2, p. 377.

carrying hostilities into China. The British likewise assured Peking that UN forces were not threatening Chinese territory.

Meanwhile, MacArthur continued his drive to the north, issuing his characteristically flamboyant and optimistic communiques as he went. One such, on November 24, stated that ". . . an air reconnaissance beyond the enemy line, and along the entire length of the Yalu River border, showed little sign of hostile military activity." American leaders remained uncertain as to whether known Chinese activity represented a full-scale attempt to drive UN forces out of North Korea or was simply an attempt to establish a buffer area to protect Chinese interests in hydroelectric power facilities along the Yalu River and to maintain some Communist control of North Korea. Analyses from hindsight suggest that Chinese concern about the power facilities was grossly exaggerated in Washington. A clue to the state of mind in the capital was Secretary of Defense George C. Marshall's personal inquiry to MacArthur early in November, ". . . do you feel that the hydroelectric and reservoir situation is probably the dominant consideration in this apparently last-minute move by the Chinese Communists, incited by the Soviets to protect their interests in the Far East?"[32] However, by mid-November a number of America's UN allied intelligence agencies had concluded that the Chinese Reds were not bluffing. The CIA in Washington remained skeptical.[33]

But there was deep concern about the possibility. On November 24 a summary prepared by the CIA stated that at the very least the Chinese would increase their operations in Korea, seek to strangle UN forces by prolonged attrition, and maintain a semblance of a Communist North Korean government. The CIA also stated categorically that the Chinese possessed sufficient military strength in Korea to force the withdrawal of UN forces to defensive positions.[34] On the same day, MacArthur dramatically announced the start of his "end the war" offensive. On November 28, two months after

[32] Quoted in Whitney, op. cit., p. 409.
[33] Higgins, op. cit., p. 70.
[34] Truman, Memoirs, Vol. 2, p. 381.

the Chinese acting Chief of Staff had told Indian Ambassador Panikkar that China would intervene, General MacArthur issued his now famous *communique* to the UN in which he declared in a surprised tone: "We face an entirely new war." From basically wrong assumptions and a classic failure in field intelligence, MacArthur's troops had been marched into a trap. The Red Chinese struck not from beyond the Yalu but from concealed positions in the mountainous terrain *behind* MacArthur's forces.

Thus both the June 25 attack and the Chinese intervention in October–November came as a strategic as well as tactical surprise.[35] In defense of the policy makers in Washington it may be said that intelligence estimating, particularly about the enemy's intentions, is a far more difficult job when one is on the defensive in a surprise-attack situation. This points a lesson to those who are responsible for planning our future security.

The Korean War intelligence experience is aptly summed up in a 1951 exchange between a Senator and a Secretary of State:

> *Senator Saltonstall:* They really fooled us when it comes right down to it; didn't they?
> *Secretary Acheson:* Yes, sir.[36]

Even more significant was the comment of the man serving as Secretary of Defense when the Communists invaded South Korea. Asked whether, when the war started in June 1950, the Pentagon thought the Chinese Communists would intervene, Louis Johnson replied: ". . . we hoped they wouldn't come in. . . ."[37]

Four major points about strategic intelligence in national decision making may be drawn from the Korean experience:

First, it reflects perhaps the commonest of all intelligence failures, the failure to comprehend a foreign power's definition of self-interest and the various pressures at work on foreign decision makers. The United States failed to under-

[35] *Department of State Bulletin*, September 18, 1950, p. 463.
[36] "MacArthur Hearings," p. 1835.
[37] *Ibid.*, p. 2630.

stand the North Koreans' and Communist Chinese (and the Russians') fears of American aggressive action and their unwillingness to see the North Korean state and its military apparatus destroyed. Intelligence estimators and policy makers also failed to give adequate attention to other aspects of Communist self-interest. Red China apparently desired to affect United States-Japanese relations in a manner favorable to China, that is, to create strains in such relations. Another factor was Peking's concern for "face" and its role in the rest of Asia. Red China was obviously threatened with loss of prestige if the North Korean Communist regime were destroyed. Yet another factor may have been internal weaknesses in China and the possible value of the war as an excuse for suppressing internal opposition groups and producing a greater degree of national unity. Red China's own revolution was not yet thoroughly consolidated. It is also possible that Russia wanted China to intervene and applied pressure for such action.[38]

These considerations received inadequate attention in Washington. Intelligence analysts and policy makers mistakenly put the foreign policy aims and aspirations of the United States above them. A corollary failure was permitting political objectives to be set by military progress on the ground, and by the military, rather than the political, logic of the situation.

Second, political leaders paradoxically put too much faith in strategic warning. In a brilliantly penetrating study of the attack on Pearl Harbor, Roberta Wohlstetter concludes that the possibility of a surprise attack always exists, since it derives from "the conditions of human perception and stems from uncertainties so basic that they are not likely to be eliminated. . . . The relevant signals, so clearly audible after an event, will be partially obscured before the event by sur-

[38] These considerations are discussed in Whiting, *op. cit.*, Chapter VIII; an excellent discussion of how these matters were viewed from the Presidential desk in Washington is in Neustadt, *Presidential Power*, pp. 123–51.

rounding noise."[39] Despite Pearl Harbor, America seems to have kept the naive faith that a reliable and unmistakable strategic warning (months or at least days in advance of a military attack) is possible. In this regard, Harvey A. De-Weerd of the RAND Corporation notes three prevailing assumptions that have developed since the Pearl Harbor attack in 1941: if we collect all possible information we are sure to catch in the net the important items; if we have a neatly organized, "coordinated," central intelligence system, all who need to know will be certain to get information; and since we need strategic warning in order to survive, we somehow will get it and respond properly.[40] In spite of the elaborate warning machinery now maintained by the United States the advantage seems more than ever in favor of the surprise attacker.[41] One must remain skeptical of the assurance given by Secretary of Defense Neil McElroy in 1959 that a surprise attack is "almost an impossibility."

Third, the Korean War represents a failure of national policy. American decision makers failed to comprehend the consequences of the nation's contradictory foreign policy. On the one hand, the United States supported the unification of Korea under a form of representative government, in face of clear opposition from North Korea, Red China, and the Soviet Union. On the other, it withdrew its troops from Korea, reduced its strategic commitments to that area, imposed strict budgetary ceilings on military preparedness at home, and placed heavy reliance upon air-atomic power that is of little use in a "limited war." In other words, the United States challenged Communist Korea and its allies at the same time that it was reducing its power to support its challenges or attain its declared policy aims. But our actions spoke

[39] *Pearl Harbor: Warning and Decision,* Stanford University Press, 1962, p. 397.

[40] See DeWeerd's "Strategic Surprise in the Korean War," Santa Monica, California, RAND Study P-1800-1, June 1962. For a more academic discussion of intelligence failures, see Benno Wasserman, "The Failure of Intelligence Prediction," *Political Studies,* Vol. VIII, June 1960, pp. 156–69.

[41] Wohlstetter, *op. cit.,* p. 399.

louder than our words to Communist decision makers. A more efficient American intelligence system might have pointed to the fundamental contradiction between our declared policies and our capabilities, and the possible consequences. But, in the end, to make any difference the political leadership would have had to be receptive to such information.

Fourth, in the Korean situation, American leaders became committed to a plan, a classic problem of intelligence. Despite "hard" intelligence indicators that the Chinese were preparing to intervene, General MacArthur's operation plan to drive north to the Yalu went ahead. More than a decade later, in the CIA-sponsored, abortive attempt to invade Cuba, the same kind of failure dominated decision making.

III

Early in 1960, ten years after the start of the Korean War, President Eisenhower and his new Secretary of Defense Thomas S. Gates announced that American intelligence had "better estimates" than before about Russian intentions to produce transoceanic ballistic missiles. Again the problem was to balance speculations about intentions against theoretically attainable concrete information on capabilities. Gates initially told a House defense appropriations subcommittee on January 13, 1960, that the new forecast of Soviet missile production was based upon "an intelligence estimate of what we believe he [Russia] probably will do, not what he is capable of doing." This, he added, represented "a very significant change" in intelligence estimating methods—a claim that startled many intelligence professionals aware of the pitfalls of leaning too heavily on enemy "intentions."

Secretary Gates later (January 25, 1960) explained to the House Committee on Science and Astronautics:

> There is obviously no intelligence whatsoever on U.S.S.R. intentions as to specific military or political policies or actions. Of course, it is impossible to have such intelligence. What we have is a refined and better set of facts pertaining to the probable, or what the Soviet ICBM may be.

Still later he made a more careful attempt to explain the

"new approach" to intelligence. In 1959 Pentagon planners had a National Intelligence Estimate, representing a government-wide intelligence consensus, of the numbers of operational ICBMs Russia might attain in given future time-periods. These were calculated for two contingencies: that the Soviet Union would pursue an "orderly" missile production program, or, that it would engage in a highly accelerated "crash" program. In 1960, additional information was acquired from behind the Iron Curtain, possibly from U-2 overflights, that seemed to suggest that a crash program was not underway, and refinements in data were made. The basis for the 1960 assertions that the Russian ICBM threat had lessened was a comparison of the 1959 estimate assuming a "crash" program with the 1960 estimate assuming an orderly missile program. This clearly demonstrates that it is not only the raw "facts" that are crucially important, but how one interprets them.

When Allen W. Dulles, as Director of Central Intelligence, gave estimates of Russian ICBM strength to Congress in January and February of 1960 his secret reports almost certainly contained such terms as "possible," "probable," and "improbable." He doubtless referred to a range of possibilities of Soviet missile strength, indicating finally the numbers the intelligence community had agreed upon as most likely now and in the years ahead.

If he had testified, for example, that by June 30, 1963, the Russians would have between 350 and 500 ICBMs ready to launch, he would have had to add: they conceivably could have more by adopting a "crash" program, or they might decide to produce fewer than their estimated potential. But, he would have explained, positive information that the Russians are training crews, building bases, or making other provisions required for deployment of a larger number of missiles is lacking.

A good deal of the defense debate in the years since World War II has involved *net* estimates of military power. These are made by a supersecret committee representing the NSC, CIA, Defense Intelligence Agency, State Department, Atomic Energy Commission, and Office of Emergency Planning after highly refined "war games" that involve the computation of probabilities and the costs and gains assigned to maneuvers in various hypothetical contingencies. The CIA's role is to supply estimates about Soviet capabilities and probable courses of action, but American capabilities and intentions are of equal importance, since the basic issue in a net estimate is the adequacy of military forces of all kinds for meeting various likely situations.

While intelligence estimates of Soviet missile production were the principal ingredient in calculating a net estimate during the 1959–61 "missile gap" controversy, there were other considerations: whether the United States conceded to Russia the first strike in an attack; whether the Soviets could strike suddenly or only after detailed and observable planning; the relative accuracy and reliability of the two nations' weapons and targeting information; the destructive power of the weapons; and the relative positions of the two countries in air defense and dispersal and mobility of forces.

Predictions of future Soviet missile strength must inevitably cover a wide range, just as predictions of intentions must be qualified by such terms as "improbable," "possible," and "probable." The calculator must choose from the lower or upper range and assume less or more favorable conditions. When President Eisenhower stated in his final State of the Union message in January 1961: "The 'bomber gap' of several years ago was always a fiction, and the 'missile gap' shows every sign of being the same," he did not mention that the "gap" was a figure projected for the future. If it did not develop, this may have been, in part, a consequence of our policy and programing in reaction to the possibility of such a gap. The Air Force Vice Chief of Staff, General Frederick H. Smith, Jr., told Congressmen in February 1962 that the Russians had the "capability" to create a missile gap, but that they "did not do what our intelligence people thought they would do."[42]

[42] House, Department of Defense Appropriations Subcommittee, *Hearings*, ". . . Appropriations on 1963," 87th Congress, 2d Session, Part 2, p. 489.

IV

The sound and fury of the missile-gap debate helped to obscure a related intelligence issue: the over-all assessment of the growth of Soviet power and projections of relative U.S.-U.S.S.R. future strength. In recent years experts, both inside the government and out, have repeatedly warned that the Soviet Union is moving ahead at a rate faster than that of the United States.

Intelligence on comparative U.S.-U.S.S.R. economic growth rates appears to be far more reliable than predictions of Russia's ICBM inventory. In November 1959 Allen Dulles as Director of Central Intelligence took the unprecedented step of appearing in open session before a Congressional subcommittee to assert:

> If the Soviet industrial growth rate persists at 8 or 9 per cent per annum over the next decade, as is forecast, the gap between our economies by 1970 will be dangerously narrowed unless our own industrial growth rate is substantially increased from the present pace.[43]

In saying publicly that the situation was dangerous, Dulles may have overstepped the dividing line between intelligence and policy making. The remark bore a close resemblance to a policy recommendation. But the implications of this type of intelligence seem to have been generally dismissed in the highest echelons of government, at least in the 1956–60 period, because they ran counter to existing policy and values. This might be termed the "intelligence gap"—the gap between available, relatively "hard" intelligence and the final, crucial step where most of the great intelligence "failures" have occurred: the application of intelligence in unpleasant or unpopular policy decisions.

[43] *Hearings*, Congressional Joint Economic Subcommittee on Economic Statistics, "Comparison of United States and Soviet Economies," November 13, 1959, p. 11.

The Gaither Committee episode provides an excellent illustration. The President and the National Security Council in 1957 appointed a special committee of experts outside of government, the Security Resources Panel, with H. Rowan Gaither as chairman, to make what was in effect a net estimate of U.S.-U.S.S.R. military power. These outside experts, aided by the highly competent Institute for Defense Analysis (a joint university corporation created to do operations analysis research for the government) and given access to secret intelligence, presumably had no interest in juggling the facts either way.

However, when the report, based upon the same intelligence reports available to the Administration, called for much higher defense expenditures, the Administration attempted to suppress it under the claim of executive privilege. President Eisenhower apparently feared that such a pessimistic report would panic the American people and pressure unwise government actions. The clamor for its release was widespread, particularly after the first Russian sputniks had gone into orbit. And someone privy to its findings felt sufficiently alarmed to "leak" them to the press.[44]

In the shadow of the missile-gap debate it is pertinent to recall some of the Gaither Committee's findings in 1957: first, that the Soviet Union's economic, scientific, and technological advances were putting it in an increasingly favorable position to pursue its economic and psychological assaults on the non-Communist world; second, that the United States was moving at an alarming rate toward a position of military power second to that of the Soviet Union; and third, that unless remedial action were promptly taken the United States would be imminently exposed to the superior threat of missiles launched from the Soviet Union. (In retrospect it appears that some of the intelligence estimates of Soviet military power were exaggerated.)

According to the newspaper stories, the report called for an urgent program to bolster national power; recommended in-

[44] See Morton H. Halperin, "The Gaither Committee and the Policy Process," *World Politics*, Vol. XIII, April 1961, pp. 360–84; also Huntington, *The Common Defense*, pp. 106–13.

creased expenditures for air and missile power, civil defense, and preparations for limited war; and suggested reorganizing the Department of Defense. But the only major action taken by the Administration was to strengthen strategic deterrence programs.

The fate of the Gaither Committee Report underlines the fact that no matter how objective the intelligence estimate, the crucial element is the way in which the information is viewed and acted upon by the final policy makers. Secretary of Defense Charles E. Wilson once identified the nub of the problem: "We know more about the Russians now than we know what to do about."[45]

In assessing the risks and costs of alternative defense policies, government leaders should ponder Winston Churchill's advice to the House of Commons in 1939:

> It seems to me that Ministers run the most tremendous risks if they allow the information collected by the Intelligence Department and sent to them, I am sure, in good time, to be sifted and coloured and reduced in consequence and importance, and if they ever get themselves into a mood of attaching weight only to those pieces of information which accord with their earnest and honourable desire that the peace of the world should remain unbroken.[46]

Had he been speaking in an American setting he might have added, after a Churchillian pause, "and that the budget should remain in balance at the existing level."

V

The fact that even the best attainable intelligence leaves the difficult choice of alternatives to the decision maker does not mean that a central intelligence system poses no threat of invisible government or irresponsible power. If, for example, central intelligence were to report to the President that there was positive intelligence that the Soviet Union would attack

---

[45] Interview with Robert J. Donovan, New York *Herald Tribune*, December 13, 1957.

[46] *The Gathering Storm*, Boston, Houghton Mifflin, 1948, p. 352.

the United States in forty-eight hours, how could he challenge the information? And the dilemma he would face would be particularly cruel because an enemy decision to attack can always be reversed, while a defensive action might, in some circumstances, itself provoke an attack.

Even more serious would be the problem presented by a defense system that, to be effective, would have to respond automatically to a warning system to, say, an intercontinental missile attack upon missile bases. Since an ICBM takes less than thirty minutes from launch to target, the reaction time must be measured in minutes. Or suppose that central intelligence suddenly advised the President and National Security Council that the Soviets had twice the number of ICBMs previously estimated. In both these cases, there would be no immediate way, outside of the intelligence system, to check or balance or evaluate the information further. Leaders and defenders of existing arrangements in the intelligence bureaucracy insist that the confederated nature of the intelligence community provides built-in checks against narrow bias. But if the nation had been continually reassured in advance that "all was well" and surprise attack "impossible" the leader's will might be paralyzed by an unprepared and unwilling public opinion.

Because certain kinds of decisions will have to rely increasingly upon intelligence, it would be unwise to leave the intelligence system as free from external surveillance and controls as it has been since 1947. Closer surveillance, by the Presidency particularly but also in a more clearly defined way by Congress, would permit better judgment than now exists as to what weight can be given to intelligence reports and other forms of often conflicting information in a given situation. And the risks involved in the system should be candidly explained to the public. Perhaps it would be useful for the President to issue periodic intelligence reports to the nation. Americans must insist that the intelligence system in all of its activities is under the firm and constant control of responsible political leaders. This problem is discussed in the next chapter.

CHAPTER VII

CIA: CLANDESTINE SERVICES
IN AN OPEN SOCIETY

I

The Central Intelligence Agency presents a particular paradox among the many stemming from the conflict between security and liberty. At the entrance to the CIA's new headquarters building near Washington is the biblical inscription: "Ye shall know the truth and the truth shall make you free."[1] Were he permitted through the entrance so decorated, a seriously inquiring citizen would, however, soon discover the agency's operating principles:

> . . . the Central Intelligence Agency does not confirm or deny published reports, whether good or bad; never alibis; never explains its organization; never identifies its personnel (except for a few in the top echelons); and will not discuss its budget, its methods of operations, or its sources of information.[2]

So the citizen, as far as CIA's managers are concerned, cannot in fact know "the truth" about a very large, expensive, and increasingly important government agency, the director-

[1] CIA's attachment to John 8:32 also reflects the belief of intelligence professionals in the existence of an objective "truth" in world affairs. If "all the facts" are gathered, they seem to assume, then the problems of policy makers are virtually self-solving. They share this myth with many policy makers.

[2] From mimeographed pamphlet, "The Central Intelligence Agency," issued on request by CIA, Spring 1961, p. 7. Existence of the pamphlet itself seems inconsistent with the secrecy policy declared therein.

ship of which has been described as "second in importance only to the President."[3]

The existence of a large, secret bureaucracy sometimes pivotally important in making and implementing national policies and strategies raises special problems. At the level of democratic ideals, the problem is the existence of a potential source of invisible government. At the level of representatives of the people—Executive and Legislative—the problem is primarily how to control a dimly seen instrument, so hot that if not handled with great skill it can burn its user instead of its adversary. The problem for the scholar is access to verifiable information for objective analysis.

The secrecy officially proclaimed by the CIA and affiliated intelligence agencies, and required by the statutes establishing them, quite obviously has not been absolutely maintained. America's open society, particularly the separation of governmental powers, the pluralism of the administrative bureaucracy, and a free press, have made complete secrecy impossible. Journalists and scholars have been able to produce a considerable amount of literature, much of it speculative.[4] The vol-

[3] Senator Richard B. Russell, Chairman, Committee on Armed Services, in that committee's *Hearing*, "Nomination of McCone . . . ," January 18, 1962, p. 30.

[4] Relevant scholarly works include: George S. Pettee, *The Future of American Secret Intelligence*, Washington, D.C., Infantry Journal Press, 1946; Sherman Kent, *Strategic Intelligence for American World Policy*, Princeton University Press, 1949; Roger Hilsman, *Strategic Intelligence and National Decisions*, Glencoe, The Free Press, 1956; Washington Platt, *Strategic Intelligence Production: Basic Principles*, New York, Praeger, 1957; Ransom, *Central Intelligence and National Security*; William M. McGovern, *Strategic Intelligence and the Shape of Tomorrow*, Chicago, Regnery, 1961; and Wohlstetter, *Pearl Harbor*.

Important journalistic accounts are: Tully, *CIA, The Inside Story*; Sanche de Gramont, *The Secret War*, New York, Putnam, 1962; Karl E. Meyer and Tad Szulc, *The Cuban Invasion*, New York, Praeger, 1962; David Wise and Thomas B. Ross, *The U-2 Affair*, New York, Random House, 1962; and William L. White, *The Little Toy Dog*, New York, Dutton, 1962.

The list of periodical sources, mostly journalistic, is longer. Notable is Allen W. Dulles, "The Craft of Intelligence," *Harper's Magazine*, April 1963, pp. 127–74, to be published later in expanded book form.

ume has increased as a result of a series of misfortunes or misadventures in recent years, particularly the U-2 incident, the defection to Moscow of two National Security Agency employees, and the abortive attempt to invade Cuba in 1961. These events removed, temporarily at least, the cloak of secrecy to an unprecedented degree. Even with these disclosures, however, our view remains a partial one. One simply cannot apply the usual rigorous standards of data gathering and documentation to this subject. But within limitations, one can analyze some of the dilemmas presented by the existence of a secret intelligence apparatus in a democratic society.

Some say this is not a subject fit for public discussion. Senator Henry M. Jackson has stated that "details with respect to intelligence should not be discussed on the floor of the Senate" because it "may be unwittingly giving aid and comfort to the enemy. . . ."[5] President Kennedy, in a message to Congress in 1961, said intelligence "is not a matter on which public discussion is useful."[6] Admittedly, government leaders or officials with legitimately secret information should not discuss it publicly. Students of government must, however, analyze any source of power within government to the extent that such analysis can proceed outside of the boundaries of classified information.[7] Disclosures in recent years make it clear that the large secret intelligence apparatus now maintained by the government can have a profound impact on the quality and effectiveness of America's role in international affairs. Certainly the existence of such an apparatus creates problems of policy, organization, and control, especially since the CIA's three major functions—the collection of information; the analysis, interpretation, and production of this mass of data into "intelligence"; and clandestine political operations overseas—are all secretly performed.

[5] *Congressional Record*, January 29, 1962, p. 927.
[6] May 25, 1961.
[7] This writer has never been a member of the central intelligence system and has never had access to classified material on intelligence.

In gathering information, Intelligence[8] must have the objectivity and detachment from policy that will assure the most forthright possible reporting on world affairs. But this detachment should not be such that Intelligence either develops its own policy preferences or loses contact with the informational needs of the policy makers. Its duty is to report objective facts without regard to whether they spell good or bad news for existing policy preferences, but with appropriate regard for policy alternatives. In its operational (political warfare or overseas counterintelligence) missions Intelligence must serve always as an instrument of foreign policy and never be allowed to make its own policy.

Knowledge, however, conveys power. Secret knowledge can become secret power. A secret intelligence apparatus, claiming superior knowledge from undisclosed sources, and operating—because of legitimate secrecy claims—outside the normal checkreins of the American governmental system can wield invisible power either in the policy-making process or in clandestine operations in other countries.

The American democratic system is inspired by the ideal of visible, identifiable power, subject to the checks and balances of popular government. Congressional representatives of both parties oversee and ultimately legitimize the executive power of government. Congress acts as the public's eye and purse. But without adequate information, the people's representatives are like rich blind men at the mercy of persuasive supplicants. Congress cannot perform its role effectively with regard to any government function whose scope and operations are mostly invisible.

Obviously, America cannot do without an intelligence apparatus. Our world-wide responsibilities and commitments require a system for keeping the complex details of world affairs under constant surveillance, sometimes by espionage or other ancient instruments of power and policy in interna-

---

[8] Intelligence with a capital "I" will be used here to denote the system; lower case "intelligence" will denote the informational "product."

tional affairs.[9] And our new world position demands an instrument for counterintelligence and secret political action overseas, although its proper use must remain a troublesome question.

The need to make the most economical use of finite resources in implementing long-range national and foreign policy objectives places heavy reliance on intelligence estimates. As a result, the intelligence system is called upon to answer a vast range of questions: What is the future of the NATO alliance? What course will Sino-Soviet relations take? What will be the course of the new nationalisms in various regions of the globe? What will be the probable consequences of various possible foreign policy actions? Answers to these can be obtained, if at all, only by a massive research effort and sometimes only by illegal methods. The wide spectrum of information required, plus any bureaucracy's tendency to amoebic growth, explains the rapid increase in the size and cost of Intelligence since World War II, until its annual budget certainly and perhaps the number of its employees exceed those of the Department of State.

Accurate intelligence information, rapidly transmitted, is an absolute requirement for an effective strategy of deterrence to which this country has committed itself. Strategic striking forces must have accurate data on potential enemy targets. "Essential elements of information" as indicators of a potential enemy's military position must be constantly available to thwart an enemy's possible surprise knockout blow and his attempts to use claimed striking power for diplomatic blackmail. With hundreds of mega-death intercontinental missiles

[9] A leading candidate for designation as America's first spy is an Indian brave named Amocis, who was sent by Emperor Powhatan to mingle with the whites and observe their activities in order to keep the emperor informed. See Captain John Smith, *A True Relation . . .* , (1608) as cited by C. C. Davis, "Speak to Me Softly," *Columbia University Forum*, Spring 1961, p. 26. Hans J. Morgenthau reminds us also that the first appropriation act adopted by the first Congress of the United States in 1789 contained in pursuit of American national interest a contingent fund for the "bribery" of foreign statesmen.

positioned for attack, Intelligence assumes a terrifying role of informational responsibility.

Essential military and political information is held in tight security by national governments behind the Iron and Bamboo Curtains. Comparable information this side of the curtains is freely available to the Communists for the asking.[10] This creates a serious strategic imbalance. It can be argued that the espionage requirements of the United States are greater than those of the Soviet Union.

II

A policy maker must contend with three major considerations in reaching a decision: First, what are the policy objectives or goals being sought and what are the risks or probable costs in seeking them, in terms of alternative values that might have to be sacrificed? In other words, if a certain value is placed on military security as an objective, must other policy objectives, such as self-determination and economic development, be sacrificed in some calculable degree? Second, what are the pressures and forces likely to shape world affairs whatever course of action is adopted? Put another way, what are the calculable facts and the most probable trends in world affairs? Third, how may one assess the potentialities and limitations of the alternative instruments by which the environment may be influenced in the most favored direction? In other words, with national objectives and world trends in mind, how can we best go about attaining our ends?

Traditionally, the intelligence services are concerned only with the second of these and not with national values, ends, or means. Yet all are inextricably entwined. Max Millikan, who served as an assistant director of the CIA in the early

---

[10] An FBI report states that one Russian defector estimated that the Soviet Military Attaché's office in the United States is able to obtain legally 95 per cent of the material useful for its intelligence objectives through government agencies or commercial publishing houses. See "Exposé of Soviet Espionage," May 1960, *Senate Document No. 114*, 86th Congress, 2d Session, July 2, 1960, p. 7.

1950s, illustrated the problem when he said, discussing predictions of Russian developments:

> A study of what is happening in Soviet society will be useful to the policy maker only if it is written in the light both of what he would like to have happen there and of the instruments he can use to affect what happens. Equally, he cannot even state his goals or enumerate his instruments with clarity except in terms of an implicit or explicit theory of Soviet evolution.[11]

An agency charged with supplying secret information about the state of affairs in the Soviet Union can be a source of great influence in the policy process. To assume that the U.S.S.R. is "mellowing" in its objectives calls for one American foreign policy; to decide that she intends to conquer the world soon, either by surprise attack or otherwise, for quite another.

There are, to be sure, checks on the growing influence of secret intelligence. In the American governmental system, long-range policies or major shifts in existing policy are determined normally only after an elaborate consensus-building effort. An intelligence estimate, no matter what its assumed degree of accuracy, cannot alone determine major policy outcomes. Yet the rapidly changing, increasingly complex nature of world politics seems to be leading to more and more Intelligence participation in national decisions. The senior intelligence professionals in the interdepartmental policy planning units, though in theory they "advise" and do not "recommend," have already come to have great influence. And since intelligence professionals are usually more permanent members of the advisory and policy planning units than are representatives from the State Department or the armed services, who are constantly "rotated" through such assignments, their prestige increases all the more.

The Laos affair is a good example of the potential power of

11 "The Relation of Knowledge to Action," *The Human Meaning of the Social Sciences*, ed., Daniel Lerner, New York, Meridian Books, 1959, p. 177.

suppliers of "blue-chip" information to government policy makers. Early in January 1961 the United States government publicly disclosed "hard evidence" of Soviet Russian and North Vietnamese participation in what the State Department announced as "Communist military operations against the Royal Lao Government and Lao people."[12] The State Department issued a detailed chronology of the "illegal Soviet and North Vietnamese airlift into Laos," even listing the registration numbers of the aircraft, which, it said, were also used by Russia in the Congo in the previous year.

This announcement came at a time when most of our allies in the Southeast Asia Treaty Organization (SEATO) were making known their doubts that such evidence existed. The Associated Press reported from Bangkok two days later that "many United States diplomats in Asia [which included men in Laos and neighboring Thailand] doubt the charges of their own government that substantial numbers of outside Communist forces have intervened in Laos. . . . One Western diplomat said it appears United States diplomats and intelligence agents are dispatching conflicting reports to Washington and the CIA reports have gained credence in the United States capital."[13]

Whatever were the true facts, it is clear that information can be decisive in determining United States reaction to events. This reaction, in turn, has its impact on the situation. In the case of Laos, this has been demonstrated since 1954, when the country was created out of a fragmented Indo-China, leaving pro-Communist Pathet Lao rebel forces unreconciled. The tragicomic opera that ensued can be laid in part to poor information supplied by the CIA that produced faulty policies in Washington for nearly a decade. Specifically, in one episode, a decision was made to support General Phoumi Nosovan, apparently chiefly on the ground that he was anti-Communist. But, as it turned out, he was politically unpopular in Laos, and his army nearly worthless. American

[12] Baltimore *Sun*, January 4, 1961; *The New York Times*, same date.
[13] Baltimore *Sun*, January 6, 1961.

policy had to be abruptly changed. The cost to the American taxpayer ran into the hundreds of millions of dollars. The chief beneficiaries appear to have been the Communists, who appeared to be closer in touch with the realities. Responsibility for policy objectives was the President's and the State Department's. But their policies could be no better than the information on which they were based; their implementation no better than the undercover political instrument for this purpose—the CIA.

In 1962, two of President Kennedy's most important decisions—to resume nuclear testing in the atmosphere, and to take action against the Soviet deployment of missiles in Cuba —were based on evidence supplied by the CIA.

The ultimate power and the ultimate restraint of democratic government is an informed electorate. While it would make no sense to publish information about legitimately secret intelligence operations, the principle must be maintained that the citizen, or at least his representatives, be as completely informed as possible. A corollary requirement is that the citizen know something about the source and process by which intelligence is produced. There ought to be public confidence in the professional competence of the intelligence services, but in recent years this has been badly shattered.

III

The product generated by the vast machinery of the loosely confederated intelligence community[14] described in the preceeding chapter is distributed according to a governmental "need to know" concept. With a few exceptions, neither the product nor the system's organization, functions, and costs are matters of authenticated public record. The rationale for secrecy is that intelligence activities are particularly sensitive in three respects: First, sources of certain types of data would immediately "dry up" if disclosed. Second, espionage and

[14] For further organizational details, see Ransom, *op. cit.*, Chs. IV and V.

other illegal forms of information gathering should not be officially acknowledged as a government function. In the intelligence tradition, governments always strive to be in a position to "plausibly disavow" espionage. Acknowledgment by top United States officials, in May 1960, of U-2 espionage flights over Russia sharply violated this precedent. Third, underground political actions, which since 1947 have been within the jurisdiction of the CIA, must be secret.

Inevitably and perhaps logically, the Executive branch monopolizes the control of information on all these activities, and within the Executive, the intelligence community has its own inner-circle monopoly. This inner circle can dole out intelligence reports or information on clandestine activities to groups or individuals having, in the opinion of the leaders of the intelligence establishment, a need to know. Although intelligence reports and estimates go regularly and routinely to important decision-making units, their flow is tightly controlled. Information on some sources and some activities, it may be assumed, is never communicated beyond a small group. Some very high-ranking government officials, it turns out, did not know of the U-2 flights over Russia.

It is often argued that many aspects of Intelligence must be accepted on faith. In 1954, Allen W. Dulles declared: "You have to look to the man who is directing the organization and the result he achieves. If you haven't got someone who can be trusted, or who doesn't get results, you'd better throw him out and get someone else."[15]

This contradicts one of the working hypotheses of democratic government: that you do not necessarily accept the management of important foreign military affairs on faith. By what criteria can one judge such invisible "results" as the role of the CIA in ousting Premier Mossadegh in Iran in 1953, in the *coup d'état* in Guatemala in 1954, in the Hungarian uprisings in 1956, in Laos, in Berlin, in various explosive Middle East situations and in numerous other clandestine activities, some of which were apparently failures? On

[15] Interview, *U. S. News and World Report*, March 19, 1954.

these specific events, speculation is the only recourse available to the outsider. Indeed, when asked about CIA's role in the ill-fated invasion of Cuba in 1961, the new Director of Central Intelligence in 1962 told Senators he could not answer because "I do not have the facts."[16]

This situation confronts the American system of government with a two-sided problem: How can there be public control over functions that require secrecy; and how can the effective operation of a two-party system of government be assured when control of the Executive branch gives the party in power a potentially exclusive access to essential information in the field of foreign military policy?

Prior to the ill-fated flight of a CIA U-2 reconnaissance plane on May 1, 1960, most citizens could name only one American spy: Nathan Hale. Now all Americans know the name of Francis Gary Powers, convicted as a peacetime spy by a Russian tribunal. Poorly trained as a spy but well trained as a technician, Powers was carrying out a Cold War mission and became a pawn in international politics. He was not executed by his captors, even though he was engaged in illegal activity of a nature most serious to the Soviet Union; he was in fact released early in 1962 in exchange for a Russian spy held by the United States. A Board of Inquiry, which reviewed his case, concluded that Powers "lived up to the terms of his employment and instructions in connection with his mission and in his obligations as an American. . . ."[17] Again, the outsider had to accept this verdict on faith. But if Powers' performance had been inadequate because of poor training by the CIA, one could never be sure that the CIA was not protecting Powers in order to protect itself.

American secret operations—both information gathering and political action—have long been well known to the Kremlin and to sophisticates in world affairs. But such activities on a large scale in peacetime are unfamiliar in the American tradition. President Eisenhower expressed a popular

---

[16] Hearing, "Nomination of McCone . . . ," p. 61.
[17] Text of official report, The New York Times, March 7, 1962.

sentiment when he described espionage as "distasteful." But he also called it a "vital necessity." Taken literally, the President was saying that the nation's life depends upon the distasteful, dirty game of espionage and associated secret operations. If this is so, few functions of American government are of such critical importance.

No longer a secret, as a consequence of "accidents," are the facts that: espionage activities and clandestine political action overseas on a large scale and by every possible means have been an expanding American government function since 1947; under the cover of weather research and in the ostensible employment of a large private aircraft corporation, American CIA operatives spied on the Soviet Union with long-range aerial cameras and other devices between 1956 and 1960; and by means of a large and complex organization comparable in estimated size and cost to the CIA, the National Security Agency has for some years been operating or supervising a massive network for electronic eavesdropping on adversaries and allies as well.

These established facts represent only the top of the iceberg.[18] Authenticated details regarding other American secret intelligence activities must be conjectural. It is difficult to cite "solid" sources as evidence for conjecture. One must therefore speak in vague terms of "undercover political action" and alleged CIA aid to various foreign rebellions. And one must resort to citing anonymous sources, such as the following comment from a retired foreign service officer of the Department of State:

. . . every senior officer of the Foreign Service has heard something of CIA's subversive efforts in foreign countries and probably most of them have some authentic information about CIA operations of this nature in some particular case. Unfortunately most of these activities seem to have been blundering affairs and most, if not all of them, seem to

[18] For muckraking speculation in detail, see Fred J. Cook, "The CIA," *The Nation* (special issue), June 24, 1961; also Tully, *op. cit.*, and de Gramont, *op. cit.*

have resulted to the disadvantage of the United States and sometimes in terrible failure.[19]

It is often asserted that the CIA has its own foreign policy. Little direct evidence can be brought forth to prove this. The more likely situation is that the CIA has moved on its own in a policy vacuum. Standard operating procedure is for the Ambassadors on the spot to be fully cognizant and in control of clandestine operations. It is hoped that this principle is forcefully applied and will always be. "Civilian control" is as important here as in the use of the military instrument for policy aims.

Certain specific questions need to be raised about the control and management of secret operations in a democratic system: Who sets the policies for such activities? Should Congress play a part in approving policies and specific programs? Is existing Presidential and Department of State authority adequate for authorizing, controlling, and auditing these highly sensitive and dangerous governmental functions?

IV

The Central Intelligence Agency's operations, like those of the National Security Agency, are financed by annual Congressional appropriations. Until the sensational disclosures of recent years, however, most Congressmen knew little about the nature and functions of either agency. They know even less about the amount of money annually expended.

Congress as a whole has voluntarily walled itself off from detailed information by statutes requiring secrecy at the discretion of the CIA's Director. In establishing the CIA in 1947, Congress prescribed its organization and functions in general terms, giving the broadest possible definition to "intelligence," in current usage a term covering a number of distinctly different functions. Wide discretion was left to the

[19] Senate, Committee on Foreign Relations, *Study of U. S. Foreign Policy*, "Summary of Views of Retired Foreign Service Officers," June 15, 1959, p. 54.

National Security Council, for which the agency was to work, and to the CIA Director. Congress made the Director responsible for "protecting intelligence sources and methods from unauthorized disclosure."

In the CIA Act of 1949 Congress went even further, exempting the CIA from existing statutes requiring publication or disclosure of "the organization, functions, names, official titles, salaries or numbers of personnel employed by the agency."[20] The Director of the Budget was proscribed from making the usual reports to Congress. The standard procedures regarding the expenditure of public funds were waived, and the Director's personal voucher alone became sufficient for expenditures for purposes of a "confidential, extraordinary or emergency nature."

The Bureau of the Budget has since established special review procedures for the CIA, and most of the CIA's funds are said to be audited in a regular, albeit classified, manner by the General Accounting Office. The unvouchered funds expended at the discretion of the CIA Director, running to tens of millions of dollars annually, are said to be audited also, but by an even more secret process. The CIA must also participate in the annual cycles of rigorous budget "justifications" within the Executive hierarchy.

In 1956 Congress considered a concerted and responsible move to change the existing system by establishing a Joint Committee on Foreign Intelligence. Earlier and less responsible moves had been made in Congress, led by the late Senator Joseph McCarthy, to investigate the CIA on charges of "Communist infiltration, inefficiency, and waste." The new move was led by Senator Mike Mansfield. With 34 cosponsors, Mansfield introduced a bill to establish a Joint Committee. This bill went as far as a floor debate and vote in 1956. But the combined opposition of the Executive branch and senior Senate leaders who felt they knew all they needed to know about intelligence operations defeated it by a vote of

[20] Public Law 110, 81st Congress, 1st Session, June 20, 1949, 63 Stat. 208.

59 to 27. Rather than risk public revelation of the CIA's operations, a leading Senator declared, ". . . it would be better to abolish the Central Intelligence Agency and, by so doing, to save the money appropriated and the lives of American citizens."[21] Since that date, each Congressional session has seen the reintroduction of proposals for a Joint Committee. But through 1962, all died in committee. On May 12, 1960, the House Rules Committee unanimously voted to shelve seventeen resolutions that would establish a Congressional committee to oversee the CIA. In 1961 the same committee devoted more serious attention to the issue by appointing a subcommittee to consider whether there should be a special Congressional investigation of the CIA following the Cuban misadventure in April 1961.[22] No formal investigation followed.

The discovery that the CIA was sponsoring aerial reconnaissance flights deep within the borders of the Soviet Union in the 1956–60 period was as much a shock to almost all Congressmen as it was to the man in the street. But the CIA leaders could cite Congressional statutes as authority for withholding such information.

Senator Willis Robertson, Democrat of Virginia, on May 9, 1960, said:

> I had been hearing testimony presented before the Committee on Appropriations by the Central Intelligence Agency for 13 years. Never during that time were we told what the money was to be used for. It was a deep, dark secret. . . . I asked a number of members of our Defense [Appropriations] Subcommittee if they knew that the Central Intelligence Agency owned and operated planes, and they said they did not. . . . it embarrassed me not to know that the CIA had planes. . . .[23]

[21] Senator Richard B. Russell, *Congressional Record*, April 11, 1956, p. 5412. For a fuller discussion, see Ransom, *op. cit.*, Ch. VII.

[22] Washington *Star*, June 6, 1961.

[23] *Congressional Record*, May 9, 1960, p. 9078.

This was not, however, a dark secret to every Congressman. A few were privy to some details. One such privileged member spoke up on the other side of Capitol Hill the next day. Representative Clarence Cannon, a Democratic Congressman since 1923, as Chairman of the House Committee on Appropriations told his colleagues that, although members were unaware of it at the time, they had earlier appropriated money for the U-2 program and other unspecified espionage missions. The ill-fated U-2 mission of May 1 was, Cannon said, "one of a series and part of an established program with which the subcommittee in charge of the appropriation was familiar, and of which it had been fully apprised during this and the previous session."[24]

To justify the fact that some senior appropriations committee members as well as the more junior Congressmen had been hoodwinked into approving camouflaged appropriations for secret intelligence operations, Representative Cannon cited "absolute and unavoidable military necessity, fundamental national defense." He explained that the privileged subcommittee that knew of and approved the U-2 flights included for the most part the same legislators who were privy to the secrets of the atom bomb in World War II. The U-2 flights were, he said, the CIA's response to insistent Congressional demands that the nation be forewarned of enemy attack. Presumably they were also in response to the Strategic Air Command's demands for better target information to bolster "deterrence." Tight secrecy about such matters was required, Cannon implied, because "some incautious member of a congressional committee or its staff" might disclose highly sensitive information.

Cannon's House appropriations subcommittee is not the only House group concerned with intelligence. A special House Armed Services subcommittee was activated in 1958 by Chairman Carl Vinson, Democrat, Georgia, amidst Capitol Hill discontent with intelligence performances. This committee is composed of four members of the majority party,

[24] *Congressional Record*, May 10, 1960, p. 9146.

three from the minority, and reviews CIA activities, according to its spokesman, "to the fullest extent it deems necessary."[25]

A similar group exists in the Senate. The Senate Armed Services Committee has, since 1955, maintained a formal subcommittee on Central Intelligence composed of five of its highest ranking members of both parties, all of whom are also senior members of the Senate Committee on Appropriations. This subcommittee receives "information on the magnitude of the CIA appropriation and the purposes for which this money is spent." Its chairman, Senator Richard B. Russell, Democrat, Georgia, said in 1960 that the CIA was "very cooperative," and that he "knew in advance of the U-2 aircraft and its capability."[26] The group, like the others concerned with the CIA, holds its meetings in secret; no record of subcommittee actions has ever been released.

From the information available about the actual extent of Congressional surveillance, it appears that the House has been more active than the Senate. The Senate group has apparently not been aggressive in seeking complete details about CIA operations. For one thing, most senior Senators have little time to devote to a largely watchdog function. For another, they are reluctant to ask questions that would penetrate the darkness in which intelligence units normally operate. As Republican Senator Leverett Saltonstall of Massachusetts put it in 1956, ". . . it is not a question of reluctance on the part of CIA officials to speak to us. Instead it is a question of our reluctance, if you will, to seek information and knowledge on subjects which I personally, as a Member of Congress and as a citizen, would rather not have. . . ." Quite a different view has been expressed by Senator Wayne Morse, Democrat, Oregon, who complained late in 1962 that Congress cannot obtain information from CIA if the Agency is unwilling to give it. "I am a member of the Foreign Relations Committee of the Senate. Not a single member of that com-

25 Letter to author from Chief Counsel, House Committee on Armed Services, October 7, 1960.
26 Letter to author, November 3, 1960.

mittee can get any information out of CIA that CIA does not want to give us. . . . That is a frightening and frightful power."[27]

Allen Dulles, as CIA Director, once said about investigations: "Any investigation, whether by a Congressional Committee or any other body, which results in a disclosure of our secret activities and operations or uncovers our personnel would help a potential enemy just as if the enemy were able to infiltrate their agents right into our shop."[28] Thus the amount of information revealed to any Congressional group is largely at the discretion of the Director of Central Intelligence whose authority comes from Congress itself.

In the investigation of the U-2 incident conducted by the Senate Committee on Foreign Relations, the committee probed as deeply as possible into events surrounding the U-2 affair and received testimony from the highest ranking officials in the CIA, the State and Defense Departments. Yet on a crucial point for Senatorial, and public, evaluation of the government's performance, absolute silence was maintained by Executive Department officials. The question: "Was the information sought by the May 1 flight of sufficient importance to justify the hazards involved?" The Director of the CIA refused to answer, even in executive session, although it was the committee's view that such information was "crucial to reaching an informed judgment."[29]

Even after Russia's return of U-2 pilot Powers, his public testimony, and the CIA's official report, many important questions remained unanswered regarding the specific flight, the pilot's training, the CIA's management of the program, and the purpose of such activities.[30]

[27] Senator Saltonstall's statement in *Congressional Record*, April 9, 1956, p. 5292. Senator Morse's statement in *Congressional Record*, October 10, 1962, p. 21775.

[28] Interview in *U. S. News and World Report*, March 19, 1954, p. 67.

[29] Senate *Report* No. 1761, 86th Congress, 2d Session, June 28, 1960, p. 22.

[30] For a competent journalistic account of the incident, see Wise and Ross, *op. cit.*

If Congress has been relatively inactive in performing the watchdog function, other *ad hoc* groups have sporadically served this purpose. Between 1947 and 1961 central intelligence was subjected to five separate special studies and investigations. Two of these were by task forces of the Hoover Commission, in 1948 and again in 1955.

The CIA was in its early stages of organization and development when the first Hoover Commission made its report early in 1949. The Hoover task force called for vigorous efforts "to improve the internal structure of the Central Intelligence Agency and the quality of its product. . . ."[31]

Another special survey was conducted by a three-man group headed by Allen W. Dulles, reporting to the President and National Security Council in 1951. The report of this group was never made public, even in summary form. Presumably it centered upon the shaky intelligence performance during the Korean War. It also provided the springboard for Allen Dulles' entry into the CIA in 1951 as Deputy Director.

Still another survey of CIA organization and performance was made in 1954 by a four-man group headed by Lieutenant General James H. Doolittle. This study came at a time when the agency was under the heavy threat of a Senate investigation by Senator Joseph McCarthy and was designed in part to head off what promised to be an unrestrained fishing expedition into the CIA's affairs. The Doolittle group made a private report to the President in October 1954. General Doolittle simultaneously issued a brief public statement that CIA was doing a "creditable job," but that unspecified organizational improvements were needed. *The New York Times* editorialized that such a verdict had to be accepted "pretty much on faith."[32]

A Hoover Commission task force headed by General Mark W. Clark made a detailed survey of the central intelligence system in 1955 which resulted in two reports. One, dealing with organizational aspects, was published. The other, dealing

[31] Hoover Commission, Task Force Report, "National Security Organization," Appendix G, January 1949, p. 16.
[32] *The New York Times*, October 24, 1954.

with secret operations, was top secret. The Clark Task Force made special note of the CIA's freedom from the public surveillance normal to our governmental system. Believing this potentially dangerous, it recommended the establishment of Executive and Congressional watchdogs. The Executive group would be a Presidential board of distinguished private citizens. The Congressional group would be a "Joint Congressional Committee on Foreign Intelligence, similar to the Joint Committee on Atomic Energy."

The Joint Congressional Committee idea was not adopted because of Presidential opposition and a similar coolness among senior legislators. But the first recommendation led to the creation, in February 1956, of the President's Board of Consultants on Foreign Intelligence Activities. Its specified duties were to "conduct an objective review of the foreign intelligence activities of the Government and of the performance of the functions of the Central Intelligence Agency . . . and report its finding to the President semiannually or at more frequent intervals. . . ."[33] The Board's jurisdiction covered not only CIA but all government intelligence agencies. The Director of Central Intelligence was required to reveal to Board members any information demanded, and Board members were sworn to secrecy.

After the 1961 Cuban fiasco President Kennedy reconstituted this Board, changing its name to the President's Foreign Intelligence Advisory Board. On May 2, 1961, James R. Killian was reappointed chairman,[34] a post he once held under Eisenhower.

Concurrently, President Kennedy summoned former Army Chief of Staff, General Maxwell D. Taylor, to make a special study of the Cuban failure and of America's capabilities for

[33] Executive Order 19656, February 6, 1956.

[34] New members added included Robert D. Murphy, veteran State Department official; Professor William L. Langer of Harvard, former OSS, State Department, and CIA official; Clark Clifford, a White House adviser to Presidents Truman and Kennedy; and Frank Pace, of broad industrial and government experience. Clifford succeeded Killian as chairman in May 1963.

paramilitary operations and guerrilla warfare. General Taylor was assisted in this study by Attorney General Robert Kennedy, Chief of Naval Operations Admiral Arleigh Burke, and CIA Director Allen Dulles. The aftermath was a delayed but major shake-up in the top leadership of the CIA. Within a year after the Cuban affair, the Director and Deputy Director had retired and were replaced by John A. McCone, former shipbuilder, Air Force official and Chairman of the Atomic Energy Commission, and Major General Marshall S. Carter, a career Army officer. Functional deputy directors for "plans" (secret operations) and "intelligence production" were also replaced within the year. But major organizational changes, as of this writing, have not been disclosed.[35]

One point to note about surveillance is that the Executive has not usurped monopolistic control of the CIA. Rather, Congress voluntarily, by statute, gave the President and the National Security Council wide and undefined discretionary authority. Only a few specific statutory restraints were placed on the agency: that it have no policy or internal security functions; that it not foreclose or usurp the foreign intelligence work of existing departments and agencies; and that it be given access to FBI files only upon written request from the CIA Director to the FBI Director.

V

Who determines specific policies and operating programs for the Central Intelligence Agency? Because the CIA is but a central unit among various overlapping, duplicating, and inevitably competing intelligence agencies, who arbitrates the jurisdictional disputes? The working constitution of the intelligence system is a set of National Security Council Intelli-

[35] While there was much speculation, after Cuba, about reconstituting CIA as an exclusively information-gathering agency, assigning clandestine political and paramilitary missions elsewhere, such radical surgery apparently has not been performed as of the end of 1962. For a provocative discussion of possible changes, see *The New Republic*, June 19, 26 and July 3, 1961.

gence Directives, stemming from Congressional statutes of 1947 and 1949. While such directives bear the imprimatur of the NSC, this may be little more than "rubber stamp" approval of working rules and jurisdictional assignments made under the leadership of the Director of Central Intelligence among the various cooperating (or competing) units of the intelligence community. These directives, codified in 1959, set forth the operational and organizational principles of the CIA and assign functions among the various other intelligence units of government. From these basic NSC directives, Director of Central Intelligence directives are formulated to guide the operations of the agency and to coordinate government-wide foreign intelligence activity, in the hope of preventing duplication or gaps in essential information.

The "public interest," then, as represented by the President, advised by the NSC; a handful of senior legislators on Capitol Hill; and the President's Foreign Intelligence Advisory Board. The latter group is not statutory and serves, on a very part-time basis, at Presidential discretion. The question remains: Is this system for surveillance adequate, given the scope and importance of the intelligence function and the potentially explosive nature of some types of operations that have come under the rubric of "intelligence"?

Before dealing with this question, it may be useful to ask: Who authorized and controlled such programs as the U-2 espionage flights of 1956–60? The available record suggests the shocking fact that neither the President, the Secretary of State, nor the Secretary of Defense knew on May 1, 1960, that our U-2 pilot was in the air over the Soviet Union. The U-2 reconnaissance project was operated by the CIA, using the Lockheed Aircraft Corporation, the Air Weather Service of the Air Force, and the National Aeronautics and Space Administration as "cover." But top policy direction for U-2 flights came from an *ad hoc* group of representatives of the Departments of Defense and State, and the White House. The Director of CIA periodically, after obtaining the "concurrence" of the Departments of State and Defense, recommended a series of alternative aerial espionage programs to the President. Thus the President, it seems, had "general knowledge" of the U-2 program, and had approved the May 1 flight as one among "several" in a continuing program of high-altitude espionage flights. It is not clear that the State or Defense Departments were consulted on this specific flight.[36] At any rate, it was clearly a Presidential responsibility.

After the flight and the subsequent collapse of the Paris summit conference, President Eisenhower told the nation: "I take full responsibility for approving all the various programs undertaken by our government to secure and evaluate military intelligence."[37] Regarding the timing of the May 1 flight, on the eve of the summit conference, the President said, "The decision was that the program should not be halted." The record is unclear as to whether deliberate and specific decisions were made not to discontinue Powers' U-2 flight prior to the Paris conference. "I had no thought of it having any possible bearing upon the summit meeting or my forthcoming trip to Moscow," Eisenhower said later.[38]

Secretary of State Herter testified that a pre-summit meeting moratorium was not discussed with anyone in the State Department. It would appear that in this instance the CIA followed its usual practice of obtaining the concurrence of the White House and the State and Defense Departments for a general espionage program and taking the specific timing on itself, subject to Presidential intervention. Reflecting on the matter some months later, President Eisenhower said that he would cancel the flight if he had it to do over again.[39]

Leaders in the Executive branch are likely to calculate the risks of such programs more carefully if they are conscious

[36] Most of these details are found in "Events Incident to the Summit Conference," *Hearings*, Senate Committee on Foreign Relations, May 27–June 2, 1960. See also Senate *Report* No. 1761 on same, June 28, 1960. See also Wise and Ross, *op. cit.*

[37] Address to the nation, May 25, 1960.

[38] Quoted in Adams, *Firsthand Report*, p. 456.

[39] A. Merriman Smith, *A President's Odyssey*, New York, Harper, 1961.

of a Congressional committee looking over their shoulders. But strong arguments can be made for or against a Joint Congressional Committee on Central Intelligence for additional extra-Executive supervision of the CIA.

Standard arguments against such a committee are: The existing system is adequate in that the public is represented by a small group of its most senior and experienced Congressional members, and the entire intelligence system functions, in theory at least, under responsible Presidential leadership. Establishment of a Congressional committee with a large and permanent staff would not only risk disclosure of the most sensitive of all government operations, but would be an annoyance to the intelligence leadership because of inevitable "second-guessing" by the Committee and its staff, some of whom might be disgruntled former intelligence employees. Furthermore, the State Department, Pentagon, Atomic Energy Commission, Federal Bureau of Investigation, and other intelligence units are already under the purview of various Congressional committees, which would be extremely reluctant to give up their jurisdiction.

Intelligence work is peculiarly a staff function without any direct political responsibility, which brings details of its activities under the heading of "executive privilege." Any change in this status, goes the argument, would do violence to the Constitutional concept of Presidential power and responsibility, particularly the President's special discretionary powers in foreign affairs. The American precept of consent of the governed need not be stretched to claim that the people have a right to know all the details about the formation and implementing of foreign policy. There are areas of legitimate secrecy, in which certain functions must be delegated to responsible leadership. Greater disclosure of intelligence activities to Congress would further complicate the already difficult problem of interallied intelligence cooperation. Most allied intelligence organizations would become even more reticent to disclose secret information to United States representatives if they thought it would be passed on to American Congressmen.

From another perspective, the principal arguments are: The government's intelligence system is too important to be left unsupervised by any group outside the Executive branch. Congress probes in depth only under exceptional circumstances, and Congressional surveillance is fractured into half-a-dozen committees, inhibiting an over-all view and promoting needless, time-consuming work within the Executive departments. The prestige of the central intelligence system is low on Capitol Hill and among large segments of the relevant bureaucracy. Public confidence, too, has been shaken by a series of apparent failures. There is a lack of understanding of the limits and potentialities of intelligence reports and estimates. A permanent well-staffed Joint Congressional Committee might serve as promoter and defender of the central intelligence system while simultaneously guarding the public interest. Such a committee might be composed of chairmen and highest ranking minority party members of the House and Senate Committees on Appropriations, Armed Services, Government Operations, and the Senate Foreign Relations and House Foreign Affairs Committees. The American system, furthermore, is based upon an unwillingness to accept government activities on "faith" without the proper institutional devices and criteria for judging whether faith is warranted.

With all the arguments, the essential question boils down to this: Are there adequate checks upon the potential power of the central intelligence system, adequate, that is, for both democratic government and efficient operation of the system? It is my own belief that the system would benefit rather than suffer from additional external surveillance, because of the inherent value within a government bureaucracy of the feeling of external responsibility and the fear of being embarrassed or called to account.

Perhaps 80 to 90 per cent of the activities of the Intelligence Community could be scrutinized by a Joint Congressional Committee to the same degree that existing committees oversee the defense establishment, foreign affairs, and atomic energy policies and programs. These fields too contain highly sensitive elements from a security viewpoint. The record of Congress in keeping secrets given to its various committees in "executive" (secret) session is good. Probably more secrets have deliberately "leaked" from the Executive branch than from Congress.

An arguable objection to Joint Congressional Committees is that they usurp Executive functions. Where there are separate Senate-House committees, this problem is alleviated, for it gives the Executive some leverage in the interplay between House and Senate. It can be argued that the large staff of the Joint Congressional Committee on Atomic Energy has made administrative life difficult within the AEC by taking over some of its executive functions, particularly by attempts to participate unduly in personnel, budgetary, and policy-making functions. The new Director of Central Intelligence is a former AEC chairman, with a long experience of working with a Joint Congressional Committee. Reportedly he had no objection to the establishment of a properly constituted Congressional Committee on Central Intelligence.[40]

Democratic government involves taking risks on the kind of individuals who turn up as leaders within the system. This includes the legislature as well as the executive. Certainly some risks are involved in regularizing Congressional surveillance over Intelligence, including, in addition to security risks, unwarranted harassment of intelligence employees and uneven or inadequate appropriations support for intelligence activities.

In her search for democracy America produced a government system that fragments and diffuses power. To recommend giving Congress a more institutionalized role in overseeing central intelligence is not to recommend more diffusion of power but less. A Joint Congressional Committee on Central Intelligence would be a center of countervailing power, and should help to focus responsibility and authority.

[40] Arthur Krock, "A Proved Breed of Watchdog Is Available," *The New York Times*, May 24, 1962.

There is also the troublesome question of whether meaningful debate can occur, particularly in national elections, when sometimes crucial information is in the control of the party in power. During the 1952 election campaign, President Truman established the precedent that the Presidential and Vice Presidential nominees of both parties receive foreign intelligence briefings from the Central Intelligence Agency. His purpose was to assure foreign policy continuity, regardless of the candidate elected. Since such information is highly classified, however, it may be used for background purposes only, and this limits debate on decisive issues. Aware of this, General Eisenhower, in accepting Truman's offer, did so with the understanding that, except for security information, it would "in no other way limit my freedom to discuss or analyze foreign programs as my judgment dictates."[41] Interesting questions were raised by the 1960 presidential election campaign in which the Democratic candidates for the presidency and vice presidency were given special intelligence "briefings" by the CIA.[42] Did this mean that John F. Kennedy as a Presidential candidate was entitled to information unavailable to him as a member of the Senate Foreign Relations Committee? Or did Lyndon Johnson receive, as a candidate, information to which he was not entitled as Senate majority leader and, incidentally, a member of the Senate Armed Services subcommittee on the Central Intelligence Agency? Presumably so. Justification for this may be that

[41] The New York Times, August 15, 1952.

[42] A controversy later arose as to the extent of Senator Kennedy's briefing by the Director of Central Intelligence, specifically as to whether the senator, as a 1960 Presidential candidate, had been informed of plans for an invasion of Cuba. Former Vice President Nixon has asserted in his memoirs, Six Crises, Garden City, New York, Doubleday, 1962, that Kennedy was so apprised and had improperly used the information, putting Nixon at a disadvantage in the 1960 campaign debates over Cuban policy. A Kennedy Administration spokesman denied that Kennedy had been so informed and this was corroborated by Allen Dulles, at the time CIA Director.

Presidential and Vice Presidential candidates are in fact entitled to special information unavailable to others—including the principal legislative leaders.[43]

VI

The foregoing analysis suggests some guidelines that may be useful in assuring that the intelligence services are as efficient as possible and under the control of responsible authority. Operational intelligence activities must, above all, never be more or less than instruments of national policy, and even as such should not be overrated. Some missions are better left to diplomats. In their informational function, intelligence services must preserve their objectivity. At the same time, Intelligence must serve policy in a staff role rather than attempt to persuade decision makers, openly or subtly, on particular courses of action. And there must be mutual understanding and a close working relationship between the policy makers and the intelligence professionals.

While the control of Intelligence must remain primarily the President's responsibility, Congress must assume a more active and clearly defined role, and the Department of State must participate aggressively in weighing gain from success against cost of failure in every proposed major secret operation. A strengthened Department of State is a prerequisite to putting Intelligence in its proper place.

The CIA is misnamed. More than an intelligence service, it has become a multipurpose organization, engaged in a number of disparate "strategic services." The informational mission of the intelligence system should be organized separately from the clandestine political mission. For when operational

---

[43] In proposing a Joint Congressional Committee on Foreign Intelligence in 1962, Senator Eugene McCarthy suggested there were always sufficient Presidential aspirants in the Senate to constitute such a committee. The Senator, in opposing the nomination of John McCone as Director of the Central Intelligence Agency, provoked a useful debate on the Senate floor. See *Congressional Record*, January 29, 1962, pp. 925–46; and January 31, 1962, pp. 1159–71.

planners also supply the ultimate decision maker with the information required to justify a plan's feasibility, great risks abound, with the self-fulfilling prophecy perhaps the most common danger. Planners and operational commanders are notoriously prone to view their proposed plan as an end in itself. As experiences in the Korean War, Laos, and Cuba demonstrate, selecting only those bits of "intelligence" that justify a given plan's practicability courts disaster.

Another problem involves secrecy and the frequent "leaks" that have occurred in this country. Certain strategic services by definition require the utmost secrecy. The United States can impose a higher degree of legitimate secrecy in two ways. First, the leadership of the intelligence community must resist the many temptations to mount the public speech-making rostrum. Wisdom suggests that they cultivate a passion for anonymity.[44] Second, a restoration of confidence in the professional quality of the intelligence system and in the *fact* of its unquestioned subordination to responsible political authority will automatically produce greater self-restraint on the part of Congress and the press.

Perhaps the most fundamental problem, reflected in the apparent bungling in recent times of supposedly secret operations, has been the lack of a clearly defined national purpose and a national consensus on American foreign policy objectives. A clarified national purpose is the most commonly recommended nostrum for the nation's ailments in foreign affairs. Intelligence has borne the brunt of criticism for many policy and operational failures. The blame ought to be shared with the Presidency, State Department, and Congress. Many

[44] In 1960–61, Allen Dulles, in evidence of his role as a public figure, received the following awards: St. George Association, Golden Rule Award; Veterans of Foreign Wars, Bernard Baruch Gold Medal; All-American Conference to Combat Communism, Vigilant Patriot Award for 1960; New York Employing Printers Association, Franklin Award; and American Committee for the Independence of Armenia, Freedom Award. To his credit, and probably on White House instruction, the new Director of CIA John McCone, through 1962 demonstrated a passion for anonymity as far as public statements are concerned.

of the problems of the intelligence system would be self-solving, given a positive consensus on foreign policy aims other than the natural concern for self-survival. In this regard the Communists have an advantage in conducting clandestine political action, for a democracy cannot enforce an ideological dogma. However, dogma places totalitarian regimes at a disadvantage—witness Nazi Germany and now Soviet Russia—because intelligence reports processed through an ideological filter are likely to be inaccurate and misleading. Even with vast intelligence services, Stalin refused to believe that Hitler was about to attack Russia in June 1941; Hitler in his later years habitually refused to hear "bad" news from his intelligence services; and more recently Khrushchev has misapprehended the United States. All leadership suffers from this malady; totalitarians perhaps to the greatest degree.

Some Americans argue that we must refrain from clandestine illegal operations overseas, adhering instead to high moral principles of conduct. While diplomacy is preferable, and usually more reliable and effective than subversion, the United States cannot realistically abstain from espionage or follow an absolute principle of non-intervention in the internal affairs of other nations.[45] Cold War is by definition a stage in international politics that is neither war nor peace. In this situation, and short of a reign of international law based upon the consent of the governed, the United States may sometimes have to engage in clandestine activities to protect the national interest. The nation cannot accept the claim, in every situation, that the existing government or regime in every foreign country is the legitimate one. The national interest and the common defense may require intervention, even though this confronts us with legal and moral

[45] For a good discussion of the problems of intervention in foreign internal politics, see H. Bradford Westerfield, *The Instruments of America's Foreign Policy*, New York, Crowell, 1963, pp. 401–91. For a sketchy treatment see Harry Howe Ransom, "Secret Mission in An Open Society," *The New York Times Magazine*, May 21, 1961, pp. 20, 77–79.

problems. The United States rarely faces comfortable alternative choices in support of foreign regimes. Often we must accept the lesser evil because circumstances fail to provide an ideal option.

America can neither unilaterally resign from the Cold War without unacceptable risk to all nations sharing democratic ideals, nor cyncially adopt an "ends justify means" rule for action. Intervention or espionage should occur only when no alternative exists, and should be undertaken with a precision and a purpose, determined always by responsible, identifiable political leaders, that have been lacking in the past.

CHAPTER VIII

SECRECY, DEFENSE,
AND DEMOCRACY

I

A principal distinction between a free and a totalitarian society is that in the latter the government controls the formal media of communication. But even in a free society government-imposed secrecy for intelligence operations and reports is regarded as acceptable practice and traditional necessity. There have always been legitimate military and state secrets in a democracy, not only in wartime but in the conduct of peacetime defense and diplomacy. The number of state secrets tends to vary in proportion to the government's concern about threats to the common defense.

Since World War II government secrecy has been extended far beyond the traditional peacetime boundaries. Democratic man's "right to know" about what his government is doing is now challenged by a new concept of "need to know" and by the government's increasing ability, in the name of national security, to manipulate the news as an instrument of policy. The burden of proof has shifted from government, once required to defend its secrecy, to Congress, the press, or the individual citizen in or out of government, who now must prove a "need to know" certain categories of information.

An ever-expanding secrecy, or its corollary—state management of the flow of critical information—is not the result of the Cold War alone. Certainly the Communists' Iron Curtain around strategic information has provoked the American government, whatever the party in power, to retaliate with greater domestic secrecy than ever before. But beyond this, the growing role of government in American life and the increasing complexity in the forms and functions of the great Federal bureaucracy impose their own secrecy requirements— not always, it must be said, to the detriment of individual freedom. The national security label has become a convenient one to apply to almost any category of information the Administration in power wants to protect from disclosure, even though at times the only "security" sought may be the security of the party in power.

Because information about defense plans, policies, programs and weapons systems, if prematurely disclosed, can be of great strategic value to a potential enemy (including domestic "enemies" of policies in the planning stage), the government has created an elaborate security system for classifying documents according to degrees of secrecy required. Such a system is not without its costs. It can actually endanger security by hampering scientific progress, alienating allies, and making difficult the existence of a well-informed electorate, or, at the very least, a knowledgeable, attentive public.

The problem was once concisely summed up by Dr. Vannevar Bush as that of "distinguishing between information which rightly and properly belongs to every man and information which for the safety and security of every man must be protected."[1] It is far easier to state the problem than to solve it.

In the contemporary atmosphere the pressures for secrecy are overpowering the pressures for disclosure. The size and scope of national security programs extend the arguments for secrecy beyond those that normally attend the growth of a giant bureaucracy, and unbalance the Executive-Legislative relationship. The expanding role of government in the economic life of the nation, bringing into government files a massive amount of confidential data on corporations, institutions, and individuals, has inevitably increased the amount

[1] Address to American Society of Newspaper Editors, April 16, 1958, Washington, D.C.

of bureaucratic secrecy. The expansion of the civil service, especially in an era that has been characterized by widespread "loyalty" investigations,[2] has produced highly personal information on the lives of millions of Americans. The increasing number of bureaucratic organizations has multiplied the amount of intragovernmental flow of confidential, privileged communications. The enormity of the task of interdepartmental coordination of defense plans and policies greatly augments the number of documents stamped "Secret."

Another factor nurturing secrecy is the fact that government agencies have become "public relations" conscious. This has led to a centralization of the public-information function in the various departments and agencies, in the hope of manipulating the departmental image in the public mind. Joseph and Stewart Alsop have termed this a "progressive *embourgeoisement*" of government departments, stemming from their desire to put up a good front and to expand their size and service. Behind the penchant for secrecy and good public relations lies the belief of most bureaucrats—this term is used here in its objective sense—that Congress and the public cannot comprehend crucial issues of public policy and should not be informed until decisions have been made. These bureaucrats also recognize that information is one of the most powerful of weapons in the interdepartmental competition over the allocation of national resources. Both the FBI and the Navy, to take random examples, would like the public to believe that their services represent the nation's "first line of defense."

Centralizing public information tends to establish an agency "party line," restricting the flow of objective information. Information is selectively released by press agents. Congressman John Moss, Democrat, California, has described one particular tactic: "Not only has the Pentagon invented dozens of ways of keeping information secret, but it has full

---

[2] This aspect of the problem, of great relevance to the impact of Cold War on democratic form and reality, is not dealt with in this book. An extensive literature exists.

time platoons of press agents managing news and attempting to dull reporters' senses through floods of handouts."[3]

Attempts to strike a balance between public disclosure and secrecy have taken the form of an elaborate system of classifying privileged information into three major categories, TOP SECRET, SECRET, and CONFIDENTIAL. There are also higher categories whose classifying labels are themselves secret. One wag has suggested that the highest security classification is: "Burn Before Reading." And there is a complex informal system for maintaining the secrecy of internal administrative information, not necessarily sensitive in the military security sense, but thought to be *privileged* in the administrative sense.[4] By means of Executive Orders, directives, and regulations, elaborate systems now exist for prior review and censorship or clearance of information emanating from the Department of Defense, the military services, and associated national security agencies.

II

The problem of controlling government security information has several dimensions. First of all, there is the question of what information should be withheld. By means of the classification system noted above, by administrative rules and regulations, and by administrative customs and practices, information emanating from the national security apparatus is officially, if not always effectively, controlled. This negative function is a form of censorship, under which certain categories of persons are privy to specified types of information, while all others are denied access.

Secondly, there is the issue of what, how much, and by what means information should be released. The Office of

    [3] Address, October 8, 1960, at Reno, Nevada. Many of these points are cogently discussed in Francis Rourke, "Secrecy in American Bureaucracy," *Political Science Quarterly*, December 1957, pp. 544–48.
    [4] A number of other categories of classification also have been widely used in the past, such as "For Official Use Only," "Strategic [Technical] Information," and "Restricted."

the Secretary of Defense and the three armed services and their subordinate units engage in the systematic distribution of information and propaganda through the public media. Each of the armed services spends about $1 million annually directly on public information, and many millions indirectly, exclusive of the internal "information and education" programs of the armed services. The Office of the Secretary of Defense in 1961 had a public information and "community relations" budget of $800,000. In addition, hundreds of thousands of military man hours and dollars are expended upon legislative liaison and almost every conceivable form of information-dispensing and propaganda.[5] This is also true in other agencies concerned with national security, such as the Atomic Energy Commission and the Office of Emergency Planning.

Third, there is the matter of handling responses to inquiries from Congress, the press, scholars, or others seeking information from national security agencies.

This and the following chapters deal primarily with the first question: What information should be withheld and what are the pressures and counterpressures affecting defense information policy?

The answer one gives depends upon the vantage point from which the problem is viewed and upon one's assessment of the comparative risks and costs of secrecy and disclosure. As a relevant example, the October 21, 1957 issue of *Aviation Week*[6] disclosed that United States missile detection and performance monitoring equipment based in Turkey had given detailed information about Russian missile testing since the summer of 1955.

Some persons high in government considered this disclosure of previously unpublished information harmful to the nation. Most vocal among them was Robert Cutler, then Special Assistant to the President for National Security

[5] For details and an analysis see Gene M. Lyons, "PR and the Pentagon," *The New Leader*, October 17, 1960.

[6] *Aviation Week*, October 21, 1957, pp. 26–27.

Affairs. According to press reports, Mr. Cutler harshly denounced *Aviation Week* at an "off-the-record" meeting of
the Commerce Department's Business Advisory Council on
October 26, 1957, in Hot Springs, Virginia, where he did not
speak from a prepared text and no transcript of remarks was
made. Later he informed a Congressional committee investigating government information policy that he had advised
Business Advisory Council members that "the publication of
this story was in a category of things prejudicial to our nation
and its people in the free world struggle for survival."[7]

Still later he told the same committee:

. . . the deliberate publication of information classified as
secret on the grounds of military security will, I hope,
lead your committee and the Congress to examine existing
law with a view to determining whether it effectively pro-
tects the people of the United States from public disclosure of information helpful to an opponent dedicated
to destroying our individual liberties.[8]

This was a thesis with which the editor of *Aviation Week*
had already demonstrated sharp disagreement. In the issue
of his magazine a week after the original story, he complained
of President Eisenhower's "continued refusal to tell the American public facts on the Soviet missile program that scientific
intelligence has been reporting to him for two years . . ."[9]
and suggested that the radar complex in Turkey by which
much of this information was gained was a secret to no one
except "the vast bulk of the American people."

Here the issue of secrecy versus disclosure was joined. From
where Mr. Cutler sat, as a close Presidential adviser on national security affairs and as the guiding force of the National

7 *The New York Times*, November 25, 1957.

8 House Committee on Government Operations, House *Report*
No. 1884, "Availability of Information from Government Departments and Agencies," June 16, 1958, pp. 19–20, 172.

9 *Aviation Week*, Editorial by Robert Hotz, editor, October 28,
1957, p. 21.

Security Council's secretariat, the *Aviation Week* disclosure was "shameful" and prejudicial to the national interest. To the editor of *Aviation Week* the opposite was true.

As a background to the discussion of how the United States has attempted to resolve such conflicting views it will be useful to trace briefly the Federal Government's defense information policies. Writing in 1813, Thomas Jefferson recalled that "the first misfortune of the Revolutionary War induced a motion to suppress or garble the account of it. It was rejected with indignation."[10]

By the time of the outbreak of the American Civil War, both the methods of war and the techniques of communication had reached a stage that presented complex information problems to civilian and military leadership. During the conflict, policy and procedure regarding censorship and the security of government information fluctuated widely. In the turmoil of press-military-government relations, many precedents were set for subsequent generations. General Joe Hooker, for example, is credited with instituting the practice of the newspaper by-line, which resulted in much-needed improvements in the accuracy and responsibility of press reporting from the battlefield. Some New York newspapers were temporarily suppressed in 1864. And Thomas E. Knox, a reporter for the New York *Herald*, was arrested by General William T. Sherman as a spy and narrowly escaped the gallows. Sherman subsequently instituted an accreditation system for war correspondents.[11]

An apocryphal cable on the eve of the Spanish-American War from a famous entrepreneur of senational journalism to his man in Cuba: "You furnish the pictures and I'll furnish the war" suggests the ascendancy of press influence in the United States by the end of the nineteenth century. William

[10] Quoted in James Russell Wiggins, *Freedom or Secrecy*, Oxford University Press, 1956, p. 94.

[11] The general freedom of information during the Civil War supported by a sympathetic though often harassed President, has been a boon to historians of the war.

Randolph Hearst's opinion of the power of the press may have been exaggerated, but by the time the United States entered the First World War, government leaders were convinced that it was important not only to impose secrecy on certain types of information but also to have a hand in shaping public attitudes toward the conflict.

During American participation in the First World War a dual public information function evolved: the *negative* (censorship) and the *positive* (propaganda). Censorship began with the promulgation of voluntary regulations by the State, War, and Navy Departments on March 24, 1917. One such regulation stipulated that "no information, reports or rumors, attributing a policy to the government in any international situation, not authorized by the President or a member of his cabinet, be published without first consulting the Secretary of State." The Espionage Act of 1917 administered by the Attorney General, and the Trading with the Enemy Act of the same year administered by the Postmaster General, were further formidable deterrents to unauthorized disclosure of security information.

Using emergency war powers, President Wilson on April 14, 1917, created the Committee on Public Information, with George Creel as Administrator, and war censorship was instituted. Creel had little faith in the effectiveness of direct press censorship; the best guarantee of military information security, he felt, was censorship at the source by the military departments. During the war the press was persuaded to apply a voluntary self-censorship. Editors were given detailed instructions by the government on the kinds of information they should refrain from publishing.

Creel's major function, however, was to generate support for the war effort, and in carrying out the propaganda program, the Creel Committee created a large government propaganda bureau to manage the flow of information in a manner calculated to produce maximum support toward winning the war. The government's propaganda efforts and the supervision of voluntary censorship were combined within Creel's central agency.[12]

Within a few days after the attack on Pearl Harbor, President Roosevelt outlined American information policy for World War II in an address:

> This Government will put its trust in the stamina of the American people, and will give the facts to the public as soon as two conditions have been fulfilled: First, that the information has been definitely and officially confirmed; and second, that the release of the information at the time it is received will not prove valuable to the enemy directly or indirectly.[13]

When Pearl Harbor was attacked, there was no organization to prevent disclosure of strategically valuable information. Each department and agency within the government was made responsible for maintaining proper secrecy of sensitive information within its domain. Some six billion documents, many of which remained beyond public reach into the 1960s, were classified in the process. The Federal Bureau of Investigation was given temporary control over external censorship. Then, shortly after the war's outbreak, Congress passed the first War Powers Act, giving President Roosevelt authority to establish censorship over all forms of communication between individuals in the United States and foreign nations, and accordingly the Office of Censorship was established on December 19, 1941. In announcing the appointment of Byron Price, an executive of the Associated Press, as Director of Censorship, President Roosevelt stated:

> All Americans abhor censorship, just as they abhor war. But the experience of this and all other nations has demon-

[12] For accounts of government information activities in World War I, see George Creel, *How We Advertised America*, New York, Harper, 1920; James R. Mock, *Censorship, 1917*, Princeton University Press, 1941; and Mock and Cedric Larson, *Words that Won the War*, Princeton University Press, 1939.

[13] Quoted in *The United States at War*, Washington, D.C., Bureau of the Budget, 1945, p. 203.

strated that some degree of censorship is essential in war-time. . . . The important thing now is that such forms of censorship as are necessary shall be administered effectively and in harmony with the best interests of our free institutions.

The Executive Order stated that the Director:

. . . shall cause to be censored, in his absolute discretion, communications by mail, cable, radio, or other means of transmission passing between the United States and any foreign country . . . in accordance with such rules and regulations as the President shall from time to time prescribe.

The Office of Censorship had two main objectives: to prevent the transmission in or out of the country of information that might be useful to the enemy; and to obtain external information from the communications examined that might be of intelligence value to the prosecution of the war. Unlike the World War I arrangement, the censorship agency was completely separated from the task of war information and propaganda. Each department and agency maintained its own unit. And several overlapping agencies were handling war information, including the Office of Facts and Figures, the Office of Government Reports, the Coordinator of Information, the public information divisions of the separate armed services, and the many emergency war agencies.[14] The resulting jurisdictional confusion led to several reorganizations, with the Office of War Information emerging as the principal informational agency, although it never attained a monopoly position.

Voluntary censorship of press and radio was instituted by a Presidential letter to Byron Price on January 27, 1942:

As President . . . I hereby authorize and direct you in your capacity as Director of Censorship to coordinate the efforts of the domestic press and radio in voluntarily with-

[14] Ibid., Chapter 8, "Informing the Public."

holding from publication military and other information which should not be released in the interest of the effective prosecution of the war.

"Voluntary codes"—largely the work of the War and Navy Departments and the Maritime Commission—were issued, stating what should or should not be published. Press and radio divisions were established within the Office of Censorship to refine, interpret, and disseminate these codes.

Regulations were revised every six months, describing categories of news not to be published unless authorized by "appropriate authority." These included: troop strengths and movement, shipping activity, ship sinkings, air attacks, disposition of aircraft, descriptions of fortifications, production contracts and capacity, weather reports, rumors on enemy damage, photographs or maps useful to the enemy, and reports of casualties.[15]

The Office of Censorship was abolished on August 15, 1945. At the war's end Byron Price summarized the principles upon which, he said, censorship had been conducted. These were enunciated by a veteran newsman with an eye toward the future.

He stated, in part, that voluntary censorship:

. . . must never base a request on any security consideration which may be questionable . . . avoid interference with editorial opinion . . . must never be influenced by non-security considerations of policy . . . make every effort to avoid multiple censorship . . . must be absolutely impartial and consistent . . . must operate openly, advising the public of every request made to the press. To do otherwise would undermine public confidence and foster unwarranted suspicion both against the Government and the press.[16]

[15] For a discussion of World War II censorship see Theodore F. Koop, *Weapon of Silence*, University of Chicago Press, 1946.

[16] See Office of Censorship, *A Report on the Office of Censorship*, Washington, Historical Reports on War Administration, Series I, 1945.

The delicate and difficult nature of press-military relationships in a democracy, even in time of war, can be further illustrated by recalling that World War II started and ended in the United States with a press furor. Just three days before Pearl Harbor, the Chicago *Tribune* printed portions of an allegedly secret war plan of the United States. The war that followed obscured the controversy over this publication, and the government did not prosecute.

At the war's end, the news of the signing of the German surrender was flashed to the world by Associated Press correspondent Edward Kennedy, in spite of a previous pledge not to release the story until a later hour. Apparently breaking the agreement, Kennedy "scooped" his colleagues, who were infuriated, and Associated Press privileges were briefly suspended throughout Europe. In fairness to the press, however, it must be said that in general the operating concept of voluntary self-restraint proved workable during World War II. The Cold War confronts the government and the press with more difficult problems.

After August 15, 1945, the communications media were free to print at will whatever information they could gather from all sources, with some exceptions. The Atomic Energy Act of 1946 continued the strict secrecy rules for information on atomic energy. For the first time in peacetime history the Federal courts were empowered to issue injunctions at the request of a government agency—the Atomic Energy Commission—to prohibit the printing or distribution of specified types of information.[17] Otherwise, such censorship as existed—until 1954—was imposed at the source through the discretionary power of the government to withhold information within its control.

[17] For a discussion of this and later statutory provisions, see Herbert S. Marks and George F. Trowbridge, "Control of Information under the Atomic Energy Act of 1945," *Bulletin of the Atomic Scientists*, April 1955, pp. 128–30.

III

The Cold War has coincided with the new cult of government public relations and with dramatic developments in communications technology. At the same time, the bipolarization of world power, an accelerating technology, the commitment to the concept of collective allied security, and the massive machinery for national defense have resulted in the most restrictive government information policies in peacetime history.

While government control of information during "hot" wars met with the general cooperation of the mass-communications media, such a high degree of press self-restraint cannot be expected in periods of ill-defined "Cold" War. Since World War II editors and reporters have complained loudly and often that the sources of independent information within the government are drying up, and that the government has been flooding the press and the public with "managed" information.

James Reston has referred to government officials' "growing tendency to manage the news,"[18] and Marquis W. Childs commented in 1954:

> Among working reporters in Washington there is a growing concern over what appears to be a concerted effort to suppress legitimate news—and with a system of rewards and punishments to see to it that only news which is favorable, or is reported in a favorable light is given to the public. Partly this is a carry-over from the big and little wars of the past fifteen years, when propaganda was an instrument of warfare. Partly it reflects the tensions of the cold war and the continuing struggle against Communist imperialism.[19]

[18] Testimony in *Hearings*, Subcommittee on Government Information, House Committee on Government Operations, November 7, 1955, Part I, p. 25. For a more recent description of conditions, see Clark R. Mollenhoff, *Washington Cover-Up*, Garden City, New York, Doubleday, 1962.

[19] United Features syndicated column, December 3, 1954.

It was, however, from a different angle that President Kennedy viewed the problem after the CIA-sponsored attempt to invade Cuba in April 1961 had failed. Speaking to the American Newspaper Publishers Association he said that this time of "peace and peril" creates a threat to national security never exceeded even at the height of any of our past wars. He observed that America's foes have "boasted openly of acquiring through our newspapers information they otherwise would hire agents to acquire through theft, bribery or espionage." Such information—on our covert intelligence preparations, on the strength, location, and nature of our forces and weapons, and details on secret missile tracking mechanisms—would never have been revealed by the press under the conditions of a declared emergency or war. But the President at this time declared no such emergency. Rather he pleaded with the mass communications media to exercise discrimination between the "facts the public deserves to know" and the news it doesn't, and to exercise voluntary self-restraint.[20] Short of declared war, can such a formula be expected? The President's response is revealing: "Perhaps there is no answer to the dilemma faced by a free and open society in a cold and secret war."

Official policies have attempted to resolve the dilemma, but the balance has been increasingly weighted on secrecy's side. Following "unification" of the armed forces in 1947, the first Secretary of Defense, James Forrestal, issued a memorandum on October 10, 1947, which dealt with public relations. In addition to restricting security information, Mr. Forrestal directed that only data "not inimical to the national security shall be released." He added that the Unification Act of 1947 established a unity principle and "the conduct of public relations is to conform to the spirit of the law." It is surprising now to read his further decree that public disclosures of "interservice controversies are to be avoided."

To this end he required *prior approval* by his office of an-

[20] Speech to American Newspaper Publishers Association, April 27, 1961. Text in *The New York Times*, April 28, 1961.

nouncements on subjects (principally general policies, budget making, and interservice disputes) that were his responsibility as Secretary of Defense. Included under this directive was any news release affecting more than one department unless the release had the agreement of all departments concerned.

Forrestal's "unity" directive was supplemented on February 4, 1948, by another memorandum to the Secretaries of the three services and the Joint Chiefs of Staff, stipulating that no speech, press release, or article touching upon a controversial subject could be released either by them or by the Under Secretaries, Assistant Secretaries, Deputy Chiefs of Staff or the Vice Chief of Naval Operations without prior clearance from the Defense Secretary's office. This directive, he said, was "intended to promote a closer and more harmonious integration of the armed forces by preventing the inevitable differences of opinion about policy matters from becoming topics of public debate and controversy." Anyone who has followed military affairs between 1948–62 knows that the directive has been something less than effective.

To administer control of such information Secretary Forrestal established, on July 19, 1948, an Office of Public Information within the National Military Establishment. A director was made specifically responsible for "developing and coordinating over-all public information matters." On March 17, 1949, Secretary Forrestal further centralized all public information activities of the military establishment within the Office of the Secretary of Defense. At the same time, he assembled various media representatives to discuss the problem of departmental "leaks" and the more prompt release of non-security technical information. He urged upon representatives of the press "an assumption . . . of their responsibility in voluntarily refraining from publishing information detrimental to our national security." He advocated a "security advisory council" of six media representatives to advise the Secretary and guide the press, but when he was unable to persuade the press of the necessity and feasibility of this proposal, he abandoned the idea[21] and designated the Office of Public Information as "the sole agency for the National Military Establishment at the seat of government for dissemination of information to media of public information." Secretary Forrestal retired from office soon after this and his successor, Mr. Louis Johnson, on April 14, 1949, announced an even more restrictive policy termed by the press a "gag rule." This was subsequently rescinded on June 4, 1949.

By June 1950, the United States was at war in Korea, and some of the atmosphere that had prevailed during World War II returned. Voluntary censorship was attempted in Korea but soon gave way to field press censorship following unfriendly press relations between General Douglas MacArthur and some of the war correspondents.[22] In December 1950, President Truman directed prior White House clearance of policy statements by high military officials. It was this requirement that Mr. Truman accused General MacArthur of disobeying when he relieved him of his command the following April.

Since 1950 the concept of security has expanded far beyond the military establishment. The Truman Executive Order No. 10-290 of September 24, 1951, spelled out censorship regulations based largely upon State Department and military censorship codes for all Federal Departments, and empowered heads of Federal agencies to designate persons within their organizations authorized to classify information.

This order drew sweeping condemnation from such organizations as the American Society of Newspaper Editors, the Sigma Delta Chi journalistic fraternity, and the managing editors of the Associated Press, on the grounds that: it extended to non-military agencies what was essentially a military classification scheme; it failed to define the precise criteria for the various categories of classification; it invested agency heads with power to delegate classifying responsibilities; it provided no system for reviewing the decisions of

[21] J. R. Wiggins, The Washington Post, May 7, 1961, p. E 1.
[22] For one view of a newsman in uniform see Melvin B. Voorhees, Korean Tales, New York, Simon & Schuster, 1952.

classifying officers; and it established no appeal system from such decisions.

President Truman, in promulgating Executive Order 10-290, admonished government officials not to abuse their new authority or use it to cover up maladministration or dishonesty. He promised that his own White House press office would handle any complaints of overclassification or other abuses. The press did not rest easily with these assurances and criticism continued.

The Truman order also incurred the ire of the President's political opponents in the Senate. On October 2, 1951, Senator Styles Bridges of New Hampshire and twenty-four other Republican Senators issued a statement, in part, as follows:

> We . . . pledge to the American people that we shall fight to guarantee that in the difficult days ahead, no man's voice shall be silenced. We shall vigorously resist any attempt to conceal the facts from the American people. We shall defend to the utmost the fundamental right of free, unlimited discussion of controversial questions in government. We shall rally to the defense of any person against whom reprisals are directed as a result of his constitutional right of freedom of speech.

Later, on September 18, 1952, the staff of the Republican Policy Committee of the United States Senate issued a long report, "The Growth of Federal Censorship under 20 Years of Democratic Administration." And the 1952 Republican Party platform contained the pledge: ". . . not to infringe by censorship or gag order the right of a free people to know what their government is doing."

Despite this pledge most segments of the press seem to agree that during the period 1953–60, secrecy in the Executive branch became more pervasive than ever. Revelations of continued progress in Soviet science and technology and of Soviet espionage activities convinced many persons that American information security was not tight enough. Many assumed, incorrectly, that the chief basis for Soviet technological achievement was information carelessly revealed by, or stolen from, the United States.

President Eisenhower attempted to correct the worst abuses of Truman's Executive Order 10-290 by substituting another Executive Order, Number 10-501, on November 6, 1953. This deprived twenty-eight Federal agencies of power to classify information on security grounds, restricting classification powers to seventeen agencies; limited the authority of agency heads to delegate this responsibility; attempted to define the various security classifications more clearly; and made provisions for appeal and review, allowing the press, for example, to appeal to higher authority an official's decision to deny access to specific information.

Although most critics believed that the new order was an improvement over prior regulations, a number felt that it was no more than "window dressing." Allen Raymond, spokesman for the press, put it this way: "Actually all this new Eisenhower order did was to placate some of the editors, temporarily, and eliminate a few of the more glaring absurdities in President Truman's directive."[23]

The fires of controversy were to burn still brighter in the two years that followed. Fuel was added by two actions of the Executive branch, one in 1954, the other in the year following.

The 1954 action came on November 5, when Secretary of Commerce Sinclair Weeks announced that at Presidential direction, as recommended by the National Security Council, the Office of Strategic Information was to be established within the Department of Commerce[24] to work with the business community in "voluntary efforts to prevent unclassified data from being made available to those foreign nations which might use data in a manner harmful to the United

[23] Allen Raymond, *Report to the American Civil Liberties Union,* October 24, 1955, p. 39. This report is an excellent review of the secrecy issue during this period.
[24] The section of the NSC directive establishing the OSI is reprinted in *25th Intermediate Report,* House Committee on Government Operations, pp. 21–22.

States." In the interest of national security, restrictions were placed upon the release to news media of certain kinds of industrial information. This provoked immediate protests from the press, from the technical and trade publications chiefly affected, and from journalism societies.

A public relations specialist, R. Karl Honaman from Bell Laboratories, was named Director of the Office of Strategic Information. Mr. Honaman had to try to balance two conflicting requirements: the need for interindustry communication—so important to technological progress—and the presumed need to protect information of strategic importance. This move by the government to institute, in effect, a fourth classification—*Strategic Information*—was criticized, particularly from within the journalistic fraternity, on a number of specific counts: a new classification had been added by an Administration pledged to a freer flow of information from the Executive branch; no clear-cut definition of "strategic information" was made; danger existed that the system could be used to discriminate against some companies while showing partiality to others by giving out information on a "need to know" basis; a new kind of censorship, albeit voluntary, was to be instituted on non-military information; and such a system would inhibit and stifle technological progress.

Commenting on the NSC-Presidential directive creating the Office of Strategic Information, Walter J. Murphy, editorial director of the Applied Journals of the American Chemical Society, told Congress:

There seems to be a childlike belief on the part of a great many people in this country—people who should know better—that (1) we have all, or practically all, of the scientific and technical brainpower of the world residing in this country. (2) If each night we lock up our store of scientific and technical reports, we will thereby curtail the scientific and technological advances of other countries.
. . . If we padlock our scientific and technical knowledge, we will be withholding it from our own scientists and technologists just as much as from a potential enemy. Anyone

who has had the slightest contact with science knows it is an elementary fact that a report of one piece of progress catalyzes further advances. . . .[25]

Under a barrage of similar criticism, the Office of Strategic Information went out of existence on June 30, 1957, perhaps because it represented a misguided effort with the unintentional consequence of effecting a closed society. The immediate cause of its demise was the failure of the Administration to obtain appropriations for its continuance in the face of strong Congressional opposition, organized and led by Democratic Congressman John E. Moss of California and his House Subcommittee on Government Information of the Government Operations Committee.

The new public relations spirit appeared to be predominating when, on March 29, 1955, Secretary of Defense Wilson issued a directive requiring officials of his department to adhere to new regulations for prior review and clearance of material to be published. The directive stated in part:

> Such review and clearance shall be related not only to a determination of whether release of the material would involve any technical or substantive violation of security but also to a determination of whether release or publication of the material would constitute a constructive contribution to the primary mission of the Department of Defense.[26]

This "positive thinking" directive specifically required that manuscripts, speeches, and news items to be released to the public through news media by military or civilian personnel of the Department of Defense be submitted for review and clearance not less than three days in advance of public release, and required all Defense Department personnel to as-

[25] From *Hearings* of April 27, 1956, in *25th Intermediate Report*, House Committee on Government Operations, *Report* No. 2947, 1956, p. 23.
[26] Department of Defense Directive No. 5230.9, March 29, 1955, p. 2, Sec. VI.

sume responsibility for their speeches, articles, and information releases being "consistent with the national security and the policies and objectives of the Department of Defense."[27]

The Defense Secretary simultaneously issued a memorandum directing each service secretary to supplant military officers with civilians as public information chiefs, and to reduce sharply service public-information personnel. These new regulations were believed to be the result of the Secretary's growing impatience with publicity about interservice rivalries. They were also apparently the result of White House pressure. President Eisenhower had become incensed on a number of occasions about the amount of unauthorized information on new weapons and defense planning appearing in the press.

The orders produced more loud protests from the press. Hanson W. Baldwin wrote in *The New York Times* that "A new kind of iron curtain, Pentagon model, is being tried out in Washington this week."[28] American journalistic societies, particularly the Freedom of Information Committee of the American Society of Newspaper Editors, made formal protests to the Pentagon, demanding a clear definition of what would constitute a "constructive contribution." The main point of the criticism was that it is the press and the public, after all, who decide what is, in fact, "constructive."[29] Many press representatives protested vigorously at a designation of a "gray area" in security information, implying the existence of information that is not legitimately a military secret but might

[27] *Ibid.*, Sec. VI. A look at the way this policy worked in practice was afforded by General Maxwell Taylor in his book *The Uncertain Trumpet*. In an *appendix* the General reprints an article he drafted for *Foreign Affairs* in the spring of 1956, but never printed because major portions were banned by Defense and State Department censors.

[28] "Pentagon Iron Curtain," *The New York Times*, April 7, 1955. Eight years later Baldwin was to be equally critical of the Kennedy Administration.

[29] Secretary Wilson discussed his new directive at length with Washington newsmen at press conferences on April 12 and 26, 1955.

prove helpful to a potential enemy, particularly when collated with additional facts.

The nub of the matter was that secrecy had been extended beyond any legitimate or necessary boundary. A striking example of the unnecessary secrecy that was being practiced is the fact that for some years the velocity at which an intercontinental ballistic missile could travel was considered secret information. Yet the word "ballistic" and the freely announced missile's range of, say, 6000 miles almost automatically spells out this velocity to anyone with the knowledge of how to calculate it.

The Harvard Library case is another example. During World War II, Harvard scientists undertook secret research for the armed services. More than a decade later the Harvard Library found itself burdened with a mass of material still labeled secret. Not only was this unavailable to Harvard scientists, there was no one on hand with "clearance" to examine the material which continued, year after year, to occupy badly needed space. Storage cost ran to $1200 per year. Congressman John E. Moss, attempting to remove the albatross, appealed to the Secretary of Defense:

> Harvard . . . is burdened with the cost of storing and protecting secret material which no one at Harvard can look at and which Harvard can't get declassified, can't return to the Government, can't give away, and can't burn. At the same time, material which would be of value to scientists and scholars is padlocked beyond their reach.[30]

A sensible classification system would be one in which such data was automatically declassified by a certain date, unless a deliberate decision were made to keep it secret. Risks would be involved in such a policy, no doubt, but gains would very likely outweigh loss.

A more difficult problem is the bureaucrat's tendency to overclassify in the initial step. Without a basic change in at-

[30] Letter of May 24, 1957, quoted in House Committee on Government Operations, 27th Annual Report, House *Report* No. 1884, June 16, 1958, p. 118.

titude it will be unrealistic to expect an individual officer to resist this temptation. No one is punished for overclassification, but there are reprimands for underclassification. The only incentives for releasing information are the protests of scientists, newsmen, or Congressmen. Until this is changed and fewer persons (over a million in 1960) have the authority to classify, the mountainous mass of documents, some perhaps permanently secret, will grow.

Many of these problems were emphasized in the Democratic Party's successful drive to capture the White House in the 1960 election. Once in office and having felt the sharpness of the dilemma's horns, the President called attention, after the Cuban fiasco of April 1961, to a "challenge of our times" which imposes "two requirements that may seem almost contradictory in tone, but which must be reconciled and fulfilled. . . . the need for greater public information and . . . the need for greater official secrecy."[31]

In a directive on May 31, 1961, Secretary of Defense McNamara promulgated four "principles" of public information policy: (1) In a democratic society the public must be kept informed of major issues, including the arguments on both sides of any major controversy. The public also is entitled to know about mistakes and ineffective administration and operations. "The public has at least as much right to bad news as to good news." (2) However, information that can materially assist the enemy must not be disclosed. And toward this end "it is equally as important to avoid overclassification—when in doubt underclassify. In no event should overclassification be used to avoid public discussion of controversial issues." (3) Public statements by Pentagon officials, civilian and military, which appear to reflect Department of Defense policy must reflect that policy in fact. (4) In their public statements, all Defense officials should confine themselves to defense matters. Specifically they must avoid foreign policy matters, a field reserved to the President and the Secretary of

[31] Address to the American Newspaper Publishers Association, April 27, 1961.

State. Otherwise there is danger that when military officers state their opinions on foreign policy matters, their words may be taken as the policy of the government.[32]

The problem reflected in the latter two "principles" was highlighted in 1962 when a special Senate Armed Services subcommittee conducted extensive public hearings on the question of what was popularly referred to as the "muzzling of the military," that is, the requirement that they submit public speeches, prior to delivery, for review by the Office of the Secretary of Defense and by the State Department.[33] While, as often happens, these hearings produced as much confusion as enlightenment, two facts seem to have emerged: that it is sound practice for Pentagon officers to submit their public speeches for policy and security review and clearance; and that censorship officers should exercise their blue pencils in a more reasonable fashion than has sometimes been the case. But one must pity the unfortunate middle-level censoring official who must try to apply policy guidance to speeches when foreign military policy has not been made clear to him. And the problem is magnified when military officers are too often called upon to make public speeches on subjects beyond their jurisdiction and competence.

At the heart of the information-secrecy issue is the question of the "privilege" of the Executive as opposed to the "rights" of Congress and the public. The "public" in this regard is represented by the competitive, free press; the Congress by its various committees, or the continuous competition of the political parties. Congress, of course, cannot always be equated with the public, for unlike the public, segments of the legislature often receive secret information in closed-door hearings. But the secrecy dividing line more often than not puts the Executive on one side and the Congress, the press, and the public on the other.

[32] Department of Defense Directive No. 5230.13, May 31, 1961.
[33] Senate, Armed Services Special Preparedness Subcommittee, *Hearings*, "Military Cold War Education and Speech Review Policies," 87th Congress, 2d Session, 1962, Parts 1–7, and *Report*, issued October 19, 1962.

Law and custom have put certain types of information beyond Congressional or public scrutiny. It is not the purpose here to describe in detail the legal basis for Executive secrecy, or the complex subject of how the Federal courts have dealt with questions of administrative secrecy, or the Legislative-Executive conflicts over access to information.[34] Suffice it to say that Congressional statutes, administrative regulations, and common law have in combination over the years supported widespread administrative secrecy.

A number of statutes explicitly prescribe administrative secrecy. Such authority has persisted since the earliest days of the Republic, when Congress first enacted in 1789 a so-called "housekeeping" statute, vesting in the heads of Executive departments discretionary control over the "records, papers, and property" of such departments.[35] Although never intended to give Executive officials authority to impose widespread secrecy on public records, this statute was so often used for that purpose that Congress came to feel it was being misused. Consequently, it was amended by the 85th Congress in 1958 to the effect that: "This section does not authorize withholding information or limiting the availability of records to the public." Interestingly, this amendment was opposed by each of the ten cabinet-level Federal departments. But it was passed by unanimous vote in the House. In signing the bill, President Eisenhower declared that its legislative history showed:

It is not intended to, and indeed could not, alter the existing power of the head of an executive department to keep appropriate information or papers confidential in the public interest. This power in the executive branch is inherent under the Constitution.[36]

[34] For a thorough analysis see Francis E. Rourke, *Secrecy and Publicity: Dilemmas of Democracy*, Johns Hopkins Press, 1961.
[35] United States Code, Title 5, Sec. 22, codified in 1875 as Revised Statutes 161.
[36] August 12, 1958.

The new law left intact some seventy-five statutes that in one way or another restrict public access to certain kinds of information in the files of Federal Executive agencies. Such broad legislation as the Administrative Procedures Act of 1946 (5 U.S.C.A., Sec. 1002) and the Atomic Energy Act of the same year (42 U.S.C.A., Sec. 1801) contain provisions authorizing secrecy for specified types of information. In the case of atomic energy, persons guilty of violating information disclosure prohibitions face stiff penalties, including in some cases the death sentence. And, as we have seen, the Director of Central Intelligence has the statutory authority to deny important information even to Congress.

While Congress has deliberately prescribed secrecy for many categories of information, it has remained skeptical of broad assertions by the Executive of his inherent authority to impose secrecy beyond statutory prescriptions. More than half the Presidents from Washington to Eisenhower have on occasion refused requests from Congress for information. A leading figure in the successful Congressional drive to amend the "housekeeping" statute, Congressman John E. Moss, in 1958 commented in the face of Presidential claims of "inherent" power to withhold information: "One of the main reasons for taking this [amendment] as a first step is to get them back to relating their claims of authority to the appropriate statutes and not to use this as a catchall for any claims they may want to assert."[37]

Since George Washington's time, Presidents have claimed that under their Constitutional "executive power" they must on occasion keep secret certain kinds of documents, even though no specific statutory authority can be cited. President Eisenhower's letter to the Department of Defense, during the Army-McCarthy controversy in 1954, prohibiting disclosure to Congress or the public of "confidential communications" within the Executive branch may be cited. Although addressed to the Secretary of Defense for a specific purpose in the Army-McCarthy investigation, the Eisenhower letter,

[37] *Congressional Record*, April 16, 1958, p. 5887.

with an appended memorandum from the Attorney General stressing "separation of powers" and "executive privilege," was subsequently used by some nineteen other government agencies as authority for withholding information. A more recent example was President Kennedy's invocation of the doctrine on February 8, 1962, forbidding the Secretary of Defense to tell Senators probing prior censorship of the public speeches of military officers the names of individual censors who altered certain foreign policy speeches proposed by military officers.[38] At the same time, the President observed that the principle at stake "cannot be automatically applied to every request for information." But there appear to be few limits to categories of information claimed to be covered by "executive privilege" at Presidential discretion.

So-called "state secrets," including diplomatic and military subjects, have been accorded judicial recognition as matters within the power of the Executive to withhold from public disclosure even in the absence of permissive statutes; and the courts have generally held that the President has discretionary authority to withhold information from the public in the national interest. But there have been no judicial tests involving Congressional claims of the right to obtain information from the Executive branch. Perhaps this will always remain within the realm of the "political questions" that the Supreme Court will leave to be solved by combat between the President and Congress. In general, the Presidency has prevailed on the basis of a broad claim of "executive privilege" —a claim normally challengeable with effect only in the political arena.

A White House point of view was expressed by President Eisenhower in a press conference on July 6, 1955:

> If anybody in an official position of this Government does anything which is an official act, and submits it either in the form of recommendation or anything else, that is prop-

[38] Text of letter to Secretary McNamara in *The New York Times*, February 9, 1962.

erly a matter for investigation if Congress so chooses, *provided the national security is not involved.* [Italics added.]

But when it comes to the conversations that take place between any responsible official and his advisers, or exchange of mere little slips, of this or that, expressing personal opinion on the most confidential basis, those are not subject to investigation by anybody. And if they are it will wreck the Government.

In an atmosphere of Cold War, the phrase "provided the national security is not involved" removes much of the practical meaning from such a statement of principle, for "national security" is hardly susceptible to a standard operational definition. If common agreement existed on what is and is not in the national security interest, the great controversy over information policy would have subsided.

Interesting cases arise when a statute seems to require release of information by the Executive branch, and it claims Executive privilege. Such a case was the refusal of the Secretary of the Air Force in 1958 to make available certain Air Force reports to the Comptroller General, General Accounting Office, an independent agency set up by Congress in 1921 to make an objective audit of government expenditures. Congress and the General Accounting Office claimed many precedents as well as a statutory right and requirement to see a copy, in this case, of an Air Force inspection report, "Survey of Management of the Ballistic Missile Program." The Air Force and the Presidency claimed that this was confidential information. The House Committee on Government Operations felt that Executive refusal was in violation of Congressional statutes. In a statement, the Committee declared:

No executive act can modify, amend, or contravene a statute. Laws can be amended only in the way they were enacted. Any attempt by the Executive to alter or supersede the law does violence to the Constitution.

When the Executive can select which laws shall and shall not be enforced; when this selective power is applied to laws providing information necessary for the legislative branch to carry out its constitutional duties; when the "executive privilege" to control information for the Congress flows down from the President throughout the executive bureaucracy, then the Government of the nation ceases to be a representative democracy. Sweeping claims of an unrestrained "executive privilege" to control the facts of Government are a step towards despotism.[39]

A number of other such cases have involved Congressional requests for information on the Mutual Security (foreign aid) Program which the Executive has claimed statutory authority to withhold but on which the Congress makes a contrary interpretation.

IV

In an age in which few government matters cannot be brought under the rubric of "national security," claims of "executive privilege" must be used with restraint. So must Congressional demands for certain types of information. Any sweeping claim by Executive departments of privilege not to disclose internal operations would threaten, indirectly at least, the autonomy of Congress. Secrecy in government is always a potential enemy of democracy.[40]

In 1822, James Madison wrote:

> . . . a people who mean to be their own governors must arm themselves with the power knowledge gives. A pop-

[39] House Committee on Government Operations, House *Report* No. 234, 86th Congress, 1st Session, March 19, 1959, p. 83.

[40] The literature of various aspects of administrative secrecy is abundant. See particularly: Maure L. Goldschmidt, "Publicity, Privacy and Secrecy," *The Western Political Quarterly*, September 1954, pp. 401–16; Rourke, *op. cit.*; Harold L. Cross, *The People's Right to Know, Legal Access to Public Records and Proceedings*, Columbia University Press, 1953; J. A. Latimer, "The Power of Congress to Subpoena Members and Documents from the Executive Branch," *South Carolina Law Quarterly*, Spring 1955, pp. 379–93; John E. Moss, "The Crisis of Secrecy," *Bulletin of the Atomic Scientists*, January 1961, pp. 8–11; Harry Street, "State Secrets—A Compara-

ular government without popular information or the means of acquiring it is but a prologue to a farce or a tragedy or perhaps both.[41]

In 1956 Walter Millis, commenting on the Eisenhower years, observed: "We have cloaked the operations of the Executive Branch of Government in veils of secrecy unknown to any previous epoch of our history."[42]

The sharp contrast between the comments of Madison and Millis raises at least two fundamental questions: whether all the principles of the Founding Fathers meet the requirements of national security in the nuclear-missile age; and whether recent government leaders, in their preoccupation with security, have forgotten the importance of a free flow of information in a democratic system.

A major bulwark of liberty is a citizenry sufficiently informed about the major issues of public policy to participate in a meaningful way in self-government; and a prime requisite for progress is a high degree of freedom of information in science and its application. Democracy and progress can both be debilitated if leaders unnecessarily enshroud government operations with a curtain of secrecy. Expert witnesses before the House Special Subcommittee on Government Information testified in 1956 that there would have been no development of nuclear power if the security regulations of 1956 had been in force in 1939.

---

tive Study," *Modern Law Review,* Vol. 14, April 1951, pp. 121–35; S. D. Warren and L. D. Brandeis, "The Right of Privacy," *Harvard Law Review,* Vol. 4, December 1890, pp. 193–220; Legislative Reference Service, Library of Congress, "Congressional Power of Investigation," Senate *Document* No. 99, 83rd Congress, 2d Session, February 9, 1954; House Government Operations Committee, "The Right of Congress to Obtain Information from the Executive . . . ," 84th Congress, 2d Session, May 3, 1956, Committee Print; and numerous hearings, studies and reports, House Government Operations Subcommittee on Government Information, 1955–62.

[41] Letter to W. T. Barry, August 4, 1822, *The Complete Madison,* ed., Saul K. Padover, New York, Harper, 1953, p. 337.

[42] *Arms and Men: A Study in American Military History,* New York, Putnam, 1956, p. 360.

But the democratic way of life may be destroyed in another way—by disclosing to a potential enemy, openly or inadvertently, special categories of information that will enable him to surpass, surprise, or deter us with modern instruments of force. And enlightened innovations in public policy can, in the discussion or planning stage, perish in the harsh glare of premature publicity. In the consensus-building process of American policy making, there are always those opponents to change of any kind who can use bits of distorted information as a weapon to maintain the *status quo*.

A central problem for democratic government, then, is to discover precisely what types of information truly deserve secrecy, and when. A high price must be paid for secrecy, perhaps an incalculable amount—in civil liberties, speed and diffusion of scientific development, and knowledge and public understanding of the realities of world politics. There is also a calculable direct dollar cost: hundreds of millions of dollars annually for guards, security measures, personnel investigations, codes, and other special procedures. These expenditures must be balanced against the potential costs of disclosure of secret data that might dry up sources of information about potential enemies, increase the efficiency of enemy weapons and countermeasures, and in general solve many of the potential enemy's strategic problems.

Aside from national security considerations, an obsession with secrecy seems to be a natural stage all bureaucracies eventually reach if they are permitted to follow their inherent tendency without adequate counterpressures. Bureaucracies err on the side of secrecy. Democratic leadership must strive to thwart this tendency.

In America's past wars, the censorship and secrecy required have been effected through the cooperation of most elements in our society. Each war, nevertheless, has left its large residue of secrecy. In the Cold War, national consensus on policy and strategy are often absent. Both the nature of the threat and the best means of meeting it are highly debatable. National purpose and objectives are variously defined by different groups, this condition being, in fact, a prime characteristic of the democratic idea.

In the Cold War most of the pressures and many of the strongest arguments have been for greater government secrecy. But as these pressures have increased, they have fortunately had to contend with ever-present counterpressures. These will be discussed in the next chapter.

CHAPTER IX

SECRECY VS. DISCLOSURE:
CONFLICTING PRESSURES

Among the counterpressures against government secrecy in American society the most important are: (1) the pressure of Congress; (2) a confederated armed services structure (described in detail in Chapter IV) characterized by rivalry among its various organizations; (3) a mass media press with energetic competition among its various components for acquiring "firsts" with the news; (4) a competitive industrial system that is a source of much information and in which information is a pivotal element; and (5) a scientific and technological community with its own sources of information and an insatiable appetite for knowledge, in which the free flow of information is an absolute prerequisite.

I

Congress, by its very nature in the American Constitutional system, acts as a catalyst for the flow of information about government. Much Congressional activity involves procuring and interpreting information from the Executive branch. The source of most Executive-Legislative conflict is the Executive claim for secrecy and the Congressional claim for disclosure, even though, ironically, about one-third of all Congressional hearings over the past ten years have been held in secret. Let us consider one broadly illustrative example, the House Subcommittee on Government Information.

An extensive Congressional probe of Executive information policy began on June 9, 1955 when the House Committee on

Government Operations created this special subcommittee, headed by Representative John E. Moss, to publicize secrecy policies in all sectors of the Executive branch. Studies by the subcommittee, pursued through the 87th Congress (1962), included detailed questionnaires, hearings, and special studies and produced thousands of pages of reports.[1] The Moss committee became an unremovable thorn in the side of many government public information officers, particularly those responsible for information policies in the Department of Defense.

In an intermediate report on July 27, 1956, the subcommittee stated that the informational practices of the Department of Defense were the most restrictive in any major branch of the Federal Government. In a 1960 report the Moss committee was highly critical of the rate of declassification of documents in the Department:

> The Defense Department and its component branches are classifying documents at such a rate that the Pentagon may some day become no more than a huge storage bin protected by triple-combination safes and a few security guards. Millions of documents each year are being added to the Defense Department's classified files, and only a small fraction are being declassified annually. . . . Unless some operative system of declassification is developed in the near future, we may find ourselves completely walled off from our past historical achievements as well as from future progress in basic science.[2]

But, as usual, the many voices in Congress have not been in harmony on this issue. Congressman George H. Mahon,

[1] See the *24th Report*, House Committee on Government Operations, 86th Congress, 2d Session, July 2, 1960, and numerous other documents of the Moss Committee in the 84th Congress through the 87th Congress. In the 84th and 85th Congresses, 1955–58, less publicized studies of "Freedom of Information and Secrecy in Government" were conducted by the Senate Judiciary Subcommittee on Constitutional Rights under the chairmanship of Thomas C. Hennings, Jr., Democrat, Missouri. See its various hearings and reports.

[2] *24th Report*, p. 89.

Democrat, Texas, in appropriations hearings for 1955, expressed a contrasting view:

> I think the damage that has been done to this country by the spies and subversives is just a tiny drop in the bucket compared to the damage that has been done by the release of public information as to national defense procedures and programs, and developments, through the Department of Defense, through the Congress and through industry, and through trade journals and so forth.[3]

In its Report on the Department of Defense Appropriations Bill for 1956, the House Committee on Appropriations complained that "Too much information has been released which is of no benefit to the American public but which is of tremendous value to our [Communist] opponents."[4] In its report on the appropriations bill for 1957, however, the same committee warned Defense not to use Congressional concern for unauthorized leaks as an excuse for "withholding legitimate information from the press and public nor as a cover-up for inefficiencies and weaknesses of administration."

Defense Secretary Charles E. Wilson's views were more in harmony with Congressman Mahon and the Appropriations Committee than with the Moss subcommittee. On August 13, 1956, Wilson, reacting to contradictory Congressional and press criticisms of Pentagon information policies, appointed a special Committee on Classified Information, headed by Charles A. Coolidge, a Boston attorney and former Assistant Secretary of Defense, and composed of a senior retired officer from each of the armed services. "I am seriously concerned over the unauthorized disclosure of classified military information," Wilson wrote Coolidge. He requested that the committee make an examination of laws and regulations, organization and procedures, and adequacy and effectiveness of the

---

[3] *Hearings*, House Subcommittee on Department of Defense Appropriations for 1955, 83rd Congress, 2d Session, March 31, 1954, pp. 558–59.

[4] House *Report* No. 493, 84th Congress, 1st Session, May 5, 1955, p. 15.

Department of Defense system in protecting security information.

After a three-month study, which included interviews with some fifty persons concerned with defense information, the Coolidge Committee issued a report on November 8, 1956, that demonstrated the fundamental secrecy-disclosure paradox by reaching the contradictory conclusions that there had been too much secrecy in the Pentagon in the past and that those who violate secrecy in the future should be more severely punished. The committee criticized overclassification of information by the Pentagon but was at the same time critical of unauthorized disclosure of classified information by high-ranking military men and civilians in the Pentagon. Some twenty-eight recommendations were detailed to cope with this dual problem.

These included: restricting visits to defense plants by reporters for trade and technical journals and requiring that officials of private industry discuss only unclassified information with them; insisting that all press interviews with Pentagon personnel be arranged through the Office of Public Information, with a representative of that office sitting in; creating a special unit within the Office of the Secretary of Defense to investigate and "prosecute" security leaks; holding the commanding officer of the service, office, or unit responsible when the source of improper disclosure cannot be discovered; taking disciplinary action against individuals who disclose information regarding interservice disputes; warning industry against disclosure of classified information in advertisements and withholding contracts in extreme cases; summoning newsmen before grand juries to disclose their sources of published classified information; and issuing a statement from the Pentagon to explain the differences between ordinary peace and Cold War.

Secretary Wilson appointed a three-man committee to study the implementation of those recommendations "found to be constructive." No doubt aware that the Moss committee was watching his every move, he expressed specific reservations about the last two recommendations, indicating at once they would not be followed. They were subsequently ignored, while various parts of the committee's other recommendations were incorporated in administrative regulations.[5]

The "constructive contribution" directive was, however, one of the early casualties of the Moss committee investigations. In August 1957, Secretary of Defense Wilson signed a revised directive (Department of Defense Directive No. 5230.9) which prescribed new criteria for publicly releasing material originating within the Department. Such material, read the new directive in part:

> . . . shall not be cleared for public release until it is reviewed for violations of security and for conflict with established policies or programs of the Department of Defense, or those of the National Government, since such material may have national or international significance. Nothing in this directive shall be deemed to authorize the refusal to clear material, otherwise releasable, because its release might tend to reveal administrative error or inefficiency.

The spirit in which the new directive was to be administered was the important element. Even the new requirement that releasable information must not "conflict with established policies and programs" left wide discretion to the information policy administrator. That is, it allowed the Office of Security Review to suppress dissent or unpleasant information by broad interpretation of this phrase.

Another change attributable to the Moss and Coolidge committees—and to the high money costs of storing and guarding classified documents—was the establishment in 1958 of an Office of Declassification Policy in the Pentagon. Since that time, thousands of cubic feet of secret documents have been declassified. More recently, in July 1960, this office announced an enlightened declassification system by which se-

[5] For a detailed report by the Secretary of Defense on implementation of sixteen of the twenty-eight Coolidge Committee Recommendations, see House Government Operations Subcommittee, *Hearings*, Part 9, 85th Congress, 1st Session, April 10–12, 1957, pp. 2321–53.

crecy labels on many categories of information expire automatically at twelve-year intervals. And on September 20, 1961, President Kennedy issued an Executive Order (10-964) liberally amending this procedure. Except for certain materials from foreign governments or international organizations and those stamped secret by specific statute, such as the Atomic Energy Act, classified information is given a lower label every three years and is completely declassified at the end of twelve years. Seeking to improve the system, the Defense Department in January 1963 announced the formation of a Directorate of Classification management to speed up further the declassification process. But the arbitrary power of secrecy remains in the background, because "extremely sensitive information"—at the discretion of the head of an administrative agency—can be put outside of the declassification procedure.

Prompted by Congressional and press criticism, the Executive branch has at least become self-conscious about secrecy. Various units of the government have begun informational campaigns to eliminate the tendency to overclassify. A persuasive note is that papers classified *Confidential* could be stored at smaller cost than those marked *Secret*. However, while these new policies will benefit future historians and researchers, they have little effect on contemporary secrecy policies.

The political party competition which issues from Congress is another counterpressure against secrecy. During the Truman years, Republicans in Congress complained loud and long at the unnecessary secrecy imposed by the Executive branch, as did Congressional Democrats under the 1953–60 Republican Administration. Senators who were particularly vocal in this period included Stuart Symington and Hubert Humphrey. "No careful reader of our press can doubt that this country is menaced by a deliberate policy on the part of our Government to withhold information from the American people," said Senator Symington in 1955.[6] Senator Hum-

6 Speech in New York City, July 7, 1955.

phrey, inserting into the *Congressional Record* a long dissertation on the problem, stated in the same year: "This shroud of silence which has descended over the Government prevents not only the American people from knowing what it is doing, but prevents the Government itself from functioning as it should."[7] Democratic campaigners in the 1960 Presidential campaign stressed repeatedly the charge that the American people were not being adequately or honestly informed by the Republican Administration about America's relative power position in the world.

When the Kennedy Administration assumed office in January 1961 and attempted to tighten control over the public statements of subordinate officials, particularly in the military services, the cycle began again. Senator Barry Goldwater, on January 30, 1961, asked whether the new Administration was to be "a Dictaphone type of 'gag rule' government bent on its own prestige or . . . a government of free speech which holds the people's interest paramount?"[8] The late Styles Bridges, Senate Republican Policy Committee chairman, resumed—after an eight-year interval—his role as guardian of the free flow of information by denouncing what he called a new "gag policy" of the Kennedy Administration. Former Vice President Nixon told the Detroit Press Club on May 9, 1961: "The whole concept of a return to secrecy in peacetime demonstrates a profound misunderstanding of the role of a free press as opposed to that of a controlled press." The President's plea for press self-restraint would "inevitably encourage government officials to further withhold information to which the public is entitled," Nixon said, and "the plea for security could well become a cloak for errors, misjudgments and other failings of government."

After the attempted Cuban invasion in April 1961, Republican Senator Hugh Scott, Pennsylvania, accused the Administration of trying to "suppress, manage, and regulate the flow of news that should be going to the American public." He

[7] *Congressional Record*, August 3, 1955, pp. 11319–29.
[8] The New York *Herald Tribune*, January 31, 1961.

charged that government information policies had taken a "drastic and dangerous turn" since Kennedy took office.[9] And in its 1961 report, Sigma Delta Chi's Freedom of Information Committee joined in these sentiments by describing the Washington information picture as "for the most part about what it was under the Eisenhower Administration, with most records and actions of the Federal Government hidden by bureaucratic secrecy."[10]

II

Congress and the competitive party politics therein will continue to serve as the most important counterpressure against government secrecy, but service differences of opinion also play a part. Competition among the Army, Navy, and Air Force fosters "end runs" to Congress and a steady leakage to the press of much officially restricted military information. An end run, in Pentagon parlance, means an attempt by an armed service to curry favor with Congressional committees by informally communicating their dissents over budgetary decisions, often by supplying secret information ("leaks") or detailed opinions that did not survive budget-making procedures within the Executive branch. As one Washington reporter has observed: "Inside the Pentagon, where a sizable chunk of the federal budget is divided up, the highest classifications of military secrecy often go out the window in the rivalry among the services."[11]

Disclosures of this type, involving opinions as well as facts, have produced some of the Department of Defense information security administrators' biggest headaches, and have instilled in many officers a disrespectful or cynical attitude toward official secrets. In testimony before the Congressional

[9] Quoted in *The New York Times*, May 12, 1961.

[10] *Freedom of Information* (FOI) *Digest*, Freedom of Information Center, University of Missouri School of Journalism, November–December 1961, p. 1.

[11] Douglass Cater, *The Fourth Branch of Government*, Boston, Houghton Mifflin, 1959, p. 10.

Joint Atomic Energy Committee in 1960, Admiral Hyman Rickover reported that a toy manufacturer had marketed a $2.98 model of a Polaris submarine complete with printed instructions based upon official Navy blueprints, thereby disclosing information worth millions of dollars to foreign intelligence services. Said Rickover: "I personally am aghast that this was done, but our internal military controversy is so great there is a tendency for each service wholeheartedly to fight the others in order to achieve its own objectives."[12]

Each of the armed services or units can be expected to have friends on Capitol Hill and among the Washington press corps who are eager to publicize the views of "parochial" experts on particular defense needs, or to kill unwanted policies by premature or misrepresentative disclosure. Presidents and their budget directors have always been equally eager to discourage such discussion as might encourage Congress to untie the strings of the budget package.

The strength and pervasiveness of the "end run" and "leak" tactics is indicated by the vigorous Presidential attempts to contain them. Such attempts are usually at the heart of "news management" controversies. The following memoranda illustrate one way in which the Truman and the Eisenhower Administrations attempted to deal with them.

This memorandum was issued by President Truman on November 15, 1946:

Memorandum for the Director of the Bureau of the Budget
  I have noticed that on several occasions certain department and agency officials have shown a tendency to seek from Congress larger appropriations than were contemplated in official budget estimates.
  The estimates which I transmit to Congress reflect a balanced program for the executive branch as a whole, and each individual estimate is considered in the light of this program, its relationship to other estimates, and the fiscal position of the Government. While agency witnesses before congressional committees must feel free to supply

[12] Quoted in *The Reporter*, July 6, 1961, p. 28.

facts in answer to questions of committee members, I cannot condone the practice of seizing upon any opportunity which presents itself to indicate an opinion, either directly or indirectly, that my estimates are insufficient.

When you notify the heads of the various departments and agencies of the amounts to be included in the 1948 budget for their activities, I wish you would include a reminder that I shall expect them and their subordinates to support only the President's estimates in hearings and discussions with Members of Congress.

On December 31, 1958, President Eisenhower's Budget Director, Maurice Stans, issued the following:

Memorandum for the Honorable Neil A. McElroy

The President will shortly present his budget for the fiscal year 1960 to the Congress. As you know, the normal process of budgeting results in recommended amounts that in many cases are less than the agency head had requested.

It is understandable that officials and employees will feel strongly about the importance of their own agency's work, and will sometimes believe that a larger budget might be in order. Such feelings, however, must be related to an awareness that our budget resources are not adequate to accommodate in any one year all of the things that might be desired. The President is responsible for reviewing the total needs of the executive branch in the light of tax and debt policy and for deciding among competing requests for priorities. Executive branch personnel are expected to support the President in his budget recommendations. . . . It is expected that witnesses will carefully avoid volunteering views differing from the budget, either on the record or off the record. While direct questions at hearings must be answered frankly, it is expected that a witness who feels that he must set forth a personal view inconsistent with the President's budget will also point out that the President's judgment on the matter was reached from his overall perspective as the head of the Government, and in the light of overriding national policy. The witness should make it clear that his personal comments are not to be construed as a request for additional funds. . . .[13]

Similar moves were visible when a new Administration came into office in 1961. Testifying on the question of secrecy on missile projects before the Senate Armed Services Committee in 1961, Defense Secretary McNamara asked: "Why should we tell Russia that the Zeus [anti-missile system] developments may be unsatisfactory? What we ought to be saying is that we have the most perfect anti-ICBM system that the human mind will ever devise." The Secretary observed that he thought it "absurd" to release the contrary truth. Critics were quick to point out the implication that he favored releasing false information, which would probably mislead the American people more than the Russians. The Secretary later denied that he favored this; rather he was concerned about the danger of letting our adversaries know of our difficulties.[14] The distinction he makes is impossible to comprehend.

The public airing of controversy as well as the actual dissents on budgetary decisions have been a main source of trouble for Defense Secretaries. Secretary of Defense Neil McElroy's announcement on April 25, 1958, that promotions to three- and four-star rank in all of the armed services would thereafter be made only after approval by the Joint Chiefs of Staff and the Secretary of Defense and that they would be based in part upon "capacity for dealing objectively—without extreme partisanship—with matters of the broadest signifi-

[13] Both of these memoranda were reprinted in the *Congressional Record*, January 15, 1959, p. 643.

[14] Quoted in *The New York Times*, May 12, 1962. For contrasting views on the "news management" controversy in the Kennedy Administration see Lester Markel, "The 'Management' of News," *The Saturday Review*, February 9, 1963, pp. 50–51, 61; Hanson W. Baldwin, "Managed News—Our Peacetime Censorship," *The Atlantic Monthly*, April 1963, pp. 53–59; and Arthur Krock, "Mr. Kennedy's Management of the News," *Fortune*, March 1963.

cance to our national security"[15] was a move to give the Secretary additional power in his continuing efforts to reduce the pressures for disclosure. At the same time McElroy announced that informational and public relations activities would be integrated through policies established by a Joint Informational Council and by the Office of Plans and Programs in the Office of the Secretary of Defense, bringing the statements and opinions of defense officials, civilian and military, under stricter surveillance before they were released to the public.

Such censorship, which could be subtly applied, caused deep concern in Congress. Congressmen knew that if they were to be partially cut off from the dissenting views about organization and strategy, they would lose still more of their power to influence policy and programs.

A minor crisis occurred when Admiral Arleigh Burke, as Chief of Naval Operations, in June 1958, made clear his disagreement with certain centralizing provisions of the defense organization bill, in testimony to the Senate Armed Services Committee. Shortly thereafter, Secretary McElroy stated publicly that he was "disappointed" in Burke, and regarded the Navy Chief's Senate testimony as "regrettable." He added, "there is too much damn foot dragging" in the armed services when the Secretary of Defense sends down orders.[16]

At this point, the Chairman of the Senate Armed Services Committee, Richard B. Russell, Democrat, Georgia, suspended hearings on the defense organization bill, commenting that Pentagon witnesses apparently could testify "only under duress." Hearings would not be resumed until he was assured that witnesses could testify "in complete candor without being threatened overtly or covertly."[17] Secretary McElroy felt obliged to guarantee Chairman Russell by letter that Pentagon witnesses would be allowed to give their honest opinions, without reprisal. The Secretary reserved the right,

[15] Quoted in *The New York Times*, April 27, 1958.
[16] Quoted in *The New York Times*, June 22, 1958.
[17] Quoted in *The New York Times*, June 24, 1958.

however, to be "disappointed or regretful that an official of the department does not support fully the recommendations of the President."[18] The Senate hearings were quickly resumed.

The controversy could hardly fail to be noticed by other Pentagon witnesses. It is not possible to say how much witnesses would be inhibited in the future by the knowledge that the Defense Secretary or the President might be "disappointed" or "regretful" if their testimony were out of line.

Secretary McElroy's successor, Thomas S. Gates, Jr., expressed the view that criticism of the nation's defense program should be limited to only those expressions of opinion that would not impair "confidence in our armed forces," thereby implicitly including not only officials of the armed services but the general citizenry as well. He declared, in a public speech in August 1960: "Constructive criticism of our methods is helpful and essential to the improvement of our defense program, but this should be within the boundaries, understanding, and belief that our defenses are strong and will be able to meet our heavy responsibilities."[19] Under the Gates formula, anyone bold enough to assume that our defenses were *not* strong forfeited the right to speak out.

Shortly after becoming Defense Secretary in 1961, Robert S. McNamara stated his rules on the subject. During policy development, he expected free and full debate. "Once a decision has been reached and a policy established representing the decisions of the President and other appropriate authorities, then all members of the department, civilian and military, will be expected to support that decision, publicly or otherwise."[20] The Secretary explained that this did not preclude honest answers by officials when queried by Congress. The trouble here, as with earlier rules, is that decisions can seldom be "finally" made. It is likely that the pressures for

[18] Quoted in *The New York Times*, June 26, 1958.
[19] Address to the national convention, Veterans of Foreign Wars, Chicago, August 2, 1960.
[20] Press Conference, February 2, 1961.

disclosure will continue, as in the past, to thwart bureaucratic efforts to impose secrecy or a "party line."[21]

III

As the main vehicle for mass communication in a democracy, a free press is another principal opponent of government secrecy. The press is a central problem for administrators and leaders of the policy process because it is, as Douglass Cater has called it, in a very important way a fourth branch of government. "Press" as used here refers to all the mass media. The daily newspaper, in fact, is becoming less important as a news source than television and radio and the weekly news magazines.

The press is not usually directly active in national policy debates. With the exception of minor participation through editorial columns and by a few widely read columnists, the newspapers serve primarily as the arena in which policy debates occur. But press canons of what constitutes news, and the large band of Washington newsmen who apply these canons, figure prominently in the national policy process. The press is recognized by the competing elements in the Executive and Legislative struggle as an often decisive weapon.

A President's usual reaction to this fact is to try to control the flow of information on important policy matters emanating from within the Executive hierarchy. Motivated by the twin news criteria of being "first" and grinding his publisher's ax, the newsman will do his utmost to circumvent Presidentially imposed controls. Because of the vast size of the bureaucracy and the many competitive interests within it, the newsman is often successful in achieving his multiple aims.

[21] A somewhat separate issue, which came to a head in 1961 in the much-publicized case of Major General Edwin Walker, involved the question of the right of the military to propagandize their political views, or to exercise their independent judgment in explaining to the troops and to the public the nature and dimensions of the Communist threat. Walker was removed from his command in Germany for his questionable activities, and later resigned from the Army.

But in the Cold War, national security crises confront the nation with special problems and dilemmas.

These were acutely plain in the Cuban crisis in the fall of 1962 when the Kennedy Administration moved, amidst a barrage of criticism, to control all government information on the crisis and to regulate the contacts between newsmen and lower echelon officials in the Departments of Defense and State. The purpose was to guarantee that the government spoke "as one voice." Assistant Secretary of Defense for Public Affairs Arthur Sylvester, on October 29, 1962, bluntly described news as a "part of the weaponry" that a President must apply in international affairs, when newsmen complained that they had not only been denied information about the Cuban crisis but deliberately misled—"used" as some put it—by the government.

During this period rules were promulgated requiring State and Defense Department officials to keep a record of contacts with newsmen and a "diary" of their conversations. This aroused strong press protests, and Congressman John Moss began to organize his House Subcommittee on Government Information for a Congressional probe of the government's behavior.

When the crisis subsided, the rules were relaxed, but the central problem of the role and conduct of a free press in the Cold War remains. On October 31, 1962, *The New York Times* editorialized: "A democratic government cannot work if news of and about the government is long suppressed or managed or manipulated or controlled." This is true; but it is also true that a democratic government cannot survive if it cannot provide for the common defense.

In more normal situations, an official, unless he is issuing information for some tactical advantage in the policy struggle, wants to avoid premature publicity of policy, while newsmen are eager to report on policy still in the making. It is not only that it is more newsworthy at this stage; the thoughtful journalist is convinced that a major policy change should be subjected to long public debate.[22] The great mass of infor-

---

[22] The exact roles of information and public opinion in national policy making involve complex and relatively unexplored questions.

mation flowing from Washington each day allows the reporter, by applying his own criteria to "news," to set the standards that determine what the public is to know about government.

If the ideals of democratic government are to be attained, the press must favor neither the government's interests nor the interests of special publics, including the Congress, which sometimes itself resorts to unwarranted secrecy. Any tendency of the United States to move even indirectly in the direction of a government-controlled press is to be viewed as a signal that the health of the democracy is in jeopardy. Too much control by the government of too many kinds of news at the source is incompatible with democratic principles. Obversely, an irresponsible press threatens both the viability of democracy and the capability of the nation to provide for the common defense. The years since World War II give cause for alarm on both these scores. Not only has there been an increasing obsession with secrecy by the giant Federal bureaucracy, but the press itself has not lived up to its responsibility to report the truly significant news available. With several notable exceptions, American newspapers continue to headline superficial "news" of fires, robberies, and rapes while giving short shrift to significant trends—as opposed to spectacular events—in world and national affairs.

By all odds the press is among the freest of institutions in the United States. It ranks with the churches and the Congress in its freedom from restraint against saying what it pleases. Our Constitutional system places as few restraints upon the freedom of the press as upon individuals. With this freedom, and with an unequalled power to inform and persuade, goes great responsibility. The press appears to be performing its role of providing counterpressure against secrecy[23]

See James N. Rosenau, *Public Opinion and Foreign Policy*, New York, Random House, 1961. The concern of journalists regarding secrecy is detailed in the annual reports of the Freedom of Information Committee of Sigma Delta Chi, the national professional journalistic fraternity. See particularly the report submitted by the committee on November 1, 1959; V. M. Newton, Jr., Chairman.

[23] For some years, numerous journalistic groups, such as the Freedom of Information Center of the Missouri School of Journalism, and Sigma Delta Chi journalistic fraternity, and individuals, V. M. New-

better than it is assuming its broader responsibility. The press must share the blame that the mass public remains badly informed on the great issues in world affairs and on the nature of the threats to defense and democracy. The public would be well served if the press were to expend on these significant issues at least as much energy as it applies to shouting "right to know."

IV

In competing for government defense contracts private industries are continually involved in the secrecy-versus-disclosure problem. Defense contractors need general information about defense plans, requirements, and programs, and intelligence information about the military programs, capabilities, and plans of potential foreign adversaries. Yet they often must shape their policies and plans without this essential information.

Industrial firms are also often the source of important data on weapons production and the capabilities of new weapons systems. These data are distributed through elaborate public relations programs and can easily be found in reports to stockholders, general advertisements, popular and technical magazines, business conferences and trade conventions, and in technical and trade journals.

As the Coolidge Committee reported to the Defense Secretary in 1956, "some companies give out damaging [to national security] technical information . . . this is especially true in connection with the production of new weapons, and it applies both to prime and subcontractors."[24] Even the casual reader of certain magazines and journals is aware of the large amount of advertising done by commercial firms boasting of their manufacturing "achievements" with defense

---

ton, Jr., J. R. Wiggins, Herbert Brucker, James S. Pope, Clark R. Mollenhoff, Louis M. Lyons, and the late Harold Cross—to name but a few—have fought a vigorous, uphill battle against government secrecy.

[24] Report to the Secretary of Defense, Committee on Classified Information, November 8, 1956, p. 20.

equipment. Few if any cases can be cited in which this kind of public relations has harmfully or prematurely disclosed information of value to a potential enemy, although the Coolidge Committee on Classified Information detected what it termed "compelling evidence of the real harm caused by information published in trade and technical journals." Some of the data disclosed in such journals represented nearly complete specifications and detailed performance information on new weapons systems. These data were said to be of great help in assisting a potential enemy in attaining superiority in some fields by possession of such information. Knowing our progress, it was argued, enabled the potential adversary to concentrate on the required countermeasures.

R. Karl Honaman, who attempted to administer the Eisenhower Administration's "Strategic Information" program, used to claim that a skillful piecing together of published industrial news, normally disclosed in great abundance in the United States, can result in a highly accurate military-industrial profile. He illustrated his case with the story of an engineer who had applied to a defense contractor for a job and while awaiting security clearance decided to survey what could be learned of the United States military missile program. As Honaman told the story:

> He consulted published information available in a public library. This included daily newspapers, technical magazines, and government publications . . . for three months . . . and wrote a report on the U. S. guided missile program. His report, forty-five pages . . . included detailed information which gave for each weapon its name, model designation, manufacturer, guidance system, method of propulsion, length, diameter, range, and maximum altitude. He also included certain reasonable deductions concerning the high level plans and policies of our whole guided missile program. The report was accurate and reasonably complete. It contained so much that it was necessary to classify it.[25]

[25] Cited in Allen Raymond, Report to the American Civil Liberties Union, October 24, 1955, pp. 48–49.

Placing a security stamp on the engineer's report was obviously useless, since large numbers of intelligence specialists in Russia can put together even more complete information from similar sources. One critic rightly argued that the new restrictions would not work "unless most of our industrial magazines and normally published data are to become so blacked out as to be useless to anyone."[26]

Advertising has been cited as influencing the policy debates over alternative weapons systems. And certainly industries with close ties to one service do join in the policy struggle by supporting propaganda for a particular strategic concept or weapons system. This tends to result in greater public disclosure of information than would occur in a monolithic economic system.

Murray Snyder, Assistant Secretary of Defense for Public Affairs in 1960, drafted a directive under which defense contractors would not be permitted by the Defense Department to make "inappropriate claims of operational availability or operational capability of products" or appraisals of effectiveness or ineffectiveness of weapons systems, where in either case:

because of timing, content, magnitude, or a combination of any of these elements, release of information could reasonably be interpreted as intended to influence the adoption, revision, or cancellation of plans, programs, or policies of the Government, including legislation.[27]

Representative Moss immediately denounced this directive, which he feared "would do a great deal to prevent intelligent discussion of defense policies which may mean life or death to the United States."[28] Claiming that advertisements of defense contractors were a valuable source of information for the public, Moss charged that this move was "another attempt to hide controversy behind a mask of conformity." The real problem at issue here is less the disclosure

[26] Allen Raymond, loc. cit., p. 50.
[27] Quoted in the Congressional Record, April 25, 1960, p. A3495.
[28] Congressional Record, April 25, 1960, p. A3494.

of sensitive information through advertising than the propriety of defense industry propaganda, usually paid for indirectly by the taxpayer, that promotes a particular weapons system in the name of the manufacturer.

V

Perhaps no professional group is as uncomfortable with a pervasive policy of government security and secrecy as the scientific community. By tradition, scientists report the results of their experimentation so that others can accumulate information for further hypotheses and experimentation. This is so vital to scientific progress that the scientists have made some of the loudest protests against narrow security measures.

Dr. Chauncey D. Leake, chairman of the Committee on the Social Aspects of Science of the American Association for the Advancement of Science, stated in 1958: "American scientists have been particularly harassed by ill-advised security regulations which have hampered their scientific activities, inhibited their scientific interests and given them a serious sense of anxiety and frustration."[29]

Anyone doubting whether Dr. Leake spoke for a majority in the scientific community should examine, for confirmation, the testimony and statements of a panel of leading scientists before the Congressional Special House (Moss) Subcommittee on Government Information, in March 1956.[30]

One eloquent witness before this committee was Lloyd V. Berkner, president of Associated Universities and a specialist in geophysics and electronics. Surveying what he believed to be the results of a policy of "excessive military security and restriction on information" in the decade since World War

[29] "What We Don't Know Hurts Us," *The Saturday Review*, January 4, 1958, p. 38.

[30] "Availability of Information from Federal Executive Agencies," Part 4, Panel Discussion on Scientific and Technical Information, *Hearings*, Subcommittee, House Committee on Government Operations, 84th Congress, 2d Session, March 7–9, 1956.

II, he found that "the free flow of knowledge of scientific progress on which really important creative ideas completely depend has been severely hampered." Excessive secrecy, he argued, has boomeranged. Aimed at the potential enemy, secrecy measures have instead restricted American scientific progress.[31]

Either an arms race or programs to limit or control armaments must lean heavily upon the *esprit*, capability, and cooperation of the scientific and technological community. But government-sponsored scientific endeavor since World War II —which includes a vast amount of current research—has been hampered by the restrictive influence of official secrecy, enforced by an often exasperating complex of security regulations. Scientists have clashed head-on with government secrecy policies, including: the excessively secret regulations administered by the Pentagon, the Atomic Energy Commission and other agencies; the multiple-clearance system that seriously inhibits interagency communication; and the "need-to-know" concept, which is insulting to scientists, as well as contrary to the basic needs of scientific progress.

Under recent security policies, a wide range of reports, studies, or other information over which the government has control has been available only on a "need-to-know" basis. Such need, in practice, must be interpreted by thousands of individual custodians of "security" information. The "need-to-know" has little to do with a person's or a company's security clearance. A person may have clearance for *Top Secret* information and yet be refused access to documents because some functionary, who is likely to be overcautious, judges that there is no "need-to-know." This can and has had ludicrous consequences, such as the actual cases in which scientists have submitted reports to government agencies and later have been denied permission to re-examine them.

What has the nation gained scientifically from its secrecy policies? Certainly not any high degree of security. America's relative status in science and technology, compared to Rus-

[31] *Hearings, loc. cit.*, pp. 752–54.

sia's in recent years, seems to suggest that the secrecy mania has been self-defeating. As the head of the Army's Operations Research Office, Ellis Johnson, declared in 1960: "We actually are keeping our secrets so closely [from ourselves] that this has aided the Soviet Union to draw ahead of us."[32]

The concepts of military secrecy and the principles of scientific discovery are incompatible. Charles Kettering has been quoted to the effect that "if he locked the doors of his laboratory to others, he would lock out much more than he would lock in."[33] Many eminent scientists believe that too many locked laboratory doors in recent years have dangerously slowed down American scientific and technological progress. Because of secrecy, we and our allies have expended great effort and monies to discover facts and to develop techniques already known to us, and apparently to our Communist adversaries as well.

It is disquieting to hear eminent scientists suggest that it may be impossible to have great developments in science under existing codes of secrecy. One of them has noted that "great developments in the nuclear field were started as a result of the free exchange of information between scientists, unrestricted information, and that is not now possible."[34] Radar is often used to illustrate the harmful effects of secrecy on military technology. Discovered about 1930, radar saw little major development in the ten years following, largely because of the secrecy that surrounded it.

Government security regulations have resulted in attempts to classify "basic laws of nature." Many have felt that the basic facts on atomic fission and fusion were too long classified as secret. Most scientists scoff at such attempts as not only unwise, from the viewpoint of advancing scientific knowl-

[32] "The Lead-Time Problem," *American Strategy for the Nuclear Age*, eds., Walter F. Hahn and John C. Neff, Garden City, New York, Doubleday Anchor, 1960, p. 246.

[33] Quoted by Dr. Wallace Brode, in House Committee on Government Operations, *23rd Report*, House *Report* No. 1619, April 22, 1958, p. 11.

[34] Dr. Otto Struve, quoted in House *Report* No. 1619, p. 11.

edge, but futile, because the whole body of scientific knowledge moves forward at about the same pace throughout the industrial world. So, scientists tell us, what is known by a few will eventually be known by all, whether they are told about it or not.

Russia appears to be lessening its own internal secrecy—especially in science. There has been a somewhat freer flow of Russian scientific and technical reports in recent years, and increased communication between Soviet scientists and scholars in other nations. And since our relative positions in military technology have been shifting in favor of the Soviets, it would appear that the time has come for America to take some risks in a freer flow of government information to offset the greater risks of secrecy.

EPILOGUE

Throughout this book central issues have reappeared: concentrated power vs. dispersed power, unitary authority vs. divided authority, unity of command vs. plural command. Applying the dual criteria of defense and democracy, shall the President have undisputed authority in foreign military affairs, or must he share this with other loci of political power? Shall decision-making authority in the defense establishment be unified in a civilian Secretary of Defense, or should the Pentagon remain a confederation of semi-autonomous, separate armed services? Should the defense budget serve as an instrument of centralized control, or as a device for reconciling or protecting the interests of a pluralistic bureaucracy? Should the Central Intelligence Agency operate behind a high wall of secrecy in all of its activities, beyond the checks and balances of the American system, or should it be subject to the more normal controls of representative government? Should government information involving national security be strictly controlled and censored by centralized authority, or be subject to the free competition of the journalistic market place?

None of these issues has led us to "either-or" answers. The real decisions involve the question of the kinds of compromise best to be made within the context of the nature of the threats to defense and to democracy. The crucial test of institutional arrangements is whether they can, within a democratic framework, produce coherent planning, effective strategies, and efficient operations. These, in the end, will be functions of national purpose and leadership, no matter how rational the organization. But it does not follow that good leadership, no matter how poor or anachronistic the organization, can produce defense with democracy.

Surely the future offers an intensification of the burdens of democratic government, with foreign and military policy always as the potential Achilles heel of democracy. For the government leader the urge to secrecy and to control of the news, with national security as an excuse, will increase, as a function of strong, purposeful Executive leadership. And national security policy will enmesh an even larger sector of public and private life. Difficulties inherent in the Constitutional separation of powers and the federal system of government will intensify the problem of providing responsible national leadership and of obtaining consensus from a pluralistic society. For the citizen the great foreign and military policy issues and the information required to understand them will become increasingly complex, the choices ever more difficult, and the risks of alternate decisions ever more frightening. Yet both government leader and private citizen must always keep in mind that *consent of the governed* is the linchpin of the American system. It is, in fact, a main question at issue in the Cold War. So we must look to our system and adjust it to the needs of the time, always keeping in mind that the most important goal is the widest possible range of individual freedom.

In every crisis period, including the present, there have been groups in America—representing the right as well as the left—that scorn the democratic way. With each crisis the power at the center of the national government—Presidential power—has increased. This is inevitable. And it may be that power corrupts, as Lord Acton said. But today we cannot survive without centralized power; our place in the world and the common defense demand it. What we must do is to look to its orderly arrangement so that power, however organized, serves as an instrument for protecting both defense and democracy.

Our choice is between controlled, purposeful change and undirected change. Controlled change holds promise of yielding specific, desired objectives while retaining in essence the most valued ideals of the democratic tradition. Undirected change is more risky, for it may result in political upheaval, or in the concentration of the kind of absolute power that corrupts absolutely.

That our system has worked well in the past is no guarantee that it will automatically work in the decades ahead. Immutability is not an attribute of man's political institutions. Change we shall have, and it will be shaped either by man's intelligence and will, or by accident and force.

As the nation becomes ever more deeply involved in programs for the common defense, America's leaders and citizens must keep in mind constantly the liberties we strive to preserve. Defense and democracy can be made mutually compatible—but only if democratic man carefully shapes his governmental institutions and policies to meet the real needs of a world in revolution.

POSTSCRIPT

Much that is written on world affairs today may inevitably suffer the fate of words written in the sand at low tide. What is stated in a time of eased international tensions may eventually be read in an atmosphere of heightened conflict. In the President's assassination on November 22, 1963, we have had the tragic and unwelcome reminder that no one really knows what tomorrow will bring.

I write these words nearly a year after the preceding chapters were completed. Work on this book ended in an international atmosphere in which the United States and the Soviet Union, for the third time in two years, had come to the brink of nuclear confrontation. Today, a year after the crisis over emplacement of Russian long-range missiles in Cuba, suggestions are heard that the Cold War is over.

International tensions have eased. Yet as 1963 comes to an end, the only thing clear about world politics is that, as President Kennedy stated on October 19, "while it's too late to say that nothing has changed in Soviet-American relations, it is too early to assume that change is permanent." Any conceivable change, it must be observed, will never be permanent. And the rays of hope for peace that can now be discovered are seen in a world still dominated by the shadows of war.

Russian leaders, and even more ominously Chinese Communist leaders, continue to reject ideological coexistence with capitalist systems and plan for and actively seek the final and complete demise of capitalism, even though the Russians say this can be accomplished by less than apocalyptic means. If contemporary crises, such as those involving Cuba, Berlin, and

Southeast Asia, subside, recent history suggests that others will quickly replace them. If this is so, the United States continues to face a protracted conflict with its accompanying challenges to the efficacy of our governmental institutions.

Whether American democracy can survive Cold War, whatever new form the challenges may take, remains—a year after this book was completed—an urgent question.

The Presidency, for example, confronting great policy challenges, and with a new White House occupant, remains in constant danger of inundation by the great bureaucracy and staff system that the Chief Executive must try to control and to use effectively. And the President's power remains under constant challenge from an autonomous, disorganized, and often recalcitrant Congress. At the moment Congress is considering legislation establishing four-year terms for the chiefs-of-staff of the armed services, thereby limiting the President's authority to set shorter terms at his discretion. This will have the effect of weakening the Presidency while strengthening the autonomy of the armed services and, indirectly, the power of Congress to dampen Executive leadership. Like the unsuccessful Bricker Amendment a decade earlier, proposing to limit the Constitutional authority of the President in foreign affairs, this would be a step in the wrong direction. It does not strengthen responsible democracy and decision making, but promises, rather, further diffusion and confusion of power.

Department of Defense organization, particularly the question of the power of the Secretary of Defense relative to the separate armed services, also remains as much at issue as ever. Indeed, civilian-military relations in 1963 became increasingly tense in the ambiguously organized, confederated defense structure. Both a revolution in armed-services roles and missions and attempts rationally to adjust traditional military institutions to the age of modern weapon technology are still going on.

The defense budget system, with all of the useful innovations of recent years, remains essentially inadequate, in part as a consequence of Congressional failure to be introspective and self-reforming. Only Congress can reform itself. And only a reformed Congress can make representative government work in the second half of the twentieth century.

The performance and control of the Central Intelligence Agency, after another year of highly publicized confusion about its role, particularly in Viet Nam, leave much to be desired. The crossed bureaucratic wires among CIA's secret agents, State Department officers, and others continued to short circuit, during 1963, the effective forming and applying of integrated foreign and military policies. The question remains: is CIA a state within a state? Clearly the dangers posed by an espionage and covert operations agency have not yet been adequately circumscribed. Nor have we solved the corollary problem of striking a proper balance between disclosure and restriction of national-security information which the government has the power to control.

With these problems in mind, I restate the major theme of this book by recalling, in the nuclear age, Edmund Burke's eighteenth-century observation that forming and preserving a free government is man's greatest challenge, for to do so, he said, we must "temper together those opposite elements of liberty and restraint in one consistent work . . ."

Achieving timely and purposeful organizational change in government continues to be, as it always will, an evolutionary art. I have, finally, two major causes for concern within the American environment: first, that some persons, holding to values of a world that is gone forever, will try to take us back to a time when centralized governmental power was dispensable; and, second, that required changes may come too slowly to protect adequately both defense and democracy in a fast-moving world.

INDEX

ANCHOR BOOKS

AMERICAN HISTORY AND STUDIES

1A

AMERICAN FICTION